U-Boat Far from Home

T0307387

U-Boat Far from Home

The epic voyage of *U 862* to Australia and New Zealand

David Stevens

Allen & Unwin

Dedicated to my grandfather, William Douglas Crawford, a survivor of SS *City of Simla* sunk by *U 138* on 21 September 1940.

Title page illustration: The *U 862* insignia

Copyright © David Stevens 1997

All rights reserved. No part of this book may be reproduced or transmitted in any form or by any means, electronic or mechanical, including photocopying, recording or by any information storage and retrieval system, without prior permission in writing from the publisher.

First published in 1997 by
Allen & Unwin Pty Ltd
9 Atchison Street, St Leonards, NSW 1590 Australia
Phone: (61 2) 8425 0100
Fax: (61 2) 9906 2218
E-mail: frontdesk@allen-unwin.com.au
Web: http://www.allen-unwin.com.au

National Library of Australia
Cataloguing-in-Publication entry:

Stevens, David, 1958– .
U-boat far from home: the epic voyage of U862 to Australia and New Zealand.

Bibliography.
Includes index.
ISBN 1 86448 267 2.

1. U-862 (Submarine). 2. World War, 1939–1945—Naval operations—Submarine. 3. World War, 1939–1945—Naval operations, German. 4. World War, 1939–1945—Campaigns—Pacific Ocean. 5. World War, 1939–1945—Campaigns—Indian Ocean. I. Title.

940.5451

Set in 10/11.5 pt Palatino by DOCUPRO, Sydney
Printed by South Wind Production Singapore Pte Ltd

10 9 8 7 6 5 4 3

Contents

Illustrations, maps, diagrams and tables

Illustrations

Maps

Diagrams

Table

Acknowledgments

A work such as this requires the assistance of a great many people over a long period of time, and I offer my sincere apologies to anyone I inadvertently neglect to mention.

First I wish to thank Albert Schirrmann, Frau Marga Timm, and Horst Bredow of the U-Boat Archive, who kindly provided me with much of the original material concerning *U 862* and really allowed the project to get off the ground. Also in Germany I should like to thank *Kapitän zur See* Hans-Joachim Krug (Rtd), *Kapitän zur See* Dr Werner Rahn, and Professor Jürgen Rohwer, who all provided valuable information.

In Australia, Joe Straczek and his staff at the Naval Historical Section and the staffs of the Australian Archives in Melbourne and Canberra, the Research Centre at the Australian War Memorial, the National Library, the Defence Force Academy Library and the Defence Library System were all particularly helpful in locating primary and secondary sources. Ian Bowring, Commander Peter Jones RAN, Brian Ogle, Professor John McCarthy, Murray McFarlane, Dudley Reynolds, the late George Rimes, Dr Alan Stephens, Errol Stevens, David Vincent and Bob Wallace all helped in their own way.

In the United Kingdom, David Brown and his staff at the Naval Historical Branch showed great understanding in retrieving many obscure references for me, while Bob Coppock willingly imparted the benefit of his own extensive knowledge of U-boats and captured German records. Still in Britain, the staffs of the Public Record Office, Imperial War Museum and National Maritime Museum and Air Historical Branch all responded patiently to my requests for information, as did Professor John Chapman,

Jak Mallmann Showell, G.V. Speaight and Commander Graham de Chair RN (Rtd).

In the United States, the staffs of the Naval Historical Center and National Archives, Air Force Historical Research Agency and Project Liberty Ship all offered guidance or material, as did Ray Laenen, Otto Giese and Captain James Wise USN (Rtd). Dr Marc van Alphen in the Netherlands, Dr Ikuhiko Hata in Japan, Professor Michael Hadley in Canada and Lieutenant Commander Peter Dennerly RNZN in New Zealand were similarly helpful.

I am particularly grateful to Jock Gardner, Commander James Goldrick RAN, Werner Hirschmann, Lieutenant Commander Doug McLean RCN, and Dr Axel Niestlé for offering to read all or a large part of the manuscript. Their specialist knowledge, suggestions and criticisms were invaluable. Despite their best efforts I alone remain responsible for the final judgments, and for any errors or omissions that no doubt remain.

Final and sincere thanks go to my family: Jonathan, Timothy, Alexandra and Benjamin. Their constant encouragement and patience over the last few years have been priceless.

Table of equivalents

In general, units of measurement used conform to the standard usage of the participants in question at the time.

Temperature

All temperatures are in degrees Celsius. To convert to Fahrenheit, multiply by 9, divide by 5, and add 32.

Weights

1 ounce (oz)	28g
1 pound	0.453 kg

Ship tonnage

The unit of measurement is the 'avoirdupois' ton of 2240 pounds. Warships are measured in displacement tons, this is the actual weight of the vessel represented by the number of tons of water she displaces when loaded with fuel, water, stores and crew on board. The displacement of submarines is usually given as a surfaced figure. Because of the great difference in their displacements when fully or lightly loaded, merchant ships are measured in gross registered tons (GRT), a measurement of volume with one ton being equal to 100 cu. ft of carrying capacity. The overestimation of a target's size was a common failing of submarine personnel.

Distance

1 foot	0.3048m
1 metre (m)	39.37 inches
1 fathom	6 feet or 1.8288m
1 kilometre (km)	0.62 miles

Unless otherwise stated, a mile in the text refers to a nautical mile (6080 feet or 1.85km)

Guns

20 mm	0.79"
3.7 cm	1.5"
7.6 cm	3"
8.8 cm	3.4"
10.2 cm	4"
10.5 cm	4.1"
12.7 cm	5"

Time

The 24-hour clock system is used throughout. Local times are used whenever possible. Times based on Greenwich Mean Time (GMT) are suffixed with the letter 'Z'. Since events in the Far East occurred 9–10 hours ahead of GMT, sources do not always agree on the date. In a signal, the time of origin of a message was invariably given in GMT prefixed by two figures to indicate the date.

Speed

One knot (kt) is a unit of speed equal to one nautical mile per hour.

German, British and American rank equivalents

Kriegsmarine	**Royal Navy**	**United States Navy**
Großadmiral	Admiral of the Fleet	Fleet Admiral
Generaladmiral	–	–
Admiral	Admiral	Admiral
Vizeadmiral	Vice Admiral	Vice Admiral
Konteradmiral	Rear Admiral	Rear Admiral
Kommodore	Commodore	Commodore
Kapitän zur See	Captain	Captain
Fregattenkapitän	Commander	Commander
Korvettenkapitän	Lieutenant Commander	Lieutenant Commander
Marineoberstabsarzt	Surgeon Lieutenant Commander	Ship's Surgeon
Kapitänleutnant	Lieutenant	Lieutenant
Marinestabsarzt	Surgeon Lieutenant	Lieutenant, Medical
Oberleutnant zur See	Sub-Lieutenant	Lieutenant (junior grade)
Oberleutnant (Ing.)	Sub-Lieutenant (E.)	Lieutenant (jg), Engineering Duties
Leutnant zur See	Acting Sub-Lieutenant	Ensign
Leutnant (Ing.)	Acting Sub-Lieutenant (E.)	Ensign, Engineering Duties
Oberfähnrich zur See	Senior Midshipman	Senior Midshipman
Fähnrich zur See	Midshipman	Midshipman
Obersteuermann	CPO (Navigation)	Warrant Quartermaster
Obermaschinist	Chief Stoker	Machinist
Oberfunkmeister	CPO Telegraphist	Radioman 1st Class

Oberbootsmannsmaat	Acting PO (Seaman Branch)	Coxswain 2nd Class
Obermaschinenmaat	Acting Stoker PO	Machinist's Mate 2nd Class
Oberfunkmaat	Acting PO Telegraphist	Radioman 2nd Class
Obermechanikermaat	Acting PO Torpedoman	Torpedoman's Mate 2nd Class
Bootsmannsmaat	Leading Seaman	Coxswain 3rd Class
Maschinenmaat	Leading Stoker	Fireman 1st Class
Funkmaat	Leading Telegraphist	Radioman 3rd Class
Mechanikersmaat	Leading Torpedoman	Torpedoman's Mate 3rd Class
Matrosenobergefreiter	Able Seaman	Seaman 1st Class
Maschinenobergefreiter	Stoker 1st Class	Fireman 2nd Class
Funkobergefreiter	Telegraphist	Seaman 1st Class (Radio)
Mechanikerobergefreiter	Able Seaman (ST)	Seaman 1st Class (Torpedoes)
Matrosengefreiter	Able Seaman	Seaman 2nd Class
Maschinengefreiter	Stoker 1st Class	Fireman 3rd Class
Funkgefreiter	Telegraphist	Seaman 2nd Class (Radio)
Mechanikergefreiter	Able Seaman (ST)	Seaman 2nd Class (Torpedoes)
Matrose	Ordinary Seaman	Seaman Recruit

Glossary

ACNB	Australian Commonwealth Naval Board
Agru-Front	*Ausbildungs-Gruppe Front*—Training Group for Operational U-boats
AMS	Australian minesweeper
Aphrodite	radar decoy
A/S	anti-submarine
Asdic	British term for sonar
ASV	Air to Surface Vessel—term for airborne radar
ASW	anti-submarine warfare
Bachstelze	(Water wagtail) Focke-Achgelis FA-330
Bali	*FuMB* 29, radar detection equipment (*Wanze*)
BdU	*Befehlshaber der Unterseeboote*—Commander-in-Chief of Submarines
BdUop	*Chef der Operationsabteilung*—Chief of Operations
Bundesmarine	West German Navy
CinC	Commander-in-Chief
CSWP	Commander South-West Pacific
CSWPSF	Commander South-West Pacific Sea Frontiers
CV	aircraft carrier
CVE	escort carrier
DEMS	Defensively Equipped Merchant Ship
D/F	direction finding
FdU	*Führer der Unterseeboote*—Commander of Submarines
FECB	Far East Combined Bureau
Feindfahrt	war cruise
Flak	*Flugzeugabwehr-Kanone*—Anti-aircraft defence guns
Fliege	(Fly) *FuMB* 24, radar detection equipment

FRUEF	Fleet Radio Unit Eastern Fleet
FRUMEL	Fleet Radio Unit Melbourne
Führer	German leader
FuMB	*Funkmess-Beobachtungsgerät*—Radar Observation Equipment
FuMO	*Funkmess-Ortungsgerät*—Radar Detection Equipment
Funk	radio
GHG	*Gruppen-Horch-Gerät*—Group Listening Apparatus
GR	general reconnaissance
GRT	gross registered tons
glückliche Zeit	happy time
HF/DF	high frequency direction finding
Hilfskreuzer	auxiliary cruiser
HMAS	His Majesty's Australian Ship
HMCS	His Majesty's Canadian Ship
HMS	His Majesty's Ship
Hohentwiel	*FuMO* 61, radar
IJN	Imperial Japanese Navy
IWO	First Watch Officer
IIWO	Second Watch Officer
IIIWO	Third Watch Officer
Kempetai	Japanese secret police
Kriegsmarine	German Navy 1935–45
KTB	*Kriegstagebuch*—War Diary
LI	*Leitender Ingenieur*—Chief Engineering Officer
Luftwaffe	German Air Force
ML	motor launch
Mücke	(Gnat) *FuMB* 25, radar detector equipment
NATO	North Atlantic Treaty Organisation
NOIC	Naval Officer in Charge
Ritterkreuz	Knight's Cross of the Iron Cross
OKM	*Oberkommando der Kriegsmarine*—Navy High Command
RAAF	Royal Australian Air Force
RAF	Royal Air Force
RAN	Royal Australian Navy
RCN	Royal Canadian Navy
Reichsmarine	German Navy 1919–35
RN	Royal Navy
RNN	Royal Netherlands Navy
RNVR	Royal Navy Volunteer Reserve
Schnorchel	Snorkel

Skl	*Seekriegsleitung*—Naval War Staff; Naval Operations Command
SWPA	South-West Pacific Area
Tunis	*FuMB* 26, radar detector equipment
U-Bootswaffe	U-boat arm
U-Boot-Fahrer	submariners
U-Bootkrieg-sabzeichen	submarine war badge
Unterseeboot	submarine
USAAF	United States Army Air Force
USN	United States Navy
USNR	United States Navy Reserve
UZO	*U-Boot-Zieloptik*—U-boat target optical apparatus
Wehrmacht	German armed forces
Wintergarten	(Winter garden) gun platform
YMS	minesweeper
Zaunkönige	(Wren) T-5 acoustic torpedo, known to the Allies as the GNAT (German Navy Acoustic Torpedo)

Preface

On a grey morning in late May 1944, German U-boat number 862 prepared to sail from Kiel harbour for the last time. The U-boat's siren sounded the familiar low-pitched signal—one long blast, one short. Then, with the shouted command *'Leinen los'*, the U-boat's commander, *Kapitänleutnant* Heinrich Timm, ordered the removal of his boat's last physical ties with the fatherland. *U 862* reversed quickly away from the wharf, beginning what was her maiden operational voyage in an atmosphere of quiet restraint. Timm had taken a U-boat to war before, but that was in more successful and confident times. Unlike the optimistic farewells of earlier years, there were now no bands and no crowds of well-wishers. The departure time was ostensibly secret, and other than a few flotilla staff and dockyard workers there was no one to see the U-boat sail. Even Timm's wife was unable to exercise her customary privilege and view the departure. The few flowers thrown to the crew and still lying on the stark grey hull marked the only concession to tradition.

By May 1944 the average life expectancy of a U-boat on operations was down to eight weeks, and few if any of the crew could expect to survive a sinking. But if the young men ceremoniously lining the hull or handling lines were aware of their likely fate, they did not show it. Instead there was an air of almost excited expectation. After seven months of hard and realistic training they were at last going into action. Not, however, against the well-defended Atlantic convoys. Instead their boat was heading for the Indian Ocean.

The crew were conscientious and proud, confident in their abilities and those of their commander. Most had sailed with Timm in his previous command and were intensely loyal both to him and to the Navy's U-boat arm. They firmly believed that if Germany's waning war fortunes were to be turned around, it would only be through the actions of men like themselves. All the crew felt up to the challenges ahead and some may even have relished the prospect of adventure. Indeed, the Indian Ocean promised to be a prosperous hunting ground, with fewer risks than the Atlantic, while farther beyond lay the unknown delights of the Far East. However, as they watched Kiel recede into the distance, none could have realised just how far they would finally travel, nor that it would be more than four years before some would set foot in their homeland again.

The details of *U 862*'s voyage to East Asia, Australia and New Zealand have for more than 50 years remained largely unknown. Though he could perhaps be termed an 'ace', Timm was not among the highest-scoring U-boat commanders, and his name and boat are seldom mentioned in the written histories of the U-boat war. Ignorance has encouraged fabrication, and the few stories that have emerged have often been wildly inaccurate. *U 862* was not on a secret mission to rescue German prisoners of war from Australia, nor did her crew ever go ashore in New Zealand to milk cows.[1]

There is no need for fantasy, as even without embellishment the cruise was a remarkable, almost epic achievement. Over the course of two operational patrols and twelve months, *U 862* travelled farther from home than any other German U-boat of the Second World War. She sank seven merchant ships, shot down two aircraft and was indirectly responsible for the loss of two others, when elsewhere the average exchange rate was two U-boats lost for each Allied ship sunk. Alone, *U 862* initiated the largest submarine hunt ever undertaken in Australian waters and then slipped safely away to sail undetected around New Zealand. She achieved all this in the last year of the war, when it was obvious that for Germany the cause was already lost, and when virtually every communication concerning the boat was being intercepted and read by her enemies.

War history is all too often written from the standpoint of the victor, neglecting the equally important role and motivations of those on the other side. During the war Allied propaganda usually characterised U-boat crews as cold-blooded murderers, the willing servants of evil.[2] In 1946 a United States prosecutor at the Nuremberg war crimes trials described them as a 'pack of submarine killers . . . conduct(ing) warfare at sea with the illegal ferocity of the jungle'.[3] Such feelings were not unique. Nicholas

Monsarrat many times witnessed at first hand the death and destruction caused by a U-boat's torpedoes. His descriptions of the battle of the Atlantic, classified by him as 'the worst of any war' and immortalised in his novel *The Cruel Sea*, paint a vivid picture of the terror experienced by those attacked. Monsarrat also believed that the U-boat crews were among the worst of those who served the German cause and their behaviour the most repellent. He conceded that they were skilful, but held no illusions about what the submariners of any nation did, 'what they actually *do*, what constitutes their life work—killing by stealth, without warning and without quarter—is evil as well as skilful; moreover, it is predominantly evil, and, when we come to our senses, inexcusably so'.[4]

Nevertheless and perhaps remarkably, Monsarrat did not speak for all Allied seamen. Many held no particular grudge against their enemy and preferred to regard the submarine crews as an amorphous opponent rather than as individuals. Most submariners were just as far removed from personal contact with their foe. As one U-boat officer later recalled, 'The one advantage we had was that we never saw a drop of blood and very rarely a dead person during the war'.[5] This lack of intimacy was hardly surprising. A fundamental difference between war at sea and war on land is that on the ocean the participants rarely come face to face. There is no opportunity to become familiar with the personal habits of one's enemy. If the opposing sides do finally meet, it is usually in circumstances where one or the other has lost his ship. Only at this moment do they both realise that they have more in common with each other than they had previously imagined.

Despite the rhetoric of politicians, the rights and wrongs of the overall struggle were not necessarily the concern of the average sailor (or soldier or airman, for that matter). Though their masters saw the U-boat campaign in terms of U-boats lost versus merchant tonnage sunk—or perhaps, less charitably, as a strategic game of chess—for the men who acted as pawns it was something much more real and personal. Whether Axis or Allied, the primary concerns of an individual crewman were instead his survival and that of his shipmates, and the safety of loved ones left behind.

This book is fundamentally devoted to an investigation into the presence of a German U-boat off Australia in 1944, analysing both the thinking behind the operation and the reasons for *U 862*'s survival when so many of her sisters were lost. It is not intended as an attempt to lionise the U-boat crews. But if the underlying horror and brutality of unrestricted submarine warfare are present in this narrative, then so too are moments of humanity and endurance. Certainly the thrill of the hunt and exultation in success were familiar feelings in the U-boats, but their crews were no more inhumane in their actions than those who fought against them. The common image of U-boats machine-gunning helpless survivors, though it was a real fear to the crews of merchant ships, is demonstrably false. In the very early days of the war, before it became too dangerous, U-boats on occasion went to extreme lengths to protect the crews of sunken vessels. Sometimes food, clothing and charts were provided to the lifeboats. At least one German commander radioed the British Admiralty in London and gave it the exact position of a ship he had just sunk.[6] Only later, when the nature of a total war had become clear, were such displays of humanity not only impracticable but also officially forbidden. As the German commander, *Großadmiral* Karl Dönitz, exhorted his U-boat captains, 'Rescue no one and take no one with you. Have no care for the ship's boats . . . care only for your own boat and strive to achieve the next success as soon as possible! We must be hard in this war. The enemy started the war in order to destroy us, therefore nothing else matters.'[7]

Simply stated, the task of a U-boat commander was to sink ships, and this Timm did with skill and alacrity. Bare statistics can often be misleading, but the enormity of the human cost of the U-boat campaign cannot be disguised. Of the more than 60 000 men who served in the U-boat arm between 1939 and 1945, 30 000 lost their lives while another 5000 were taken prisoner.[8] The U-boat men had sworn to fight to the last and this they did. Ultimately, however, whether the men of *U 862* were evil or simply doing what they believed to be their duty will be up to the reader to judge. After all, submarines are as much a part of today's navies as they were 50 years ago. If Monsarrat is to be believed, it would seem that we have still not come to our senses.

A note on sources

As far as possible, this book has been based on the original reports of the participants, both German and Allied. Unless otherwise noted, place names have been standardised to modern usage. Though few official records from *U 862* have survived, I have been fortunate to obtain access to copies of the journals of crew members *Oberleutnant zur See* Günther Reiffenstuhl and *Obermaschinenmaat* Rudolf Herrmann. These diaries, together with the postwar recollections of *Maschinenobergefreiten* Albert Schirrmann and *Bootsmaat* Friedrich Peitel, provide a detailed picture of the day-to-day life of the U-boat and its operations. All German conversations quoted have come directly from these sources.

1 Unterseeboot 862

In war, only submarine commanders who possess distinctive tactical knowledge and ability will be successful in the long run. In order, however, to understand and master the tactics (i.e., of submarine warfare), it is necessary to be thoroughly familiar with the weapon, and its characteristics and peculiarities; for it is on these that the tactics depend.

—*U-boat Commander's Handbook,* 1943 edition

In the plans developed by the German Naval Staff during the seventeen years between the end of the First World War and the repudiation of the Treaty of Versailles in March 1935, the building of another U-boat fleet received only cursory attention. After experiencing the destruction wrought by the U-boats during the war, the victorious Allied powers had ensured the treaty forbade Germany from ever again building or employing submarines. Those U-boats remaining at the cessation of hostilities were either handed over to the Allies as reparations or destroyed. The Navy's U-boat Inspectorate and U-boat Office were dissolved.

Many in the German Navy, known since 1919 as the *Reichsmarine,* in any case harboured doubts over the continued utility of U-boats. Though they had been very successful against independently routed ships in 1916 and 1917, the introduction of the convoy system by Britain had robbed the U-boats of their chance for decisive victory. One U-boat commander was later to describe the dramatic change in circumstances: 'The oceans at once became bare and empty; for long periods at a time the U-boats, operating individually, would see nothing at all; and then suddenly up would loom a huge concourse of ships, thirty or fifty or more of them, surrounded by a strong escort of warships of all types.'[1]

Lacking effective radio communication, the U-boats could only attack alone, and a single boat could do little against massed ships surrounded by a strong escort. The postwar introduction of the active sound location device Asdic—which detected submerged submarines from surface ships—had also influenced naval thinking. To some it appeared that the submarine had lost its prime advantage of invisibility and was perhaps even obsolescent as a weapon of war. Thus it was not surprising that only a small amount of secret research work was undertaken in Germany during the 1920s, usually by companies covertly funded by the Navy. Nevertheless, the *Reichsmarine* did not renounce the U-boat, and Germany did manage to maintain some limited production experience. Between 1927 and 1933 boats for Turkey and Finland were designed and built in foreign shipyards.

It was not until the end of 1932 that firm plans evolved to include U-boats in the *Reichsmarine*'s own reconstruction program, and even then they did not receive specific precedence. At various times the German High Command regarded France, Poland and the Soviet Union as the most likely future antagonists, and this foreshadowed a continental struggle. Actions at sea were expected to have only a peripheral influence on the general outcome of the next war. Though a modern navy was seen as desirable, it was not given the highest priority, while a revived U-boat service was seen as only one 'comparatively unimportant part' of a balanced fleet.[2]

Only after Adolf Hitler's National Socialist, or Nazi, Party came to power in 1933 and announced Germany's intention to rearm, did preparations to recommence U-boat construction gather pace. In October 1933 plans and finance became available for the first 22 U-boats. Appropriate contracts were soon signed with shipyards, and components and materials were prepared. By August 1934 the parts for at least six submarines were ready for assembly. *Generaladmiral* Erich Raeder, Commander-in-Chief (CinC) of the *Reichsmarine*, had already asked Hitler if assembly work could start. At this stage, however, Hitler still sought to avoid unnecessarily provoking France and Britain. The *Führer* was still consolidating his position and hoped to prove to Britain in particular that Germany, despite her new navy, had no intention of threatening the Empire's interests at sea. To this end, negotiations continued towards a new naval agreement, one in which Germany would voluntarily accept a limitation on naval armament, but one which might yet permit the construction of U-boats. Hitler demanded that Raeder maintain complete secrecy for the

U-boat program and at first refused to authorise the *Generaladmiral*'s request.[3]

Reflecting its new-found purpose, on 21 May 1935 the German Navy officially became known as the *Kriegsmarine*. As Hitler had hoped, the Anglo-German Naval Agreement was signed the following month. This treaty, while fixing the total tonnage of the *Kriegsmarine* at 35 per cent of that of Britain's Royal Navy, at last recognised Germany's right to rebuild a submarine fleet.[4] So confident was Hitler that the treaty would be accepted that he had pre-empted the agreement and given Raeder permission to commence U-boat assembly in February. Preparations were so far advanced that the launching of *U 1*, the first of the new U-boats, occurred three days before the agreement was signed. By the end of the year fourteen U-boats were in commission.

Appointed as the first head of the revived U-boat arm, or *Führer der U-Boote* (*FdU*), was 44-year-old *Kapitän zur See* Karl Dönitz. A veteran U-boat commander of the First World War, Dönitz was at the time one of the few military men who foresaw that any war fought on the continent must also be fought against Britain. Dönitz was also firmly convinced that the U-boat would again become the vital factor in such a war. Unlike some other ex–U-boat officers, he refused to accept that the fighting power of the U-boat had in any way been diminished. Against an overwhelming superiority in British surface forces, only the U-boat could launch a sustained and direct attack on sea communications. It was only by severing these links, Dönitz argued, that Britain could be defeated.

Dönitz was given neither instructions nor guidance on the type of training he was to provide, so he could immediately implement his own ideas. He began a tough and thorough training program, designed to remove any sense of inferiority from the minds of his U-boat commanders and their crews. Dönitz wished instead to imbue his men with a supreme confidence in their boats. The tactics that he believed would overwhelm the convoys and regain the U-boat's rightful advantage were refined and perfected. As Dönitz recalled in his memoirs:

> A U-boat attacking a convoy on the surface and under cover of darkness, I realized stood very good prospects of success. The greater the number of U-boats that could be brought simultaneously into the attack, the more favourable would become the opportunities to each individual attacker. In the darkness of the night sudden violent explosions and sinking ships cause such confusion that the escorting destroyers find their liberty of action

> impeded and are themselves compelled by the accumulation of events to split up. In addition to all these practical considerations, however, it was obvious that on strategic and general tactical grounds, attacks on convoys must be carried out by a number of U-boats acting in unison.[5]

Early German production plans had settled on three different U-boat designs—Types I, II and VII—with preference going to the Type II and Type VII, small and medium-sized U-boats, of 250 and 500 tons standard displacement respectively. Short-ranged, but quick to build, the boats would allow a rapid expansion in fleet size on mobilisation for war while at the same time allowing for more boats to be built under the tonnage limitations of the Anglo-German Naval Agreement. Being larger and more expensive, and taking longer to construct, only two of the Type IA ocean-going boats were to be acquired. The Type I was in any case considered inadequate, with poor diving characteristics that demanded expert handling. However, as planning matured, it was possible to give less attention to considerations of assembly time and more thought to the specific military requirements of future U-boat construction.

The Type VII came closest to meeting Dönitz's conflicting requirements of technical efficiency, fighting power, handiness, inconspicuousness and radius of action. With continuous modification, it was to form the backbone of the U-boat fleet during the Second World War. However, the maximum range of the original Type VII was only 4300 nautical miles, and though later variants increased this range considerably there were still physical limits to the amount of fuel oil that could be carried. Thus by late 1935 a requirement had been identified for a larger submarine; one that could operate farther afield, cutting the important sea lines of communication between Germany's European enemies—primarily France—and their overseas territories.

The new U-boat needed to have sufficient range for a lengthy stay in the western Mediterranean, high cruising speed to limit the time spent in transit, and a large torpedo armament to ensure the maximum effect was achieved while on operations.[6] To reduce development time to a minimum it was decided to use the unsatisfactory Type IA design as a starting point. Increased surface speed would be achieved by fitting larger, supercharged diesel engines, dimensions would be increased to allow an additional 60 tons of fuel to be carried, and the upper deck would be widened to make room for additional torpedoes. The new project

U 862 *sailing from Trondheim on 28 May 1944, showing the long, low lines of the Type IXD2 U-boat. Though lengthened, the general internal arrangements corresponded to those of the earlier versions of the Type IX and the inner pressure hull maintained the same diameter. The big boats were slow to ventilate, especially when diving in bad weather conditions, and possessed an unfortunate tendency to 'hang' on the surface before finally going down.* (U-boat Archive, Cuxhaven)

became known as the Type IX, and in June 1936 Raeder ordered the first eight boats to be built.

In the original Type IX (later altered to IXA), diving and underwater performance were sacrificed in the interests of good seakeeping characteristics. The U-boat was 76.5m long, with a surface displacement of 1032 tons, and had a range of 10 500 nautical miles at 10kts. It incorporated a double-hull structure, which meant that the inner, cylindrical, pressure hull was surrounded by a floodable outer casing. The space between the hulls provided room for ballast tanks, fuel oil bunkers, and extra weapons stowage. Being comparatively slow to dive and hard to manoeuvre, the Type IX was unsuitable for convoy battles, but this was never intended to be its role. It was instead to be a solitary raider, laying mines off foreign coasts or using its high speed and endurance to catch the fast, independently routed merchant ships encountered in distant waters. *U 37*, the first of her class, was commissioned in August 1938 and by the outbreak of the war in September 1939 there were seven in service. Generally referred to in the *Kriegsmarine* as *'See Kühe'* (sea cows), over the next six years another 187 Type IXs of all sub-versions would be commissioned.

Even before the war began, modifications were in hand to improve surface performance and increase the Type IX's range still farther. The Type IXB, first ordered in 1937, was slightly enlarged to allow greater fuel capacity, while the Type IXC, though of similar dimensions, squeezed in another 43 tons of fuel by altering the cross-sectional shape. But even the IXC's unrefuelled range, which approached 13 850 miles, was insufficient once Britain had committed itself to the war. Now Dönitz suggested the need for a boat that could apply 'strategic pressure in very remote territories'.[7] The development of a completely new U-boat would have entailed significant delays and further stretched the building yards, already overloaded with wartime production. Instead, it was decided to enlarge the existing Type IXC. This solution would offer cost advantages and have far less impact on the overall construction schedule.

The result was the Type IXD, designed in 1940 specifically to take the U-boat war into the far reaches of the South Atlantic and Indian Oceans. To achieve the necessary range, the outer hull was widened and the fuel capacity doubled compared to the Type IXC. Two of the new type were built as experimental high-speed boats, fitted with six motor torpedo boat engines and designated D1.[8] The even longer-range Type IXD2 was developed in parallel. These boats incorporated two diesel dynamos to provide a separate method of charging the batteries. Together with the increased fuel capacity, these measures pushed the theoretical range to a record 31 500 miles.[9] Officially designated a *U-Kreuzer* (U-Cruiser), the Type IXD2 U-boats were more commonly known as '*ÜberseeKühe*' (super or overseas cows). Twenty-nine of this type, including *U 862*, were eventually commissioned.[10]

It should be kept in mind that even after modification there was nothing revolutionary about the Type IX U-boats. Developments between the wars had provided improvements in fire control, torpedoes, communications, diving depth and shock resistance, but the basic design remained conventional. In most areas the Type IX was only slightly superior to Germany's large ocean-going U-boats of the previous war. Thus the boats that Germany had in service in September 1939 were submersibles rather than true submarines and could not compete with the rapid advances in anti-submarine techniques that occurred during the course of the conflict. By August 1943, with U-boats forced to spend longer and longer periods submerged, all the pre-war types were

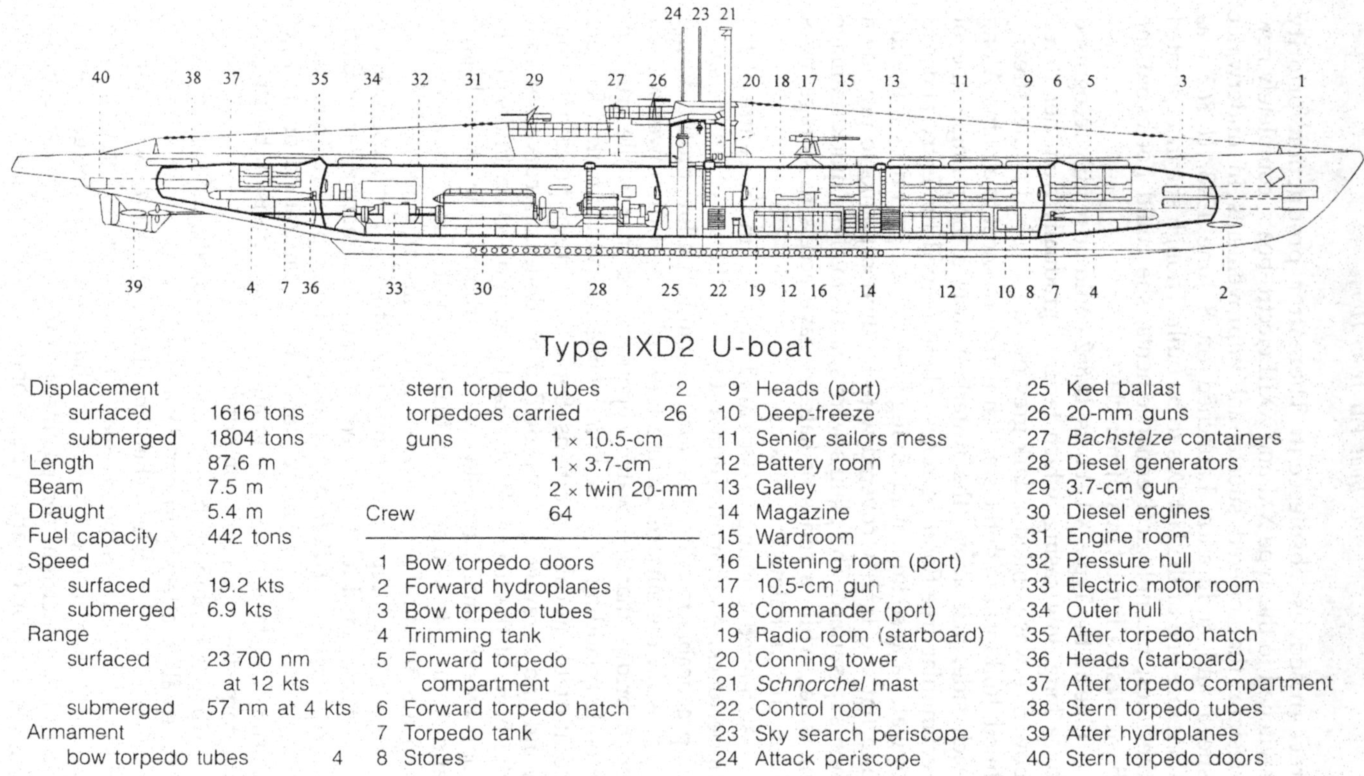

Type IXD2 U-boat

Displacement	
surfaced	1616 tons
submerged	1804 tons
Length	87.6 m
Beam	7.5 m
Draught	5.4 m
Fuel capacity	442 tons
Speed	
surfaced	19.2 kts
submerged	6.9 kts
Range	
surfaced	23 700 nm at 12 kts
submerged	57 nm at 4 kts
Armament	
bow torpedo tubes	4
stern torpedo tubes	2
torpedoes carried	26
guns	1 × 10.5-cm
	1 × 3.7-cm
	2 × twin 20-mm
Crew	64

1 Bow torpedo doors
2 Forward hydroplanes
3 Bow torpedo tubes
4 Trimming tank
5 Forward torpedo compartment
6 Forward torpedo hatch
7 Torpedo tank
8 Stores
9 Heads (port)
10 Deep-freeze
11 Senior sailors mess
12 Battery room
13 Galley
14 Magazine
15 Wardroom
16 Listening room (port)
17 10.5-cm gun
18 Commander (port)
19 Radio room (starboard)
20 Conning tower
21 *Schnorchel* mast
22 Control room
23 Sky search periscope
24 Attack periscope
25 Keel ballast
26 20-mm guns
27 *Bachstelze* containers
28 Diesel generators
29 3.7-cm gun
30 Diesel engines
31 Engine room
32 Pressure hull
33 Electric motor room
34 Outer hull
35 After torpedo hatch
36 Heads (starboard)
37 After torpedo compartment
38 Stern torpedo tubes
39 After hydroplanes
40 Stern torpedo doors

recognised as obsolescent. Thereafter production priority switched to the Type XXI and XXIII electro-boats, completely new designs that offered substantial improvements in underwater speed and endurance. Launched on 8 June 1943, *U 862* was therefore one of the last D2s to be built. Though she incorporated the latest technological enhancements, she could not avoid the basic design limitations of her class.

Like all the Type IX U-boats, *U 862* could be readily recognised by a long, low casing, which tapered gradually from her flared bow. She was painted a dark grey overall and had a fine, streamlined, hull form with the stern drawn out almost to a point. Along each side, just above the waterline, was a long single line of rectangular free-flooding holes. These helped the entry and exit of water and so improved diving speed. The upper deck was wide and flat and largely covered with hardwood planks to provide a non-slip surface. The planks were spaced to allow quick drainage of water, while a series of hatches gave access to storage areas immediately below the deck.

A stepped conning tower stood squarely in the centre of the upper deck. As in most German U-boats, the tower was as small as practicable to allow the boat to maintain a low profile during attacks on the surface. At the forward end of the tower was an open bridge that the watchkeepers would man while cruising. Wooden cladding was fitted on the internal wall to make life more comfortable in cold conditions. Some measure of protection from wind and spray was also provided by deflectors curved around the front of the tower. A retractable radio direction finder (D/F) loop was mounted in a slot on the starboard side of the bridge and behind this was a ventilation shaft. Right forward and beneath the bridge lip were conning instruments including a compass, voice pipe and engine indicators. Aft of these was the cylindrical stand for the *U-Boot-Zieloptik* (Submarine Target Optical Apparatus or *UZO*). A pair of special high-powered binoculars were clipped on top of the stand and when trained on a target during a surface attack, would automatically transmit bearings to the torpedo-fire control computer.

Directly behind the bridge were the two extendable periscopes. The smaller, attack periscope was used for the final submerged approach on a target, when minimum exposure was desired. Forward of this was the sky search periscope, raised when a wider field of view was needed. A single hatch on the bridge gave access to a small watertight compartment in the conning tower containing the seat for the attack periscope and the torpedo-fire control computer. From here the U-boat's commander could direct the final stages of a submerged attack. Another hatch on the deck of this compartment led down into the control room and the main pressure hull. At the after end of the tower were two stepped gunnery or *Flak* platforms. These platforms were enclosed only by railings and the area as a whole was known to the crew as the *Wintergarten* (winter garden).

Binoculars were still the primary means of detecting ship or aircraft targets while on the surface, but for night or conditions of poor visibility, *U 862* was fitted with the *FuMO* 61 *'Hohentwiel'* radar. A large 'bedspring' aerial, housed in a well on the port side of the bridge, could be raised and rotated manually from the control room. In fleet trials the radar had achieved a maximum detection range of 10km against a ship of 5500 GRT. Unfortunately, the radar's minimum range of 2km prevented its use for torpedo-fire control.

Despite the fitting of radar, *U 862*'s most important electronic assets were for warning rather than surveillance. The inability to detect radar transmissions from Allied aircraft had led to many U-boats being surprised on the surface and destroyed. Early detection was therefore vital to allow the U-boat sufficient time to dive before the attack could take place. To provide the required warning, *U 862* carried two types of passive radar receivers. For the earlier British metric wavelength radars (ASV Mk I and II), a fixed pressure-tight Bali aerial for the *WAnz* G2 (also *Wanze*) was mounted between the periscopes.[11] For the later centimetric radars (ASV Mk III and V), an antenna for the *FuMB* 26 Tunis was fixed on top of a wooden rod and attached to the periscope standards or into the D/F loop.[12] The Tunis provided counterdetection at ranges between 50km and 70km, but the aerial was not watertight and had to be dismounted before diving.

When submerged and below periscope depth, the U-boat became blind and the crew relied on passive hydrophones for knowledge of what was going on around them. Known as the *Gruppen-Horch-Gerät* (Group Listening Apparatus or *GHG*), the system was directional and detected underwater noise using a series of receivers mounted flush with the hull at the forward end of the keel. By electronically comparing the time difference between noise reaching the various receivers it was possible for the operator keeping watch to determine an accurate bearing of the source. Its location could only be guessed at, since the distance at which a sound could be detected varied considerably according to acoustic conditions in the water. In favourable circumstances a

A detailed overhead view of U 862's *bridge and gunnery arrangements with containers and flying-off platform for the* Bachstelze *in the centre of the picture. Cylindrical containers for ready-use ammunition are set into the deck close to each of the guns.* (U-boat Archive, Cuxhaven)

single ship might be heard at 20km and a large convoy at perhaps 100km.

U 862's final surveillance asset, and a feature unique to her class, was stored in two large watertight cylinders in the after part of the conning tower. Folded here was the small Focke-Achgelis FA-330, more commonly known as the *Bachstelze* (Water-wagtail). The *Bachstelze* was an unpowered, single-seat autogyro. The pilot sat on a metal frame against an aluminium mast on top of which were three cloth-covered blades, each about 3m long. Before being launched, the machine first needed to be assembled on a small platform abaft the storage containers. When ready, the U-boat would head into the wind until the relative velocity was sufficient to turn the rotor blades at between 130–360 rpm. As the *Bachstelze* rose, a towing cable would be pulled slowly from a third container beneath the launch platform. Thus tethered, this precursor of the helicopter effectively gave the U-boat a 100–150m viewing platform. The pilot was provided with a parachute and passed messages to the tower on a telephone. Though it had the potential to extend the U-boat's horizon to between 35 and 45 km, the *Bachstelze* prevented the U-boat from diving quickly and hence could only be used in remote areas, where Allied air patrols were unlikely.

Recessed in a channel on the starboard side of *U 862*'s upper deck lay a thick mast known as the *Schnorchel*.[13] The 8m mast contained air induction and exhaust tubes and could be raised or lowered using a hydraulic ram operated from inside the boat through a system of levers. When the mast was raised to the vertical, an opening in the centre joined to a bell-shaped housing on the conning tower which connected the *Schnorchel* with the normal intake and exhaust pipes of the diesel engines. Until the widespread introduction of the *Schnorchel* in mid-1944, U-boats had proceeded and attacked mainly on the surface. They could only cruise under water on their electric motors, whose batteries needed frequent charging. The *Schnorchel* allowed them to proceed on their diesel engines or charge batteries at slow speed while still at periscope depth, making them much less vulnerable to air attack.

At the top of the *Schnorchel* was a float valve that closed when the top of the mast went under the surface, preventing water from entering the intake tube. Unfortunately, when this occurred the diesel engines would draw their air directly from inside the boat, causing serious fluctuations in air pressure. Such rapid changes created intense discomfort for the crew, making accurate depth-keeping essential and limiting the ability of the boat to *Schnorchel* in rough weather. Even in good conditions the average pressure inside the U-boat would be well below atmospheric pressure. If the *Schnorchel* was incorrectly handled, after about three hours using it the crew would become listless and suffer severely from ear troubles. In the worst case, water pressure might exceed the pressure of the exhaust and the gases would flow directly back into the boat.

Also forward of the tower was a 10.5cm quick-firing gun for use against enemy shipping. In the North Atlantic, where Allied air power prevailed, there was little opportunity to use this weapon, but in more distant theatres it could still be useful. U-boats preferred to avoid Allied aircraft by diving, but in case she should be forced to fight *U 862* also carried a heavy anti-aircraft defence, comprising a single-barrelled 3.7cm fully automatic cannon and two twin 20mm cannon. The 20mm weapons were positioned either side of the upper *Flak* platform, just abaft the periscopes. The 3.7cm had its own platform farther aft and one level below. A hatch in the deck allowed the gun's crew to rapidly man or stand down from their weapon without having to pass through the conning tower.

As her prime anti-shipping weapon, *U 862* could carry a full load of 26 54cm torpedoes, each with a 280kg warhead. The torpedoes were referred to as *Aals* (eels) by the crew and, being the U-boat's *raison d'être,* were treated with the utmost care and attention. Most of the weapons were straight-running electric or air-driven torpedoes, but a proportion were of a new type, the *Zaunkönige* (Wren) T-5. This had an acoustic homing head that automatically steered in towards the noise produced by its target's propellers. All torpedo types had a combined magnetic non-contact or impact pistol that exploded either on hitting the target or on passing through its magnetic field. There were four torpedo tubes mounted in the bow and two in the stern. These were normally kept loaded, and another nine reloads were available in the forward and after torpedo compartments, split six and three respectively. The remaining eleven weapons were stowed in pressure-proof containers installed along the sides of the upper deck.

These torpedo tubes marked the ends of the inner pressure hull, a welded steel cylinder 4.5m wide and 68m long. Stretching the length of the boat, it was known to the crew as *die Röhre* (the tube). Ribs, bulkheads and the sides of tanks all added to its rigidity. The cylinder was split into five watertight subsections, with a single principal deck level. The main compartments were distributed along this deck, with the heavy batteries for the electric motors stored below. Within these confines the designers had crammed machinery, electronics, stores, provisions, and living, sleeping and working spaces for more than 60 men. There was no separate passageway, so all traffic forward or aft was funnelled through the centre of each compartment. At change of watch there would be constant movement, while at mealtimes, with the tables up in each mess, passage would become virtually impossible.

In the centre of the boat, connected to the conning tower by a single ladder, was the *Zentrale,* or control room. This was the U-boat's nerve centre. Against one bulkhead stood the navigator's chart table, which doubled as the attack table during action. Here also were the valves that controlled the flooding and venting of tanks, the handwheels that operated the hydroplanes, the two

The starboard side of the control room of the Type IXC U-boat, U 532. *In the centre of the picture are the large handwheels for controlling the forward and aft hydroplanes, while above them are gauges to determine diving angle and depth. To the right is the trimming panel The black cat was the crew's mascot* (IWM A28765)

periscope shafts, the depth gauges and a multitude of other switches, dials, valves and controls that directed every aspect of the boat's movement. The control room was separated from the forward and after ends of the boat by two large, curved, watertight bulkheads. Entry and exit could only be made through two small circular hatches, which would be sealed off in combat.

The primary living spaces were forward of the control room. The first part of the compartment contained the commander's cabin and listening room to port, and the radio room to starboard. These spaces needed to be centrally located so the commander had rapid access to information and could keep abreast of what was going on around his boat. The listening room contained the hydrophone equipment, while the radio room functioned as both a communications centre and a display area for the radar and electronic warfare equipment. The radio room also held the boat's gramophone and record collection.

All German U-boats were designed with wartime operations in mind and crew comfort was given only secondary consideration. Though not expendable, the boats were only expected to have a short service life. The commander was the only man onboard to have his own cabin and it served as both office and sleeping space. There was no door, and the cabin was separated from the main passageway by only a heavy green curtain. The remaining officers shared a small wardroom that spread across the full width of the hull. A drop-side table, used for meals, work and recreation, took up the majority of the available deck space. Oak panelling on the bulkheads and cabinets provided the sole concession to aesthetics. Further decoration was at the whim of the officers. In some boats there might be a portrait of Hitler, more often a picture of Dönitz or a humorous sketch. One set of double bunks to port and two sets to starboard provided sufficient sleeping space for each officer carried.

A small galley separated the officers from the rest of the crew. An electric range occupied most of the area on one side of the passageway, and the coolroom took up the other side. Two small ovens, several cupboards and a sink completed the arrangements. The entire work space had an area of just over 3 sq. m. Yet despite the conditions a great effort was made to serve the best foods, and here three meals a day were prepared for everyone on board, usually with two or three, and on special occasions even four courses.

Beyond the galley were the separate messes for the *Feldwebels*, or chief petty officers, and *Unteroffiziers*, or petty officers. As in the wardroom, there was some timber panelling and the occasional picture, but here the utilitarian nature of the U-boat became even more obvious. The sixteen available bunks were insufficient for all the non-commissioned officers carried. The solution was to share, and as a man crawled out of his bunk to go on watch, another coming off watch would crawl in.

Accommodation for the remainder of the crew was split between the forward and after torpedo compartments. The forward compartment was normally known as the 'Lords compartment' from the nickname given to the 'ordinary seaman' ratings. It was separated from the *Unteroffiziers'* mess by a watertight bulkhead and dominated at the forward end by the exposed portions of the torpedo tubes. Overhead was the handling equipment for moving the reload torpedoes stored above and below the deck plates. On either side of the compartment were two rows of three folding bunks, which were again shared between the watchkeepers. To sit down at mealtimes, it was necessary to raise the upper bunks so the lower ones could be used as seats. The few personal effects

British sailors search the forward torpedo compartment of U 532 *after the U-boat's surrender in May 1945. Note the torpedo stowage under the deck plates and the luggage crammed in wherever possible.* (IWM A28773)

allowed each crew member were stored in the wooden lockers lining each side of the hull. Arrangements in the after torpedo compartment were similar, though as the hull was narrower they were even more cramped.

Washing and toilet facilities were also rudimentary and shared by everyone on board. There were no purpose-built showers, but on occasion the crew would rig a seawater shower in the diesel engine compartment. Arrangements in the forward section simply consisted of two sinks and a toilet, commonly referred to as 'Tube 7'.[14] There was another toilet aft, but this was usually filled with stores and hence added pressure was placed on the waiting list for the first. Like most aspects of U-boat life, use of the heads was strictly regulated. A red light burned in each compartment whenever the toilet was occupied. Waiting was bad enough, but the operation of the flushing controls required particular skill. The order of opening and closing valves and operating the pump had to be committed to memory, and even then there were idiosyncrasies.[15]

Moving aft from the control room brought the crew into the engine rooms. The deck here was lower to allow full access to the machinery, which nearly filled the available space. A narrow walkway split the compartments along the centreline. First came the two six-cylinder diesel dynamos, a unique feature of the Type IXD2, which charged the batteries independently and more economically than the larger propulsion engines could. Next aft were the two 2200hp, nine-cylinder, MAN diesel engines, mounted side by side on substantial foundations. The engines, directly driving twin shafts, were designed to produce a speed of more than 19 kts on the surface, though this was seldom approached at sea. Finally, beyond another bulkhead, were the two 500hp electric motors for submerged running. Design specifications suggested a dived range of approximately 57 miles at 4kts, or a burst of 6.9kts for short periods, though again these capabilities were somewhat reduced in practice. A series of clutches allowed the configuration of the diesel and electric motors to be rapidly changed depending on whether the boat was diving, surfacing or charging batteries. Two separate electric and diesel compressors provided the air for blowing tanks and firing torpedoes.

The U-boat dived by opening vents and sequentially flooding the ballast tanks from forward to aft. When stationary, it took approximately 50 seconds to reach periscope depth, at which time there was some 10m of water above the hull. More commonly, however, submergence would be accomplished by a combination of flooding and dynamic diving using the U-boat's forward movement and the bow and stern hydroplanes. A quick-diving tank was used to further reduce delays, and an efficient boat could cut diving time to around 35 seconds. Once below the surface, the hydroplanes remained in use to dynamically alter the depth. When the desired depth had been reached, the boat was brought level and trimmed by adjusting the amount of water in the ballast tanks and forward and aft trim tanks to maintain neutral buoyancy. Trimming the boat was not an easy task and was the responsibility of the chief engineering officer. Any shifting of weight within the boat could upset the balance. This imposed certain restrictions on crew movement but provided another way to dive faster in an emergency. When ordered to crash-dive, all free crewmen raced forward, where the extra weight would rapidly increase the downward angle of the bow. To surface, compressed air was blown into the ballast tanks in a reversal of the process for diving.

This then was *U 862*, a home and workplace for her crew for up to sixteen weeks at a time, an integrated weapons system with one purpose, the destruction of Allied merchant shipping.[16]

2 Kapitänleutnant Heinrich Timm

He was a fan of classical music and a good fellow too, I believe.

—*Frau* Marga Timm

Perhaps more than in any other type of naval vessel, it is a submarine commander who fashions his boat's character from his own personality. Life in a submarine is a world apart, with men living sometimes for months at a time in a confining steel tube with little to tell them whether it is night or day. Personal space and privacy do not exist and everyone aboard is subordinated to the team. Thus, unlike his surface counterpart the submarine commander is completely integrated into the life and routine around him. Yet everyone on board still looks to him for guidance and it still falls upon him to distance himself, bring a sense of order to proceedings, and motivate his men to perform beyond endurance. Ultimately it is upon the commander that the success of a patrol depends, and it is often his skill alone that determines whether his crew will live or die.

Nikolaus Heinrich Timm, *U 862*'s first and only commander, remains something of an enigma. Few documents exist, and with the passing of the years the memories of the men who served under him have mellowed. Undeniably, Timm earned the undying loyalty and devotion of his crew, and those who survive still regard him as 'one of the best German U-boat commanders of the Second World War'.[1] To other U-boat men he was 'a happy-go-lucky chap', exceedingly well-liked by all who crossed his path.[2] There is also no doubt that Timm was passionately serious about his interests and that he was a congenial man who later took

Korvettenkapitän *Heinrich Timm photographed in summer full dress uniform and wearing the Knight's Cross of the Iron Cross.* (M. Timm)

particular pleasure in exaggerating his exploits in the presence of his former foes. As a whole, Timm's service record demonstrates that he was capable and successful. He was, after all, one of only 145 members of the *U-Bootswaffe* to be awarded the coveted *Ritterkreuz*, or Knight's Cross of the Iron Cross. But specific incidents also show that Timm was a man of extremes. At times he appears to have operated his boat with intemperate caution, at others with almost foolish recklessness.

Born in the port city of Bremen in 1910, Timm was named after his father, a *Kapitän* in the German merchant marine.[3] At the age of eighteen, and after completing his secondary education, he too joined the merchant navy. Timm started his instruction on board the sail training ship *Oldenburg*, and here his true acquaintance with the sea began. The routine was hard and physically demanding, but it confirmed Timm's desire for a life afloat and gave him a good grounding in the fundamentals of seamanship. After two years he graduated to steam ships and spent the period from 1930 to 1932 gaining practical experience in the vessels of the *Nord Deutsche Lloyd* (North German Line) of Bremen. It was during this time that Timm first visited the Far East and almost certainly sailed the shipping routes farther south, even into Australian waters.[4] In 1933, he returned to the German Nautical Academy in Bremen, where he commenced advanced training in navigation.

Timm would probably have remained in the merchant navy had not the *Reichsmarine* suffered its worst peacetime disaster in the summer of 1932. The naval sail training ship *Niobe,* struck by a sudden squall in the Baltic, capsized and sank. Sixty-nine men were drowned including 36 cadets, more than half the regular officer class of 1932 (Crew 32). The loss of so many young officers was disastrous to a navy about to embark on a period of fleet reconstruction and already seriously understaffed. Among other measures the *Reichsmarine* was forced to look to the merchant navy to fill the ranks. The first two years of both training schemes were similar enough to allow the merchant marine officers to be grouped with their Navy counterparts immediately after indoctrination training. After a successful experiment with twenty merchant officers in late 1932, the *Reichsmarine* decided to take on double the number the following year. With the Great Depression forcing German shipping lines to drastically reduce their services, Timm was one of many who took advantage of the opportunity to apply for transfer.

Timm entered the basic infantry training school at Stralsund in October 1933. At 23 he was somewhat older than the regular cadets, yet like them he began his naval career with the usual six months of intensive instruction designed to rapidly instil the essentials of military life. Kitted out in field-grey uniform and steel helmet, Timm soon grew to understand his position as a warrior within Hitler's Third Reich—'destined to achieve great deeds' and committed to order, discipline and thrift and to serving the state before all else.[5] On completion of basic training, Timm and his merchant colleagues were integrated with Crew 33 and spent a further year on torpedo, communications and navigation courses at the naval school in Flensburg-Mürwik and on board the light cruiser *Leipzig.*

In September 1935, after completing his final practical training in the pocket battleship *Admiral Scheer, Oberfähnrich zur See* Timm was posted to the torpedo boat *T 190* as a junior watch officer. Subsequent postings took him through several vessels of the First Minesweeping Flotilla, where he gradually acquired greater responsibilities. By the time war was declared, Timm had risen to become commander of one of the flotilla's vessels, the minesweeper *M 7,* in the rank of *Oberleutnant zur See.* During the first eighteen months of the war he and *M 7* saw active service during the invasion of Poland, in the North Sea and the Baltic, and off Norway. The most common employment for *M 7* was on anti-submarine patrols, and those in the Heligoland Bight proved particularly effective.

On the morning of 9 January 1940, *M 7* was operating 40 miles northwest of Heligoland when she was sighted and attacked by the British submarine HMS *Starfish*. The attack failed, but the attempt had inadvertently betrayed *Starfish*'s presence.[6] Sighting the submarine's attack periscope, Timm sped towards it and rapidly counterattacked with two depth charges.

Starfish was badly shaken. Though no internal damage was caused to the submarine, both sets of hydroplanes were put out of action. *Starfish*'s commander, Lieutenant T. A. Turner RN, ordered the motors briefly stopped and bottomed his boat, hoping the Germans would lose contact and give him an opportunity to slip away. Unfortunately for the submarine, *M 7* was able to maintain a firm echo on her sound equipment and Turner found that as soon as he started the motors the minesweeper would launch a new attack. In desperation, he ordered complete silence until dusk.

Knowing that his opponent was stopped and probably damaged, Timm made the most of his psychological advantage. He continued to maintain pressure on the British commander and dropped a further 26 depth charges throughout the day. In mid-afternoon one of these attacks released a large air bubble and the spot was marked with buoys. With *Starfish*'s position betrayed precisely, the depth charging became more accurate. By early evening internal damage and flooding were serious and Turner decided that his only chance, however slight, lay in surfacing and attempting to escape in the darkness.

Starfish surfaced directly under the glare of *M 7*'s searchlights and the minesweeper at once opened fire with machine guns. Realising his situation was hopeless, Turner showed a white light and ordered the submarine scuttled and his crew to abandon ship. Timm immediately ceased fire and lowered a dinghy to recover the men who had jumped overboard. However, the majority of the British crew decided not to risk the freezing water and remained on the submarine's deck. Timm deftly manoeuvred *M 7* alongside to take them off. A line was fastened to *Starfish* but it was obvious to Timm that she was sinking too fast to be boarded safely. With all of the British on board, *M 7* lay off and watched the submarine sink stern first. Remarkably, and thanks primarily to Timm's actions, not one of Turner's crew was lost.

The sinking of *Starfish* provided welcome news for the *Seekriegsleitung* (operations division of the German Naval War Staff, or *Skl*), which noted in its war diary:

> A most gratifying success, which is to be valued especially highly after the recent destruction of the submarine *Undine*; this will give our subchaser units more confidence and certainty and, it is hoped, will convince the British submarine arm of the dangers of operating in the Heligoland Bight. The sinking will be kept secret in order to leave the enemy in doubt as to the type of German anti-submarine measures used.[7]

The Germans were quite correct. With three submarines—*Starfish*, *Undine* and *Seahorse*—all lost in the same area in less than a week, the British temporarily abandoned submarine operations in the Heligoland Bight. Timm's flotilla commander had been on board *M 7* during the action and was suitably impressed by his handling of the incident. The day after the sinking Timm was awarded the Iron Cross Second Class and a month later he was promoted to *Kapitänleutnant*. In May 1940, after involvement in the German occupation of Norway, Timm's efforts in command of *M 7* were again recognised—this time with the Iron Cross First Class. As a successful and decorated officer, Timm could probably have expected further advancement, but instead he decided to look for a new challenge: he volunteered for service in U-boats.[8]

The exact reasons for Timm's decision are not known, but by the end of 1940 it was clear to everyone in the *Kriegsmarine* that a war against the British Empire would be a long one. Though other branches of the Navy might view the prospect more soberly, if Dönitz was to be believed, only the U-boats were going to have any influence on the course of events. Moreover, many of Timm's classmates from Crew 33 had by now established a reputation in the Atlantic battle. U-boat 'aces' such as Günther Prien, Wolfgang Lüth and Reinhard Hardegen were idolised like film stars in the German press.

Under Dönitz's untiring and inspired guidance, the fledgling *U-Bootswaffe* (U-boat arm) had developed in only a few years into a remarkable fighting force. Imbued with the spirit of an elite corps, its members were young, proud, well-trained, and enthusiastic. They had an unshakeable belief in themselves as part of the finest and most efficient arm of the German *Wehrmacht*. The

U-boat commanders were aggressive and full of initiative. They believed implicitly that only they could strike the decisive blows against Britain's vital sea lanes. This *espirit de corps* was in no small measure due to the outstanding and persuasive personality of Dönitz himself. A 'model officer' and disciplined leader, he engendered eternal loyalty in the vast majority of his men. Dönitz was variously known as *der Löwe* (the Lion) and *Onkel Karl* (Uncle Karl) and, as one biographer has noted, these nicknames give an indication of 'the mixed awe and affection in which he was held'.[9]

Though *Großadmiral* Raeder had regularly repeated assurances from Hitler that war with the British Empire would not come until 1944, Dönitz felt it his duty to prepare for every possibility. Thus, unlike the wider German Navy, which was not mentally or materially prepared for a war with the British in 1939, the *U-Bootswaffe* had at least prepared to the best of its ability. Nevertheless, only 56 U-boats were in commission in September 1939, of which from one-third to a half were either school boats or undergoing training. In consequence the U-boat Command entered the war with very clear ideas as to how the battle was to be waged, but with a completely inadequate fleet.

With limited numbers of operational boats, conflicting priorities, unrealistic political restrictions and some technical problems with torpedoes, it was a year before the U-boats could deliver their expected potential. Not until the autumn of 1940—after the U-boats had gained access to the Atlantic from French and Norwegian ports, and when the first organised anti-convoy operations commenced—did the training and innovative tactics employed by Dönitz's commanders begin to pay off. The U-boats, employed as torpedo boats which dived only when in immediate danger, took maximum advantage from their low silhouette and high surface speed. Allied convoys, with few escort ships and no long-range air patrols, found their defences easily overwhelmed. During the day the U-boats would remain on the surface, shadowing the convoys just out of sight. They would then close at night, when they were practically invisible, attacking either individually or preferably coordinated using the *Rudeltaktik* or 'wolf pack' method.

During the second half of 1940 the sinking rates of Allied shipping soared. Germany's ultimate victory through cutting Britain's oceanic lifelines seemed within reach. For the U-boat men the period became known as the first *glückliche Zeit* or 'happy time' of the battle of the Atlantic. Morale in the *U-Bootswaffe*, and in the nation as a whole, was at its peak.

Dönitz had by this time been promoted to *Konteradmiral* and his position, as it increased in importance, had been renamed *Befahlshaber der U-boote* (Commander-in-Chief for Submarines, or *BdU*). Buoyed by his early success, Dönitz believed he only needed more U-boats to win the war of attrition, and throughout the conflict he pressed for increased priority to be given to their production. But the boats alone were not enough; they had to be manned. The *U-Bootswaffe* had started the war with 3000 well-trained men. However, the increase in U-boat numbers, coupled with the considerable loss of men in action, meant that the pool of suitable personnel with sea experience was diminishing. Later, it was found necessary to use conscripts, but in the early years volunteers could still be carefully selected. As befitted an elite service, only the best and healthiest applicants were considered.

Heinrich Timm's existing experience in small vessels and his well-tested leadership skills obviously made him an attractive prospect. He was readily accepted for transfer and in March 1941 was sent to the 1st U-boat Training Division at Pillau in East Prussia. Timm qualified in August 1941 and within a month assumed command of the newly built Type VIIC U-boat *U 251*. That he was posted directly to command of a U-boat without probationary time as a watch officer reflects not only Timm's competence and the high regard in which he was held by his superiors, but also, perhaps, the consistent shortage of suitable candidates for command.

A single-hulled submarine displacing only 769 tons on the surface, the Type VIIC had its main ballast tanks positioned in the form of saddles either side of the pressure hull. It had a theoretical range of 8500 miles at 10kts and a maximum surface speed of 17.6kts. Firepower consisted of four forward and one aft torpedo tubes and one 8.8cm deck gun. The weapon load was normally 14 torpedoes.

Almost every U-boat carried an unofficial insignia, the only source of individuality in an otherwise uniformly grey fleet. Sometime early in his career Timm had acquired the nickname *'Tüte'*, which referred to a cone-shaped paper bag used to hold sweets. Timm had an overwhelming fondness for classical music, and would loudly play the best recordings of symphonies, sonatas and piano concertos. His hobby did not always endear him to his peers and the resemblance of an old-style gramophone horn to a *Tüte* prompted them to christen him after the bag. The continuous playing of classical music over their boat's loudspeakers also grew wearing on his men, but in honour of their commander, Timm's crew made his nickname an integral part of *U 251*'s and later *U 862*'s insignia. Painted on either side of the conning tower was a *Tüte* from which emerged a rather stern-looking torpedo, the primary weapon of the *U-Bootswaffe*. Over the bag strode a smiling chimneysweep. A sweep's broom was traditionally waved when a boat returned from operations, and the meaningful combination of elements proved a popular mascot and a considerable source of pride.

After six months of realistic exercises in the Baltic, Timm and his new crew of 44 were assessed as ready for front-line operations or *Frontreif* and sent to the northern theatre as part of the 11th U-Boat Flotilla. They arrived in Norway in April 1942 and over the next year *U 251* made nine operational patrols under the control of Naval Group Command North, headquartered in Narvik.

The years 1942 and 1943 were marked by some of the hardest-fought battles surrounding the Arctic convoys carrying Allied arms and supplies to Russia. Starting just two months after the German invasion of 22 June 1941 the convoys were simply aimed at keeping Russia in the war. Though the aim was achieved, it came at a high cost in Allied men and ships.[10] Not only did the convoys face some of the harshest weather in the world, but because they passed close to Norway, there was an almost continuous threat of attack from German aircraft, surface warships and U-boats.

U 251 began her first *Feindfahrt* (war cruise) in late April 1942, sailing from a fiord near Narvik. She was immediately ordered into operations against two Allied convoys: QP.11, heading west from Murmansk with thirteen ships, and PQ.15, heading east from Iceland with 50 ships. *U 251* was only one of seven U-boats allocated to the task.[11] Attacking in conjunction with German torpedo aircraft and destroyers, the U-boats intercepted the two convoys between Bear Island and North Cape. On 1 May Timm manoeuvred *U 251* into position against one of the destroyers escorting QP.11: his first torpedo attack of the war. The shot missed. It was not an auspicious start, but Timm remained in the vicinity and was soon to make amends. Just before midnight on 2 May he was surprised to find a group of ships suddenly emerging from a thick mist. *U 251* was on PQ.15's beam and there was little time to set up an attack. Timm dived and, at the relatively long range of 3500m, fired a spread of three torpedoes into the centre of the convoy.[12]

After a considerable wait a single torpedo was heard to

detonate, followed by a much larger explosion. Even underwater, *U 251* was shaken by the shock wave. Timm could not see the results, but his torpedo had blown up the SS *Jutland*, a fully loaded ammunition ship of 6153 GRT.[13] With this success and the sinking of *Starfish*, he became one of the few men in history to have such intimate experience of both sides of the submarine warfare equation—experience that he would continue to put to good use.

Retaliation from the escorts followed rapidly. The depth charges, though, were not accurate and within an hour the sounds of explosions had faded away. *U 251*, unscathed, began her return to base. The following morning *U 703*, another member of the wolf pack, investigated the scene and found large amounts of wreckage and six empty lifeboats.[14] Timm's claim for a sinking was confirmed, and his crew painted their victim's estimated tonnage onto their first victory pennant.

The permanent daylight of Arctic waters in summer provided the U-boats with little cover and made operations particularly hazardous. Opportunities to recharge batteries were all too brief. Despite several attempts on other convoys, it was not until July, during *U 251*'s fourth war cruise, that Timm scored again. Taking part in Operation *Rösselsprung* (knight's move), *U 251* was allocated with five other U-boats to a wolf pack known as the *Eisteufel* (Ice-devil) Group.[15] The boats were ordered to form a patrol line to the east of the ill-fated convoy PQ.17. On 4 July this convoy had been ordered to scatter after the British Admiralty had learned of a possible threatening sortie by a German surface force that included the battleship *Tirpitz*. It was decided that the more widely the convoy was dispersed the better the chances for individual ships to escape. However, the Germans' intelligence was also incomplete and they eventually decided not to risk their bigger ships. *Tirpitz* and her consorts returned to Narvik and left the destruction of the convoy to the *Luftwaffe* and U-boats.

After scattering, the merchant ships were without adequate escort or even mutual support and most were picked off individually. In the worst convoy disaster of the Arctic campaign, only eleven of the 36 ships that had originally sailed reached their destination. At least ten were claimed by the U-boats. Just after midnight on 10 July, Timm had his turn when *U 251* came across a small section of the convoy that had managed to retain an escort. The first fan of three torpedoes was aimed at the largest ship of the group. There were no hits, but Timm followed up immediately with a single shot against two overlapping steamships. This time a torpedo detonation on the leading ship was clearly seen.

The Type VIIC U-boat U 251 *returns to Narvik after her successful patrol against convoy PQ. 17. The U-boat displays the lighter colour scheme used by boats operating out of Norwegian bases and a victory pennant flys from her attack periscope. The Type VII in all its subversions was the most numerous U-boat in Germany's underwater fleet: 704 saw service during the war and 437 were lost in action. Between 1940 and 1944 660 Type VIIC were commissioned.* (USN Historical Center 71344)

Dönitz believed that the essence of submarine tactics was the offensive. Following his Admiral's exhortations to 'always keep attacking', Timm ordered *U 251* turned hard about and attempted a long-range stern shot against the right-hand escort, 'trusting to luck', as he noted in his war diary.[16] This missed, but the 5255 GRT Panamanian freighter SS *El Capitan*, which had been Timm's earlier target, was already sinking. Continuous depth-charge attacks followed, but again *U 251* escaped undamaged. Six days later she returned safely to base, welcomed back by a large group of officials and a Navy band, her second victory pennant flying proudly from her attack periscope.

In August, *U 251* embarked fuel oil from the *Admiral Scheer* before departing with the pocket battleship on Operation *Wunderland* (Wonderland), an anti-shipping sortie into the Kara Sea. *U 251* and *U 601* at first provided ice reconnaissance ahead of *Admiral Scheer* as she proceeded eastwards past Cape Zhelania. Later, while the battleship's guns bombarded Dikson Island, *U 251* added her own meagre firepower by shelling a Soviet radio station on an island to the east of Novaya Zemlya.

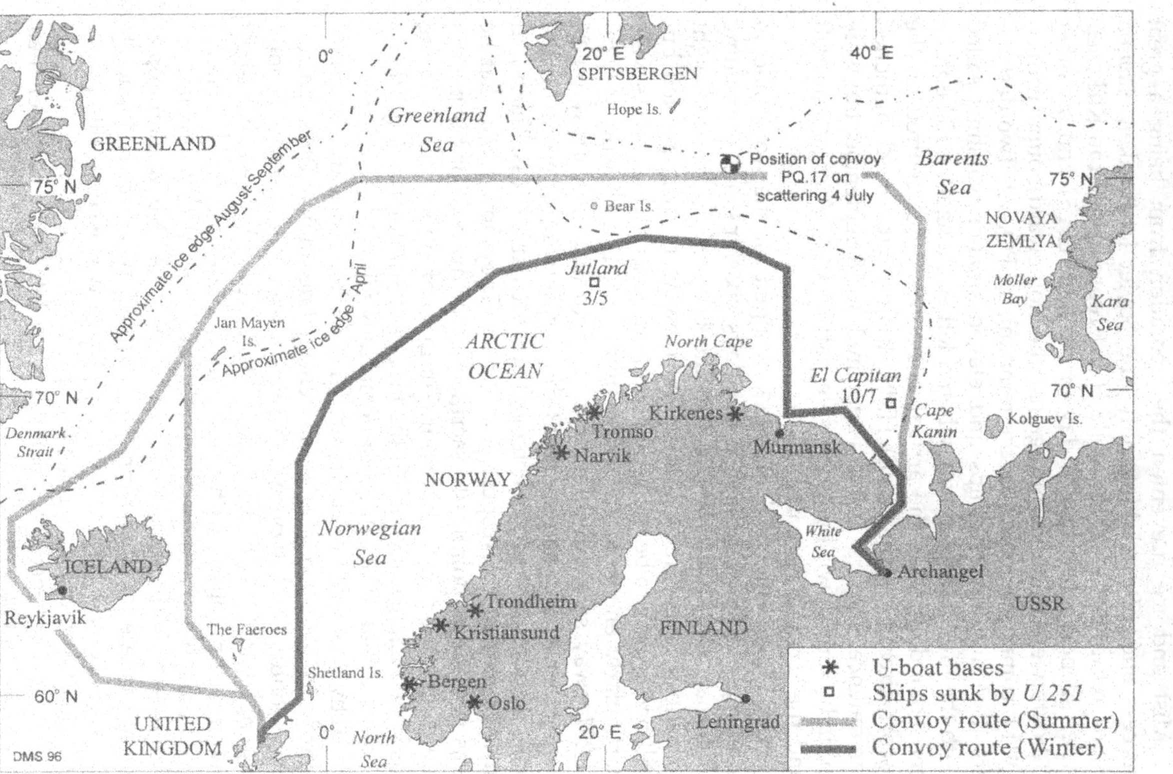

The Northern Theatre 1942

Mist and ice prevented the operation from being a great success and, after sinking only one Soviet ice-breaker, *Admiral Scheer* returned to Narvik while *U 251* reprovisioned in Kirkenes. After spending less than a day in harbour, *U 251* and six other U-boats were ordered out against the homeward-bound convoy QP.14, composed mainly of the remnants of PQ.17.[17] Two destroyers, two anti-aircraft ships and eleven smaller warships sailed with the fifteen-ship convoy when it left Archangel on 13 September. Four days later, the arrival of another force centred on the escort aircraft carrier (CVE) HMS *Avenger* further strengthened the defence. The first U-boats appeared on 18 September but were initially kept down by aggressive patrols from *Avenger's* aircraft and the screening escorts.

On 20 September QP.14's luck changed for the worse and in a running battle over the next two days, six ships and a patrolling Catalina flying boat were lost to the U-boats. Timm fired eight torpedoes but scored no hits. The crew were disappointed but still had reason to be thankful. Counterattacks by the escorts were particularly energetic and only Timm's skill in evasion brought *U 251* away safely. By the time she returned to Norway on 26 September, *U 251* had spent 43 days underway, a record for the boat. Though he had not achieved spectacular success, Timm had at least earned the respect of his crew. They now knew that he was not one to pointlessly sacrifice either his boat or his men in the pursuit of personal honour. Timm's apparent ability to bring his boat back undamaged in the face of continuous enemy attacks became a matter of almost superstitious faith.

Activity slowed over the winter months, and it was not until March 1943 that *U 251* recommenced operations. Three patrols were conducted, but no Allied ships were encountered and nothing noteworthy achieved. Two of the patrols were cut short because of problems with the starboard diesel engine. The engine problems worsened until finally in June, *U 251* returned to Trondheim with a cracked mounting plate. Norwegian repair facilities were poor, so Timm was ordered to sail his boat back to Germany. *U 251* returned to Königsberg two weeks later, where she was taken out of service for an extended refit. Timm and his crew were removed, but they were not left long to ponder their next assignment.[18]

3 Die U-Boot-Fahrer

I think the officers could be divided into three types—the young ex-Hitler [Youth] super-Nazi type, aged 22–23, who were perfectly bloody; the slightly older, and presumably pre-war Kriegsmarine, *who were very 'correct' and not very forthcoming; and the ex-reservist type, perhaps from the Merchant Navy, who had knocked about the world a bit. These latter were quite pleasant.*

—senior British officer in charge of disarming U-boats 1945

Though the Arctic convoys and operations in the northern theatre were important to both sides, the decisive convoy battles were still being fought on the transatlantic supply lines. In fact, Dönitz had argued several times with Hitler over the latter's insistence on keeping a U-boat flotilla in Norway.[1] Dönitz saw Allied shipping as 'one single, great entity', so did not care where an enemy ship was sunk.[2] At the same time he did not wish to see his forces either unnecessarily dispersed or operating where conditions were unfavourable.

Until the first months of 1943, the advantage in the Atlantic battle had seesawed as each side introduced or responded to the other's measures. Allied monthly shipping losses to U-boats peaked in March 1943 at just under 500 000 GRT.[3] But to achieve this result Dönitz, now promoted *Großadmiral*, and since January 1943 CinC of the *Kriegsmarine*, had required 193 operational U-boats, with an average of some 116 at sea each day.[4] The prey was becoming more difficult to catch and the average tonnage sunk per boat per day at sea, upon which Dönitz relied to chart his progress, was declining rapidly, from more than 400 GRT in the first half of 1942 to 127 GRT by April 1943.[5] The tide of battle was turning inexorably against the *U-Bootswaffe*.

Stronger and more effective anti-submarine defences were now maintained around the Atlantic convoys throughout their voyage. In particular, long-range, radar-fitted aircraft provided coverage across the entire breadth of the North Atlantic. The U-boats could no longer use their superior surface speed to gather around a convoy for a pack attack. To be caught on the surface meant assured destruction. The U-boat commanders found themselves lagging hopelessly behind the convoys with little chance of success. Those that did attack were confronted by experienced escorts, fully prepared to hunt a submerged U-boat to exhaustion. A crisis arose for the German effort. In May 1943 38 U-boats were lost, more than 32 per cent of those at sea. With only 42 ships sunk in return, such losses were insufferable. On 24 May Dönitz temporarily withdrew his U-boats from the North Atlantic.

With the increasing losses of boats and their crews, the experienced complement of *U 251* could not be left idle. In August 1943, after a short period of leave, Timm and most of his men were ordered to Bremen and the building yards of Deschimag AG Weser. There they stood by during the final assembly and fitting out of the Type IXD2 *U 862*. In the next few weeks they would learn everything about the inner workings of their new boat as she was put together. She was slightly faster, more than twice the displacement and 26m longer than their old boat, but if the men from *U 251* were expecting more comfortable accommodation they were to be disappointed. The extra space was taken up by larger storage areas and the additional crew members carried.

At 1000 on 7 October, *U 862* was commissioned in a short formal ceremony. Later the crew, still in their full dress uniforms, gathered around the U-boat's tower for an official photograph. Several had been decorated and proudly wore the Iron Cross; many more had been awarded the *U-Bootkriegsabzeichen* (submarine war badge) for having proven themselves on two or more patrols against the enemy. The men of *U 862* no doubt took great pride in their brand new U-boat, but it is unlikely they appreciated how the nature of the U-boat war was changing. *U 862* was assigned at once to the 4th U-boat Training Flotilla operating in the Baltic.

In addition to *Kapitänleutnant* Timm, *U 862* carried six other officers. Second in command and first watch officer (IWO) was *Oberleutnant zur See* Günther Reiffenstuhl.[6] The son of an Austrian doctor, he had joined the *Kriegsmarine* in October 1939 directly

U 862's *entire complement pose for a formal portrait on 7 October 1943, the day of the U-boat's commissioning in Bremen.* (U-boat Archive, Cuxhaven)

from school in Baden. Like Timm, he had first spent time in small ships and it was not until August 1942 that he had commenced training as a U-boat officer. Reiffenstuhl joined *U 251* as IWO in May 1943, just in time for her last northern patrol. Only 22 years old and relatively junior, he was not in an uncommon position. With the increasing shortage of men having even limited sea time, Reiffenstuhl's experience was seen as more than adequate. By 1943 U-boat commanders were often as young as 23, and in the normal course of events Reiffenstuhl could have expected command of his own U-boat within a year.[7] As IWO, Reiffenstuhl was head of the underwater weapons department and also had responsibility for communications.

Oberleutnant zur See Karl 'Kuddel' Steinhauser, 25, was *U 862*'s second watch officer (IIWO). A former officer in the merchant marine, and a member of the naval reserve, Steinhauser had only begun full-time service in April 1940. Starting as a *Matrosengefreiter*, he had risen rapidly through the ranks and had reached *Obersteuermann* when he began U-boat training in May 1942. In July, after successfully completing his basic course, he was promoted to *Leutnant zur See*. Steinhauser had served as IIWO in *U 251* since November 1942. In *U 862* he was also head of the gunnery department and, perhaps not surprisingly, was once described by Günther Reiffenstuhl as having a voice like a foghorn. Interestingly,

(Left) *IWO* Oberleutnant zur See *Günther Reiffenstuhl shows the strain of many weeks at sea.* (Right) *IIWO* Oberleutnant zur See *Karl Steinhauser on watch during the passage through the Polar Sea.* (U-boat Archive, Cuxhaven)

he was the only one of *U 862*'s officers to later admit to being an active member of the Nazi Party.[8]

Sharing the bridge watch-keeping responsibilities with Reiffenstuhl and Steinhauser was the third watch officer (IIIWO), and junior seaman officer, *Leutnant zur See* Walter Spieth. Nick-named 'Gaucho' by his fellow officers, he was one of the few members of the crew not to have served with Timm in *U 251*, and he did not join *U 862* until after her commissioning. Spieth did not survive the war and little is known of his background.

U 862 also carried two engineering officers. The *Leitender Ingenieur* (chief engineer or *LI*) was *Oberleutnant* (*Ing.*) Hugo Seggermann, 29, a native of Bremerhaven and another ex-merchant marine officer. After serving on the America run he had joined the *Kriegsmarine* as a reserve in October 1936 and started at the U-boat school in November 1940. On completion of his training he joined *U 251* and served with Timm throughout the latter's time in command. At sea the commander needed to place absolute faith in his *LI* for everything from the proper functioning of machinery to maintaining correct trim. Even in harbour the busiest officer would normally be the engineer. Timm clearly thought very highly of Seggermann, and later wrote, when recommending him for an award:

> He has served both U-boats [*U 251* and *U 862*] from the time of their commissioning and in the face of the enemy has always shown quite exceptional resourcefulness in action as well as courage and determination and as senior engineering officer has always conducted himself well even in dangerous situations. He is credited with a full share in the U-boat's successes.[9]

Assisting with maintaining *U 862*'s technical readiness was Seggermann's subordinate, *Leutnant* (*Ing.*) Walter Spindler, 23. A mechanical engineer in civilian life, Spindler began his naval career in early 1941 as an engineering sailor in fast torpedo boats. He transferred to U-boats as an *Oberfähnrich* (*Ing.*) in mid-1943 and joined *U 862* in January 1944 direct from the U-boat training flotilla in Gotenhafen.

The final member of the wardroom was the doctor, *Marineoberstabsarzt* Jobst Schäfer, 32, known to everyone onboard as 'Mumps'. He had the longest experience both with the Navy and with U-boats, and was also the only one of *U 862*'s officers to have come from a naval background; his father having served in the Imperial Navy. Entering the *Reichsmarine* in August 1932, Schäfer had undergone the same initial training as his fellow officers, only later moving on to study medicine at Kiel University. After graduation in 1938 he had spent several years in the naval hospital at Kiel. In 1940 he was posted to the U-boat tender *Wihelm Bauer* and later to the requisitioned, ex-Turkish U-boat *UA*. Before joining *U 862* in November 1943, Schäfer had spent two and a half years as medical officer to the 8th U-boat Training Flotilla.[10] As a nominally non-operational member of the crew, the medical officer was often the target of practical jokes, but in an interesting mix of responsibilities, in *U 862* Schäfer doubled as the *Bachstelze* pilot.

In addition to her seven officers, U 862 carried 57 non-commissioned officers and men. The senior sailor on board was *Obersteuermann* Kirchner. The *Obersteuermann* (chief quartermaster or chief helmsman) in a U-boat held a position of particular responsibility. Normally older than the watch officers, he enjoyed an especially close relationship with the commander. Often he was the wise old man aboard, 'injecting common sense into an otherwise ra-ra-ra atmosphere'.[11] In smaller boats the *Obsteuermann* acted as IIIWO, but experience in the Type IXs during the first long-range patrols had shown that key personnel were susceptible to exhaustion. Thus in the big boats there were now three commissioned watch officers and the *Obsteuermann* was relieved from regular watches to allow him to concentrate on his other duties.

These included responsibility for navigation, controlling provisions and lots of paperwork. Kirchner was also an essential member of the command team during an attack, plotting the bearings provided from the periscope or *UZO* and calculating the target's movements.

The remaining crew were broadly divided into 'seaman' and 'technical' ratings, then further split into their specialisations as diesel, electrical and control room engineers, radio operators, torpedo mechanics and seamen. Almost all were aged between 18 and 24 and by 1943 were experienced U-boat men.[12] Having survived longer than many of their compatriots, they were as a group older than the average U-boat crew, which tended to grow younger as the war went on.[13] Most of those who had come from *U 251* had been promoted, and with only a few new additions *U 862* soon became known as the *'Boot der Obergefreiten'*. Many of the men came from the coastal regions of northern Germany, but other parts of the Reich and Austria were also represented.

The political and social attitudes of these young men can never be known for certain. However, they were almost certainly well indoctrinated. Compulsory entry into the Hitler Youth began in 1936 and even the older crew members would have spent the major part of their teenage years exposed to National Socialist values and rhetoric. Erich Topp, an ex–U-boat commander, has written that his men were 'conditioned by their upbringing in a totalitarian state to accept as natural a philosophy of all-out, total war'.[14] A contemporary American intelligence assessment went so far as to say the U-boat men had received 'a moderate amount of training, and a great deal of German propaganda build-up'.[15]

Allied interrogation reports of captured U-boat officers often portray their subjects as 'fanatical', 'ardent' or 'typical Nazis', adding trite descriptions such as 'arrogant', 'unpleasant manners' and 'conceited'. Even an 'amiable and rather broad-minded' officer could still be classified as 'essentially a Nazi'. Captured sailors tended to be grouped together as 'simple-minded' or 'easily confused' and possessing 'below average' or 'low intelligence'.[16] An Admiralty review of the year 1944 managed a little more respect but still took essentially the same line:

> It must be emphasised that the average U-boat rating remains as tough a fighting man as ever . . . the great bulk are simply disciplined ratings who obey all orders without question to the last; off duty, many are reasonable by nature and quite pleasant, but once in uniform they become absolute automatons who carry

> out an order given to them without the slightest consideration of the consequences to themselves, their friends or their country.[17]

Much of this stereotyping had more to do with the prevailing attitudes of the times and the interrogators' own biases and expectations than with any objective assessment. Despite their indoctrination, the majority of the *U-Boot Fahrer* were not politically inclined and even the Admiralty had to admit that at most 10 per cent could be classified as 'Nazi fanatics'. They were neither less intelligent nor more keen on fighting than any other similar group of military men.[18] Though a number undoubtedly believed in what they were fighting for, any attempt to introduce political ideology on board would normally be met with deep resentment, and a somewhat passive attitude to the 'cause' was actually more common.[19] What these men did possess, though, were high principles of comradeship and a fundamental and shared will to survive.

From mid-1941 manpower shortages had resulted in engineering and technical personnel being assigned to U-boats on an 'as required' basis, but most of the crew were still volunteers, if not for the *U-Bootswaffe* then at least for the Navy. In many cases they had no doubt been influenced by the intensive recruiting campaigns, which, unsurprisingly, stressed the glorious myth rather than the stark reality of submarine warfare. The armed services held a privileged position in Hitler's Germany and submariners in particular had a special place in public opinion. According to one ex–U-boat officer, this was nothing to be sneered at: 'We were young, out for adventure, medals, girls and dedicated to doing our duty as professionals.'[20] Higher pay, longer leave, better food and greater opportunity for advancement added further inducements, as did the likely alternative of induction into the infantry and a draft to the eastern front.

Those men who had previously served in *U 251* knew well the risks and severe conditions under which they would have to work. They were probably more cynical than the new crew members, who had either succumbed to the patriotic call of the recruiting posters or simply chosen what seemed to be the lesser evil. Notwithstanding the hardships, the U-boat crews were undoubtedly better off than many, and the shared conditions were thought to weld a crew together into the Shakespearian image of a 'band of brothers'. After 1943 British intelligence reports often highlighted evidence of declining morale among U-boat survivors, but again much of this was wishful thinking. The *U-Bootswaffe* as a whole remained a determined and dedicated force right to the end of the war, and though some had started to have doubts they did not feel they had been defeated and their cohesion and special spirit was never broken.

Whether Heinrich Timm held doubts or misgivings about the new Germany is not known. Political conversations were not part of wardroom etiquette, while bitterness against the leadership would never normally become 'a subject of conversation, even if it existed in the odd officer's or sailor's mind'.[21] Timm nevertheless appears to have held a realistic attitude both to Dönitz and to the party as a whole. He clearly intended to honour his oath of allegiance to the *Führer* and fulfil his duty to the last, but would certainly not let the passing whims of the Nazis influence his musical tastes. The internal loudspeakers of *U 862* often broadcast the recordings of composers banned in the Fatherland.[22] On a more serious level, after the attempted assassination of Hitler in July 1944, Dönitz attempted to demonstrate his Navy's continued loyalty to the regime by ordering the *Deutscher Gruß* or Nazi salute—an outstretched right hand and cry of *'Heil Hitler'*—adopted throughout the fleet. In the cramped confines of *U 862* the order was naturally greeted with a degree of cynicism.[23] Timm and his crew continued to use the traditional naval salute.

No matter what his age, every U-boat commander was the *'Alte'* (Old Man) to his men. Timm was a popular *Alte* and not simply because of his ability to bring his boat back safely from operations. He took time to look after his crew. Like the best U-boat commanders and Dönitz himself, Timm had faith in those who worked under him and made their welfare a priority. He was not averse to bending the rules for their benefit. After the commissioning, for example, there was a strict official ban on travel and leave while the U-boat was working up. Despite this, Timm managed to arrange short errands out of Kiel to obtain spares and equipment parts. A sailor from the relevant locality would be chosen, and if he did his errands quickly, he would manage to fit in a few hours at home.

Timm would also vigorously stand up for his men in disciplinary hearings. On another occasion in Kiel, the newly joined *Bootsmaat* Friedrich Peitel fell asleep on watch, was reported by the base duty officer, and faced a possible court-martial. Timm intervened with the flotilla commander and, by holding a summary hearing, managed to obtain a reduced punishment of fourteen days confinement. As there were no cells on board a U-boat, the punishment was effectively ignored.

It was always clear to Dönitz that inadequately trained crews would lead to greater losses in action. The basic training scheme for new U-boats therefore remained a high priority throughout the war, even at the expense of U-boats allocated to active service. *U 862* spent the period from October 1943 to May 1944 undergoing acceptance trials and, like *U 251* before her, on intensive exercises in the Baltic. Special training flotillas had been established to work the boats up and apply the lessons learnt from actual operations. The program was designed to forge the crew into a single unit and comprehensively test them under 'war conditions'. In these circumstances it was not uncommon for a U-boat to be damaged or occasionally even lost. Exercises in keeping contact and reporting, gaining bearing without disclosing the U-boat's presence, depth-charge attacks, torpedo firings, breakdown drills, interminable diving practices, all continued for days on end until these skills were automatic.

Perhaps the most important routine was for crash-diving: clearing the bridge of watch personnel and securing the hatch before the U-boat's tower dipped below the surface. Speed in accomplishing this task would in future become a matter of life or death. An electric bell gave the alarm. The first man down was the petty officer of the watch, who went to his action station at the forward hydroplanes. He was followed by the port-quarter lookout, who assisted the commander in the conning tower. Next down was the starboard quarter lookout, who manned the after hydroplanes. Last to go below was the watch officer, whose duties included removing the Tunis aerial from its mounting and closing the hatch. He then went to his action station in the control room.

Everyone in the U-boat's complement was a specialist in his field to the almost complete exclusion of other skills:

> Everybody knows exactly what to do in an emergency, without any shouting or panic. That is exactly the moment, when one loses one's fear and is totally occupied with the task at hand. Nobody has to ask, where the fuses are. The one who is responsible for replacing fuses knows where they are and exchanges them in quiet efficiency. He does not wait for the Chief Engineer to tell him when and how to do it. Chaos and panic are the conditions a submariner cannot afford, if he wants to survive. To prevent scenes of this kind, was the prime objective of all our training.[24]

The final tactical exercise run by the *Ausbildungs-Gruppe Front* (Training Group for Operational U-boats or *Agru-Front*) was the most severe test of all and included attacks against a convoy protected by an anti-submarine screen and air escort. Familiarly known in the U-boat service as 'the fifth column', officers from the *Agru-Front* travelled on board during the exercise to introduce their own unexpected emergencies.[25] For *U 862* this last trial ran from 24–26 April and covered a wide sweep of the Baltic.

For those who had not served in *U 251* it was a reassuring feeling to join a crew who were already working as a team. The solidarity provided a certain safety and security, a confidence in their ability to perform as required. This, however, did not always mean that everything went smoothly. Once, one of the new engineers forgot to pull out the bolts from the ventilation valves at the stern when getting the boat ready for sea. When the boat came to dive the bow tanks were flooded, but air could not escape from the stern tanks because the vents could not open. At an angle of 45 degrees, *U 862* plunged into the Baltic, descending 20m every 30 seconds. There was precious little time to recover before the boat reached her maximum diving depth of 100m; much deeper than that and her hull would have been crushed by the water pressure. One of the electrical engineers managed to drag himself back up the deck and remove the bolts, while the water in the forward tanks was blown out again. The boat slowed in her dive and was gradually brought back under control. The guilty party escaped with a lecture from '*Tüte*' Timm.

With the successful completion of the training program, *U 862* was at last declared '*Frontreif*'. In late April she returned to Kiel for fitting and final tests on her *Hohentwiel* radar and was then reallocated to the 12th U-boat Flotilla (operational). The deteriorating war situation meant that there would still be no time for anything other than local leave. On 11 May 1944 Timm made the last entry in his boat's war diary before submitting it to *BdU*. He simply noted, 'Equipping for the frontline has begun.'[26]

4 Group Monsun

It was decided that, as soon as they became operational, all subsequent Type IXD boats should first be sent to the Indian Ocean. Never did any scheme fail so badly as this.

—*Fregattenkapitän* Günther Hessler, chief staff officer to *BdU*

Among Hitler's entourage Dönitz held a specially favoured position, and during the last two years of the war he was the *Führer*'s most trusted confidant. Despite the defeat suffered in the North Atlantic during the 'black May' of 1943, both Dönitz and Hitler agreed that the U-boat war still offered the best chance of delaying the Allied build-up for a European invasion. Of at least equal importance, by threatening their vital sea lanes, the U-boats remained the only practical means of waging an offensive battle directly against Great Britain and the United States. However, with the U-boats now unable to maintain concentrated attacks, it would be necessary to substitute a policy of dispersal—independent U-boats continuing to tie down Allied defences by harassing shipping in remote areas.

Such a course could only be regarded as a diversion rather than the main blow, but Dönitz reasoned that new weapons and equipment were on their way which might yet win the advantage back for the U-boats and allow the campaign to continue at its previous level.[1] Until that time, the strength of the *U-Bootswaffe* had to be conserved and unnecessary losses avoided. At a conference in late May, the *Großadmiral* explained to Hitler that he would send new submarines as they were commissioned to 'more distant areas', where he hoped the planes were not yet fully equipped with radar.[2]

Großadmiral *Karl Dönitz was regarded by his admirers as the greatest of all German war leaders and by his detractors as a man corrupted by an evil system and ultimately responsible for the death of more than 30 000 members of his beloved* U-Bootswaffe. (US National Archives 208-PU-52P-1)

These distant areas included the Caribbean, and the Brazilian and West African coasts. Here the convoy escorts were less numerous, and the escort vessels themselves were regarded by the U-boat crews as inefficient and 'harmless' in comparison to those in the North Atlantic.[3] An area perhaps offering even more opportunities, however, was the Indian Ocean. Not only was this within reach of the newer versions of the Type IX U-boats, but available intelligence also indicated that much of the shipping still proceeded as if in peacetime, with few if any escorts.

Though primarily designed for the North Atlantic, the *Kriegsmarine* was not unfamiliar with the Indian Ocean. The *Admiral Scheer* had made a successful anti-commerce cruise in 1940–41 that had reached as far as the waters north of Madagascar. Several armed merchant cruisers or *Hilfskreuzers* had also been independently roaming the Indian and Pacific Ocean shipping lanes since 1940. These sorties had achieved some early successes, but the ever-increasing strength of Allied maritime power ensured that operations by independent surface ships could not continue indefinitely. After the loss of the battleship *Bismarck* in May 1941, the Germans made no further attempts to use their capital ships as long-range commerce raiders. The *Hilfskreuzers* lasted somewhat longer, but with the sinking of the *Michel* in October 1943, raider operations effectively ended.[4]

The operation of U-boats in the Indian Ocean was likewise not a new concept for the German Navy. Raised at least as early as 1916, the idea was soon shelved owing to the difficulty in maintaining supplies to remote areas and the lack of a suitable operating base—German colonies in the Far East having been captured during the opening phase of the First World War.[5] In 1939 Germany had even fewer immediate concerns with the region. Yet only a week after the Second World War began, Dönitz expressed his desire to go ahead with production of the long-range Type XB mine-laying U-boats, specifically for use outside European waters, and operating as far afield as Singapore.[6] Shortly thereafter Hitler gave his approval to the leasing of U-boat bases in the Pacific from the Japanese, and the *Oberkommando der Kriegsmarine* (Navy High Command or *OKM*) made an official request for information. Possible bases, it was stipulated, 'should be in the neighbourhood of Japan, the Aleutians or in the South Seas, if possible uninhabited and without cable or radio connections, off the main shipping routes, navigationally possible also for battleships, and with sheltered bays for good anchorage'.[7]

The Japanese duly responded, and on 9 January 1940 they held a conference that included the German naval attaché in Tokyo and two representatives from the Imperial Japanese Navy (IJN). Five sites were suggested by the Japanese as being suitable for U-boat bases, including two in the Caroline Islands and one each in the Aleutian, Marshall and Amchitka Islands. For a number of reasons, nothing came of these early initiatives.

To begin with, there were simply not enough of the large, long-range U-boats available, priority having been given to production of the medium-range Type VII. Second, Dönitz did not wish to dilute the impact of his campaign in the North Atlantic while successes were still being achieved and adequate targets were available. Third, so long as the *Hilfskreuzers* were satisfactorily achieving their objectives Dönitz was under no pressure to assist them. Finally, once they had actually entered the war in December 1941—an event which came as a surprise to the Germans—the Japanese showed themselves to be less than supportive of a free-ranging German presence. They were, after all, ultimately seeking to reduce the influence of all the Western powers in East

Asia. They regarded the Indian Ocean as Imperial waters and felt that offensive operations there were primarily a Japanese concern.

Notwithstanding these restrictions, the operation of U-boats in the Indian Ocean was clearly an option for the Germans and they had made some practical preparations. The most significant included voyages by 'Z-ships'; merchant vessels specially converted to supply provisions and munitions to surface raiders and U-boats in operational areas. Cargoes unloaded from these ships, and the few *Hilfskreuzers* in the Far East, provided a small but important resource for later attempts to establish more permanent basing facilities.

Japan had not finally joined with Italy and Germany in the Tripartite Pact until September 1940, and even then she did not do so unconditionally. In particular, she made certain that she still 'retained the freedom to choose the timings and objectives of her war effort'.[8] The arrival in Berlin of a large Japanese commission at the beginning of 1941 led to some exchanges of ideas and a closer alliance, but the two principal Axis partners were never able to develop or implement a common war strategy. Nevertheless, some definition of operational boundaries and spheres of influence was obviously necessary. The first naval agreement, drawn up in December 1941, established the area of German U-boat operations as west of 70°E longitude, effectively restricting the Germans to the waters west of Bombay.[9] Amendments to the document a year later further limited the Germans to the area south of 20°S latitude.[10] Thus, when Dönitz finally agreed to allow the first Type IXC U-boats of Group *Eisbär* (Polar Bear) into the Indian Ocean in October 1942 they operated only between Cape Town and Madagascar.

Dönitz had consented to the despatch of the *Eisbär* Group after receiving agent reports of an accumulation of Allied shipping around the Cape of Good Hope and when the US coast lost its value as an operational area. Between October 1942 and May 1943 Dönitz sent four separate groups of Type IXC U-boats to operate in the area and the first of the new Type IXD2s. Overall these 28 boats claimed at least 116 ships sunk, totalling almost 600 000 GRT. With only three U-boats lost in return it was a considerable success. Indeed the British Prime Minister, Winston Churchill, was by March 1943 asking for explanations, declaring himself 'shocked at the renewed disaster . . . off the Cape'.[11] Supplied with fuel and provisions by U-tankers and later by the two surface tankers *Charlotte Schliemann* and *Brake*, even the shorter range Type IXC boats were able to remain on station for double the standard patrol time.

Coinciding with the increasing German presence around the Cape, the Japanese began to reconsider their earlier attitude. Japanese war strategy had been based on expectations of a relatively short one- or two-year conflict. In these circumstances, they saw the tonnage war fought by Dönitz as less important than securing naval supremacy. However, by the end of 1942 a succession of Japanese defeats and growing American pressure on their defence perimeter pointed to a prolonged war. As *Vizeadmiral* Paul Wenneker, since March 1940 the German naval attaché in Tokyo, was to report back to Berlin, 'The triumphant ecstasy at the beginning of the year has now given way to complete disillusionment.'[12]

Japan's submarine strength was too weak to apply effective pressure on Allied sea communications in all areas of Japanese interest. Strategic cooperation with the Germans, the Japanese reasoned, might be their best chance to delay defeat. In December 1942 the Japanese Naval Staff finally conceded that they were anxious for another Axis naval power to make itself felt in the Indian Ocean and were 'accordingly willing to grant either Italy or Germany a U-boat base, either at Penang, Sabang, or a port in the Andaman Islands, along with the necessary fuel supplies'.[13]

Though the *OKM* staff were suspicious of this sudden change of heart, they nevertheless found it very attractive. With the Mediterranean closed to merchant shipping, the entire Allied logistics effort in support of the North African campaign was passing around the Cape and through the Indian Ocean to the Red Sea and Suez Canal. It was a line of communications 11 500 miles long, at the end of which the British were maintaining a million men. U-boat operations might also offer a real chance of dislocating fuel and war material destined for India, and more importantly Russia.

Of the bases offered, Sabang and the Andaman Islands had no dock facilities or workshops and were immediately rejected as unsuitable. At Penang, however, there were already local workshops for minor repairs and the Japanese said they would provide other vital equipment. For major repairs and docking, they offered the extensive facilities of the nearby Singapore naval base, which they had captured virtually intact from the British in February 1942. After taking these factors into consideration on 28 December, *OKM* asked the Japanese to proceed with technical preparations for basing U-boats at Penang.[14] Three months later *Korvettenkapitän*

Wolfgang Erhardt, former executive officer of the raider *Michel*, became the first commander of the new base.

Dönitz, though, was still in no hurry to make a firm commitment—deploying his U-boats to the Far East could not be lightly undertaken. He continued to feel that the vast distances involved would render such an undertaking 'unprofitable' and was later to write that he had refrained from accepting the Japanese basing offers 'as long as opportunity to sink ships in the Atlantic existed'.[15] Dönitz also wished to ensure that his boats would be fully supported and awaited Japanese assurance that the necessary stocks of fuel, lubricating oil, consumable stores, spare parts and above all suitable provisions would be available.

In January 1943 Hitler became personally involved in the formulation of plans. Wishing to demonstrate solidarity with his most powerful ally, and hoping that the Japanese might yet participate in the war against Russia, he told their ambassador in Berlin:

> if assuming that the war becomes a long one, you should like to concentrate more on submarine warfare, we Germans want to help you as much as we possibly can. You know that it will take about a year to get ready, but if you Japanese want to wage this kind of undersea battle, we Germans are ready to ship you as a gift two new type submarines.[16]

The Japanese accepted the offer, saying they would like to copy the U-boats' design. Dönitz, however, was most reluctant to transfer the boats, believing the Japanese incapable of producing them in any worthwhile numbers. Only at Hitler's insistence did he eventually agree to send one Type IXC U-boat, *U 511*.

Designated *'Marco Polo'*, and under the command of *Kapitänleutnant* Fritz Schneewind, *U 511* left Europe in May 1943. She reached Penang safely on 17 July, having sunk two ships in the Indian Ocean during the passage. *U 511* then went on to Japan, where at a ceremony in Kure she was handed over to the Japanese as a personal gift from Hitler to Emperor Hirohito.[17] Schneewind and his crew returned to Penang, where they added to the nucleus of German base personnel and provided spare crew for following U-boats.

In the meantime Dönitz had finally accepted the need to acquire some practical experience of the Penang base. In April 1943 he agreed that *U 178*, one of the U-boats already heading for the area south of Madagascar, could continue to Penang on completion of her patrol and check the facilities there. Commanded by the experienced and capable *Korvettenkapitän* Wilhelm Dommes, the U-boat entered Penang at the end of August.

These first tentative steps were rapidly overtaken by the crisis of May 1943. Wide-ranging operations in the Indian Ocean now became a much more interesting prospect for Dönitz. The northern Indian Ocean had never before been visited by U-boats, and a sudden hammer blow might well catch the Allies off guard, perhaps even repeating the successes achieved off North America in early 1942. With Penang available as a base the U-boats could continue east after the mission if necessary. After refuelling and rearming they would then be suitably positioned to carry out further offensive operations on the way back to Europe.

Dönitz at the time had six U-boats patrolling southeast of Africa, but these had only about half their torpedoes remaining. The boats would also have arrived in the Arabian Sea during the monsoon season, which, with the prevailing heavy seas and bad visibility, would hamper successful operations. Dönitz instead ordered that an additional force of nine Type IXC and two Type IXD2 U-boats be immediately prepared to sail from Europe. These boats would arrive in the new operational area in late September, in favourable weather and ready to carry out a series of surprise attacks. The eleven U-boats allocated to the new mission were given the collective name of Group *Monsun* (Monsoon) and independently sailed from Norwegian, French and German ports at the end of June and beginning of July 1943.[18] To refuel the group in mid-Atlantic, the U-tanker *U 462* was also ordered out.

Though the new dispersive strategy avoided the dangers attendant on concentrating around a convoy, there still remained two areas in which the U-boats came together, and hence invited an attack. The first was the transit to and from port, particularly in the Bay of Biscay. Unfortunately for the Germans the suspension of U-boat operations against North Atlantic convoys had released a large number of Allied aircraft and surface units from escort duties. In the summer of 1943, during what became known as the 'Biscay Offensive', these forces were used to reinforce and intensify patrols of the restricted area through which the U-boats had to pass. The second area of vulnerability was the mid-Atlantic refuelling rendezvous, on which most cruises to distant areas were still dependent. Only the Type IXD boats had sufficient range to conduct operations in transit and still reach Penang unrefuelled.

Group *Monsun*'s departure coincided with the height of the Biscay Offensive, and its problems reflect the contemporary experience of the entire *U-Bootswaffe*. The first of the operational boats to depart, *U 200*, was sunk by British aircraft south of Iceland on 24 June. Next to sail was *U 847*, which attempted to evade air patrols by sailing through the Denmark Strait, but struck an iceberg and was forced to return to Norway.[19] On 8 July, *U 514* succumbed to a British rocket attack 20 miles off the Spanish coast. During the next four days *U 183* was damaged and *U 506* sunk, both at the hands of the US Army Air Force (USAAF). On 15 July it was *U 509*'s turn, destroyed south of the Azores by aircraft from the CVE USS *Santee*. The U-tanker *U 462* left France on 19 June, but after two attempts to break out of the Biscay blockade she was so badly damaged by bombs that she had to return for repairs. A replacement tanker, *U 487*, was allocated, but before any fuel could be supplied, she was in turn sunk by aircraft from the CVE USS *Core* on 13 July.

The loss of operational boats was serious enough, but the loss of the U-tankers put the entire operation in jeopardy. U-boat command was reluctantly forced to use one of the *Monsun* boats, *U 516*, as an emergency tanker. In late July, after pumping most of her fuel over to *U 532* and *U 533*, *U 516* reversed course for home. The remaining three boats, *U 168*, *U 183* and *U 188*, received fuel from another outward-bound U-boat. Thus, by the end of August, only five of the original *Monsun* boats had survived to round the Cape and enter the Indian Ocean.

The high loss rate was not simply due to a preponderance of Allied maritime air power. In the vast reaches of the Atlantic Ocean the ability of the Allies to time and again find and sink U-boats created great anxiety in the German Naval Command. Treason was suspected, as was a compromise of communications, or a new and undetectable airborne radar. However, repeated investigations failed to find evidence of any definite cause. Security was nonetheless tightened, and Dönitz was repeatedly assured that the complexity of the U-boat's Enigma cipher machine made a break into the communications system impossible. Dönitz himself put Allied successes down to a 'new direction finder' and the use of 'auxiliary aircraft carriers'.[20] In fact, a combination of factors caused the reverses.

The close coordination of human and scientific resources was obviously crucial to Allied success, as was the skill and patience of air crews, the adoption of the new centimetric radar, and an overall material superiority. Nevertheless, it was a highly developed and efficient intelligence system that provided the greatest advantage. The British Naval Intelligence Division at its peak employed some 2000 people and the Operational Intelligence

Centre (OIC) in London became the nerve centre of the whole naval war. The centre of the anti-submarine war was a separate Submarine Tracking Room within the OIC. Information was gathered from many sources, the most important of which was radio or signals intelligence (Sigint). This allowed the development—at no risk—of an accurate portrait of enemy operations from material provided by the enemy himself. The tools of Sigint included traffic analysis and radio direction finding, but of special interest was 'Ultra' intelligence derived from the direct decryption of German communications.[21]

Assisted by a fatal German complacency, the British cryptanalysts at the Government Code and Cipher School in Bletchley Park had since mid-1941 achieved considerable success in breaking into the *Kriegsmarine*'s ciphers. As a result even the Germans' improvements to the Enigma machine in July 1943 only caused a three-week blackout in decryption of 'Triton', the principal U-boat cipher.[22] Though gaps and delays in decryption still frequently occurred, even when incomplete, intelligence appreciations usually provided identification of U-boats, early warning of movements, and tactics to be expected. The supply U-boats were a particular priority. Refuellings at sea by necessity generated considerable signal traffic and, guided by this, a growing number of CVE task groups were successfully deployed on offensive operations.[23]

After reaching the Indian Ocean the five remaining *Monsun* boats rendezvoused with the tanker *Brake* on 11 September, 450 miles south of Mauritius. The refuelling was accomplished without problems, but the original intention of a sudden attack in the northern Indian Ocean was abandoned. Reflecting again the lack of coordination between the Japanese and Germans, the IJN had been operating its submarines in the Arabian Sea since August. The Germans had not been warned of this operation, and they appreciated that Allied defences would now be fully alerted to the submarine threat. With hope of surprise lost, the U-boats were given approval to begin attacks immediately.

Results were mixed and certainly not at the levels expected. *U 533* was sunk by Royal Air Force (RAF) aircraft in the Gulf of Oman without having scored. *U 183*, which operated between British East Africa, the Seychelles and to the south of Bombay, made one attack on an independent ship but two of the three torpedoes fired failed to detonate. *U 168*, operating in the same area, reported six sailing vessels sunk by gunfire and one freighter torpedoed, but was later criticised, together with *U 183*, for failing 'to exploit their opportunities', Dönitz apparently considering that their commanders were 'unequal to the mental and physical strain of the long voyage'.[24] *U 188*, meanwhile, sank one ship, damaged another, and made an unsuccessful attack on a convoy leaving the Gulf of Oman. The last boat, *U 532*, commanded by *Fregattenkapitän* Ottoheinrich Junker, achieved the best results, sinking four ships and damaging one more between the Chagos Archipelago and southern India.

After these efforts the *Monsun* boats made their way to Penang, and all four survivors had reached the new base by mid November. Despite the overall lack of success, the reports sent back to Germany confirmed that opportunities were still far more favourable in the northern Indian Ocean than in the Atlantic. Dönitz therefore made the fateful decision that all subsequent long-range Type IXD2 U-boats should be sent to the Indian Ocean as soon as they became operational. Their commanders were generally selected from those who had already distinguished themselves in the Atlantic, Mediterranean or Northern theatres. No doubt Dönitz felt this experience would increase their chances of success, but the subsequent losses only served to hasten the overall decline in effectiveness of the *U-Bootswaffe*.

The second group of *Monsun* boats left Europe between September and November 1943, running the same gauntlet and suffering as badly as their predecessors. Of the four boats deployed, only one, *Kapitänleutnant* Alfred Eick's *U 510*, survived the outward passage. Eick joined with the boats operating from Penang, so that by February 1944 the Germans had at least five to six boats operating in the Gulf of Aden and between India and Mauritius. This time results were much improved, with *U 188* sinking seven steamships, *U 510* five, and *U 183*, *U 168* and *U 532* two each. Only *U 178* failed to score. The destruction would have been greater had not the boats been plagued by weapons failures. Unfortunately for the U-boats, many of the torpedo batteries had deteriorated after long storage in the hot and humid conditions. Weapons running slow or failing to detonate were to be common occurrences for the *Monsun* boats. Nevertheless, Dönitz regarded the successes achieved as 'gratifying', and sinkings in distant areas made up more than 80 per cent of the total tonnage sunk in the first half of 1944.[25] Unfortunately, torpedo stocks in the Far East were limited, so the boats returning from Penang invariably carried insufficient torpedoes. It was therefore up to the boats from Europe to fully exploit the opportunities for attack, and so,

A Type IXD2 U-boat U 848 *caught on the surface and under attack by Liberators of the USN's VB-107 Squadron southwest of Ascension Island on 5 November 1943. Like many of the* Monsun *U-boats,* U 848 *was never to reach the Indian Ocean having been sunk in this attack. After drifting for four weeks one survivor was eventually rescued by an Allied warship, only to die soon afterwards.* (US National Archives 80-G-208282)

despite the disastrous loss rate, the *U-Kreuzers* continued to be sent east.

U 177 was the first boat to depart in 1944 and was sunk in the mid-Atlantic in February. Another twelve operational U-boats had followed by the beginning of May. Of the five that survived to reach the Far East, two went directly to Jakarta (also known by its Dutch colonial name of Batavia) in the Netherlands East Indies, which had, after Penang and Singapore, been set up as the Germans' third East Asian base in mid-1943 under *Korvettenkapitän* Kandler.

Of the boats lost on passage to East Asia, *U 852*, commanded by 28-year-old *Kapitänleutnant* Heinz-Wilhelm Eck, deserves special mention. *U 852* sailed from Germany on 18 January 1944 with orders to attack shipping between Aden and Bombay. Eck brought *U 852* safely into the Atlantic and on 13 March, off the coast of Liberia, sighted and torpedoed the Greek freighter SS *Peleus*, which broke apart and rapidly sank. The U-boat surfaced and, after a brief interrogation of two survivors, Eck and five of his officers—including the doctor—spent five hours cruising through the wreckage, firing machine guns and throwing hand grenades at survivors on rafts and in the water. According to Eck, he was simply attempting to remove all traces of the sinking so the

U-boat would not later be discovered by searching aircraft. If so, he failed in his objective: after a 35-day ordeal, three men from *Peleus* were eventually rescued.

U 852 sank another steamer off Cape Town in April, but in early May was damaged and forced aground by British air attack off Somaliland. The bombing killed seven of the crew, but the remainder were captured by an armed party from the sloop HMS *Falmouth.*[26] Having themselves suffered under Eck's brutality, the German ratings were almost unanimous in condemnation of their superiors, who were then tried for war crimes after the war.[27] Found guilty, three, including Eck, were executed by a British firing squad, while others received lengthy prison terms. It has since been argued that Eck was following Dönitz's secret instructions, only 'given orally to commanders', to annihilate Allied crews.[28] The case is far from proven, and Eck himself claimed that he had acted on his own initiative, and to the last denied ever receiving direct orders to shoot survivors.[29] Despite Allied propaganda this was the only documented atrocity attributed to the *U-Bootswaffe* during the war.[30]

In early 1944, U-boat operations in the Indian Ocean had been severely hampered by the successive sinkings of the *Charlotte Schliemann* and *Brake.* Sigint had revealed to the British the extent of the refuelling activities being undertaken off the Cape of Good Hope, and they were able to concentrate searches on each of the three different rendezvous areas used by the Germans. The *Charlotte Schliemann* was finally sighted by an aircraft from No. 259 Squadron RAF on the afternoon of 11 February, and sunk by the destroyer HMS *Relentless* just after midnight.

A month later the Germans made another attempt to resupply three of the *Monsun* boats from *Brake* in an isolated position 1000 miles southeast of Mauritius. *U 532, U 188* and *U 168* were on their way home, and to prevent an occurrence similar to the loss of the *Charlotte Schliemann* they undertook a preliminary reconnaissance out to 200 miles from the supply point. Finding no evidence of Allied forces, they made the rendezvous on 11 March.[31] Despite their precautions, the following day an aircraft was sighted and the U-boats crash-dived. The aircraft, a Fairey Swordfish, had come from a hunting force centred on the CVE HMS *Battler.* One of the screening destroyers, HMS *Roebuck,* was soon on the scene and *Brake* was scuttled while under fire. The U-boats were close enough to be shaken by the explosions, but had already used up their torpedoes so could do nothing in response.

The interruption of the resupply operation in an area so remote from air and naval bases clearly suggested something was wrong. *Fregattenkapitän* Junker in *U 532* had been about to fuel from *Charlotte Schliemann* when the tanker was discovered. Now, after, seeing *Brake* go down before he had completely provisioned, he was exasperated, and signalled bluntly to Dönitz, 'Presumably provisionings have been systematically compromised.'[32] *BdU* and the Chief of Naval Communications conducted further investigations into the possibilities of treachery and compromise of codes. Again nothing conclusive was established, and though emergency procedures for modifying Enigma settings were introduced, Allied success was again put down to efficient D/F. However, the loss of the last tanker was real enough. In the short term, it forced the return to Penang of both *U 168*, which had embarked the *Brake* survivors, and *U 532* which carried out an emergency refuelling of *UIT 24*. The longer-term implications of shortened time on patrol and reduced sinking rates were self-evident.[33]

At the beginning of 1944 Dönitz also attempted to relieve the critical torpedo situation in the Far East by sending out two torpedo transport U-boats. These boats, *U 1059* and *U 1062*, were designated Type VIIF, with displacement increased by some 400 tons over earlier Type VIIs so each could carry 39 torpedoes as well as other essential stores. *U 1062* reached Penang in April, but in March *U 1059* had already become yet another victim of Allied aircraft in the Atlantic.[34]

Torpedoes were not the only cargo carried in U-boats. The more general transportation of freight was the final element of German submarine operations in the Far East and, in the final reckoning, probably the most futile. Even before the Japanese entry into the war the Axis partners had made regular attempts to break the blockade imposed by the Allies and exchange raw materials, technical information and intelligence. This venture had initially been undertaken exclusively by merchant vessels, and until mid-1943, 47 voyages had been attempted in both directions, of which 31 had successfully reached their destination.[35] But as in the case of the U-boats, Allied patrols by long-range aircraft and carrier groups began to prove more effective: in the following six months only five voyages were attempted, and only one was successful. With the availability of suitable vessels declining and losses unacceptably high, the Germans decided in January 1944 to discontinue the use of surface vessels and rely exclusively on submarines.

The first dedicated cargo-carrying U-boats had been obtained the previous year from the Italians. In early 1943 the Italian Naval

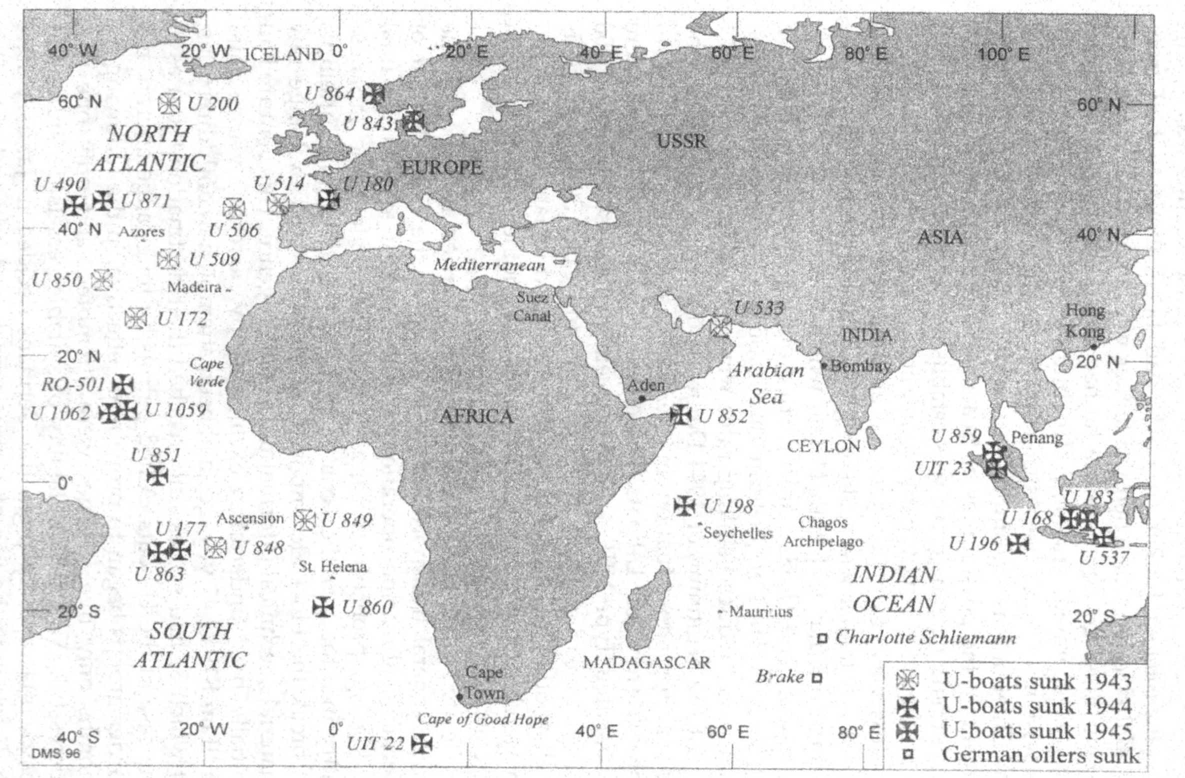

Losses of U-boats allocated to the Far East, 1943–45.

Command sanctioned the use of its few remaining submarines in Bordeaux to transport freight to and from East Asia. Between April and May four were lost in the Atlantic, but by the end of August three had reached Singapore. On Italy's capitulation in September 1943 all the Italian submarines in Singapore and the last two in France were taken over by the Germans, renamed *UIT 21* to *UIT 25*, and given the collective code name *Merkator*. Of the two boats in France, *UIT 21* had so many defects that she never became operational, while *UIT 22* was sunk south of Cape Town on her first voyage out. The boats in Singapore fared little better. *UIT 23* was sunk on 14 February 1944 by the British submarine HMS *Tally Ho*, one day out from Singapore. *UIT 24* attempted passage to Europe in February, but the sinking of *Brake* prevented her refuelling and forced a return to Penang. Both *UIT 24* and *UIT 25* then spent time in Japan undergoing extensive refits. Neither was ready to attempt another trip until August 1944, by which time there were no surface tankers or suitable U-boats available to refuel them. Their sailings were cancelled and the two boats were later used solely for local transport missions within East Asia.

The German need to carry freight to and from the Far East was so great that even operational U-boats were used. After January 1944, all operational boats carried cargo in the keel in place of ballast. The principal cargoes for Japan were mercury and lead, while boats returning to Europe carried tin, wolfram, rubber, molybdenum, opium and quinine. With careful stowing it was possible for the Type IXC or IXD2 to carry about 110–130 tons of bulk cargo in the keel and outside the hull, and another 20–30 tons inside the boat.[36] Also carried were important exchange personnel, plans and examples of electronic equipment, weapons and ammunition, motor parts, precision optical goods and medicines. Nevertheless, the U-boats were fundamentally unsuited to the task and the total cargo carried by this method was much less than the capacity of even one surface blockade-runner.

Back in Kiel, *U 862*'s crew moved out of their boat and into the accommodation ship *Milwaukee* while the final preparations for their voyage took place. Although storing the U-boat took up much time, there were still hundreds of points to be checked or examined on the boat itself. Officially no one yet knew its final destination, but it did not take long for the crew to make an educated guess. Packing cases containing tropical uniforms provided an obvious clue, as did charts of the Far East. *U 862* was already referred to as a *Monsunboot* in the dockyard and town.

Some sixteen tons of foodstuffs came on board—all in tins, or wrapped in waterproof packaging. Hanging overhead were hundreds of sausages. In every compartment, wherever they found a space or corner the provisions would be tucked away. But there was nothing haphazard about the arrangements and everything was stowed according to a detailed plan. The *smutje* or cook needed to be able to reach a selection of items to allow a varied diet. The stores also needed to be distributed evenly so the boat would keep trim while dived, and firmly secured so they could not shift in heavy seas.

Torpedoes and ammunition, fuel and lubricants were all embarked in the final few days. Behind one of the diesels in the engine room there was even a stack of Christmas packages and letters. Originally destined to travel to the Far East in a surface blockade runner, these articles were now almost two years overdue. Fully provisioned for the long voyage, the men of *U 862* felt like moles as they crouched or crawled along the narrow passageways. Now at last their first *Feindfahrt* could begin.

5 Erste Feindfahrt

The U-boat fleet is still of impressive size, nevertheless the U-boats remain the hunted rather than the hunters. They have been attacked from the Arctic to the Indian Ocean, aircraft playing a great part with the surface forces. This pressure will be maintained until all chances of a revival of the U-boat campaign are killed, whatever may be the new devices and methods developed by the enemy.

—Churchill to Roosevelt, proposed monthly report on U-boats, 5 August 1944

Though not recorded, it is possible that Heinrich Timm paid a call on Dönitz in Berlin before he sailed. It was a feature of the *Großadmiral*'s leadership style that, even after he became CinC *Kriegsmarine,* whenever possible he still liked to give his U-boat commanders a personal briefing. As an experienced commander still alive and at sea Timm was in an increasingly uncommon position and no doubt worthy of personal attention.[1] Nevertheless, whether Timm's briefing came directly from Dönitz, from his chief of staff, *Konteradmiral* Eberhardt Godt, or from another member of the small *BdU* organisation, the message would not have been different. Obsessed as he was with the continuance of the U-boat war, Dönitz would not fail to reiterate its vital importance at every opportunity, and knew that his staff would do the same.

During the first few months of 1944 the percentage losses of U-boats at sea had shown a steady increase while the number of operational U-boats had shown an even steeper decline. By May, *BdU* assessed that only 70 per cent of the boats which sailed were returning from their patrols. Successes were becoming rarer and the battle was now almost one of endurance alone. Yet despite these depressing statistics, Dönitz could still see a positive aspect. He did not express dismay at the reports of increasing numbers of Allied aircraft, escort vessels and carrier formations. Instead Dönitz regarded them as firm evidence that his campaign of 'tying down enemy forces' was succeeding. His submarine situation report for 1 June provides a useful summary of his reasoning:

> The present successes and those attainable in the future with the old submarine types do not alone justify the high expenditure in labour, armament and material on submarine warfare at home, and especially the high toll of life in the battle of the Atlantic. Operation and expenditure are nevertheless unavoidable for various reasons.
>
> The submarine war cannot be allowed to cease, since once it has finally succumbed it would not be possible to take it up again. To parry with the enemy is, although a proverb, a tactical, technical, and above all a psychological necessity. The submarine arm has shown itself capable of withstanding the most difficult times. Once again she must carry her self-assertion into battle with new weapons—even in the face of heavy loss, and without having abandoned the cause even temporarily.
>
> It has been established beyond doubt that the enemy has thrown in a total of many thousand aircraft and many hundred escort vessels—from destroyers to trawlers—for the protection of merchant shipping against submarines.[2]

To Dönitz, relinquishing the U-boat war would mean that these well-trained air and sea forces would be brought into battle directly against Germany. Furthermore, large sections of Allied industry could then be turned from the manufacture of anti-submarine equipment to the reinforcement of other areas of operations. Dönitz realised, though, that for the U-boat men themselves, the job of tying down the enemy was especially difficult. Already some of the younger and inexperienced commanders were displaying defensive inclinations, sometimes failing to press home attacks for fear of interception. However, Dönitz remained confident that the thorough training and innate quality of his 'human material' would ensure that morale remained untouched.[3]

What the *Großadmiral* misunderstood or ignored was that by 1944 the vast scale of Allied production rendered the tying up of any forces in anti-submarine warfare largely irrelevant. In any case, Allied technical and scientific superiority had already made the continuation of the U-boat war a senseless sacrifice. Undoubtedly, Dönitz was beholden to Hitler to continue the fight, but the

Großadmiral's unshaken belief in the greater importance of 'fighting spirit' and 'will' could not alter the inevitable result of this last 'defensive phase'. The final year of the U-boat war would essentially be a vain and empty gesture. It was with the added stress of thoughts such as these that Timm must have approached his first war patrol in command of *U 862*.

U 862 sailed from Kiel on 21 May 1944 in convoy with several other U-boats. Her crew were keenly aware of Dönitz's expectations, both of them and of the U-boat war, and there is no evidence to suggest they were not intent on fulfilling their role. The Propaganda Ministry played on the Allies' demand for Germany's unconditional surrender, and ensured that the outcome of defeat was feared more than a last desperate defensive battle. However, there can have been few among Timm's men who held high hopes for their survival. The failure of so many U-boats to return could not be disguised, and though *U 862* would not have to transit the Bay of Biscay, an even larger percentage of boats was now sunk while on passage through the Central Atlantic.

Following in the wake of a minesweeper for protection from air attack and assistance with passage through the defensive minefields, *U 862* threaded her way carefully north along the Danish coast. While still in Danish waters Timm read out the contents of the boat's operation orders to his crew. None were surprised when they heard that Penang would be their ultimate destination, or that on the way they would be carrying out offensive operations in the Indian Ocean. However, because of the importance of the cargo, only low-risk targets were authorised to be taken; moreover, to avoid unnecessarily provoking air patrols, *U 862* was prohibited from making any attacks in the North Atlantic.[4]

After successfully negotiating the Kattegat minefields the escort departed, and *U 862* was left alone to perform her diving and trimming trials then continue the passage to Kristiansand in southern Norway. Here the boat refuelled and picked up another escort for the short run to Flekkefjord. From Flekkefjord Timm headed out alone into the North Sea, planning to take his boat around the Faeroe Islands and to the south of Iceland.

The bank between Iceland and the Faeroes was known to the Germans as the '*Rosengarten*'. It was about 30 miles in radius and, despite the threat of mining, had become the normal way-point for U-boats entering the Atlantic. U-boat commanders had generally found that mines posed no particular obstacle to their passing through the bank either surfaced or submerged, but liability to aircraft attack was another matter. From this point of view passage of the *Rosengarten* was 'regarded as the worst part of a U-boat's first patrol'.[5]

Though *U 862* was proceeding submerged for most of the time—surfacing only briefly at night to ventilate and charge the batteries—it was very soon clear to Timm that he could not go on. *BdU* had recently warned of increased levels of enemy air patrol, but Timm found it even more intense than expected. Patrols by RAF Coastal Command's 18 Group rose from an average of ten a day to 25 or 30 a day in the second half of May.[6] Detections of aircraft radar were constant. Within seconds of the alarm the bridge watch would tumble through the conning tower hatch and down into the control room, always expecting to be followed by the blast of a depth charge. Timm believed that he had already been sighted repeatedly; it was only a matter of time before the boat was caught out and attacked.

The long hours of daylight in these latitudes provided no assistance with concealment, and though the *Schnorchel* lessened the risks, it did not remove them. The device produced its own small wake and reduced submerged speed, while the noise of the diesels both deafened the U-boat's hydrophones and made the craft more vulnerable to listening enemies. The *Schnorchel* was in any case still a novelty, and the U-boat commanders, not entirely certain of its capabilities, were reluctant to entrust their safety to it alone. On 26 May, just two days after leaving Norway, Timm signalled U-boat Command and, after citing the strength of air defence and the valuable equipment on board, received permission to turn back towards Bergen.[7]

Having failed in his first attempt to break out, Timm sought authorisation to continue farther north, as far as the latitude of Narvik. Here he planned to alter course to the westward to pass north of Jan Mayen Island and into the North Atlantic by way of the Denmark Strait. By first proceeding through the inner leads of the Norwegian coast and then hugging the edge of the Greenland ice pack, Timm hoped to confuse radar searches and avoid contact with air patrols. The passage would be considerably longer than planned and the ice would be a danger, but *BdU* approved the proposal, noting, 'The Commander has had much experience of navigation in Northern Waters so that damage to the boat by ice is unlikely.'[8]

After spending the night at Bergen, *U 862* sailed on 27 May and began a series of short hops up the Norwegian coast. Everything seemed clear until shortly after leaving Trondheim, when a

U 862 *gathers sternway as her commander reverses away from the wharf at Trondheim on 28 May 1944. The connection for the* Schnorchel *tube is visible on the starboard side of the tower and the difference in size between the attack and search periscopes can also be clearly seen. By unwritten tradition the U-boat's commander was the only officer permitted to wear a white cap cover.* (U-boat Archive, Cuxhaven)

bridge lookout noticed a trail of oil spreading out astern. An oil slick was extremely dangerous for a U-boat. Besides the loss of fuel it also provided an easy track for a hunter to follow, no matter whether the U-boat was surfaced or dived. There was no choice but to declare an emergency and take the boat into Narvik for repairs. In the meantime Timm closed up additional lookouts to assist in the search for aircraft.

However risky, it was not an oil slick but German signal traffic that allowed *U 862*'s progress to be followed by the Admiralty's Submarine Tracking Room. The U-boat made its first appearance in the special intelligence summary for the week ending 29 May.[9] There she was listed as arriving at Trondheim, and noted as the eighth *U-Kreuzer* currently scheduled to operate in the Indian Ocean. From this moment onwards the Allies would monitor *U 862*'s voyage more closely, and often with greater accuracy, than the Germans themselves.

U 862 finally secured alongside the accommodation ship *Stella-Polaris* at Narvik early on 30 May.[10] A split was found in one of the fuel bunkers—not large, but hazardous enough—and the U-boat moved to a floating dock to have the leak repaired. By now *U 862* had travelled more than 2000 miles while constantly under threat, and the strain on the crew was beginning to tell. No one objected to the opportunity to spend a few extra days in harbour. Workmen finished repairs just before midnight on 2 June and the U-boat immediately moved out of the dock and alongside the stores ship *Ostmark*. After completing her final top-up with fuel and provisions, *U 862* put to sea and within ten hours had again reached the open sea.

Still travelling submerged for the most part, Timm tried to recover lost time. During the few hours on the surface he pushed *U 862* to the limit. The U-boat was soon alone and racing at high speed through the Norwegian Sea, but there was nothing remotely appealing in her passage. The wind freshened. Waves built up and began to break over the low tower structure. The bridge watch, now consisting of four lookouts and the watch officer, were fully clothed in heavy leather suits and oilskins. They ducked and cursed whenever the sea crashed over them. The clothing was the best protection the U-boat arm could provide, but still offered little relief from the drenching, icy water, which unfailingly managed to penetrate every crevice. At the end of a watch the sodden leather suits would be removed and taken into the engine room to dry. By the time they were needed again, they were as stiff as boards, and covered with a salt crust.

If those on the bridge suffered badly from the wet and cold, the conditions for those left below were not much better. The air inside the hull soon became damp and stale. The stench produced by unwashed, sweaty human bodies, oil fuel, and rotting vegetables permeated everywhere and everything. The crew simply ignored the dirt and liberally splashed on cologne to neutralise the odour. The bulkheads dripped with moisture and beneath the grime men's skins became pale and drawn. As only those on watch were allowed on the bridge, access to fresh air became an incalculable luxury. During periods on the surface, only one man at a time was permitted into the conning tower below the bridge, and this was also the only place smoking was sanctioned. Sometimes the queue stretched to the galley.

The unending cycle of watchkeeping dulled the senses, while the perpetual noise and activity along the main passageway prevented rest. Even in the bow and stern compartments there could be no peace, for the electric torpedoes had to be regularly withdrawn from the tubes for examination and maintenance. And behind this clockwork routine lay the ever-present danger. The sound of explosions and the swift inrush of freezing water might well be the first and only indications of an attack. It was a stressful existence, lubricated by continuous cups of strong coffee, and the U-boat men had to adapt both physically and mentally.

In the damp atmosphere the fresh provisions rapidly became mouldy. Often only the centre of an item could be consumed. Not surprisingly, the abilities of the cook were particularly important in maintaining morale and *U 862* was at least well served in this respect. Despite the basic conditions the cook provided an attractive and varied diet and the crew had few complaints. Goulash, corned beef with onions, sausage salad, sausage in vinegar, and oil and onions were all popular items on the menu. One of the few consolations on board was that as the stocks of food in the passageway and messes were gradually reduced the conditions in the compartments became marginally better. Soon the men would be walking upright again.

As the boundary marking the limit of the Greenland ice pack drew closer the stormy wind relaxed, though it remained bitterly cold. Timm sailed as close to the ice as he dared, then on 6 June altered course to follow the ice edge round to the south. While the focus of world attention centred on the Allied invasion of France, *U 862* quietly zig-zagged through snow, mist and icefloes on her way to the Denmark Strait. In this deceptively stark and peaceful seascape, hundreds of seals and birds were the only other signs of life.

For three days *U 862* made her way along the edge of the Greenland ice pack, repeating in many ways the successful breakout of *Bismarck* and *Prinz Eugen* into the Atlantic just three years before. Nevertheless, *Bismarck* had been run down and sunk a few days later, and the conditions now were even more difficult. Declared British minefields stretched out northwest from Iceland, and at this time of year the width of navigable water in the Strait was still only 30–40 miles. Iceland was also a vital base for aircraft supporting Atlantic convoys. Naturally the waters surrounding the island were heavily patrolled and the Tunis equipment repeatedly detected aircraft radar. Though no attacks had yet developed, Timm must have appreciated how slim were his chances of continuing unscathed.

Then the fog came. Like a shroud it enveloped the U-boat. Visibility reduced to barely 100m and in the thickest patches, not more than 5–6m. These were the conditions Timm had been hoping for, as even with radar, aircraft would have little chance of finding him. The *Bachstelze* was assembled and prepared for flight. Once airborne the machine was put out just far enough to provide a view above the misty sea. After confirming that all was clear Timm gave the command to Reiffenstuhl to proceed, and in the dense mist *U 862* broke through between Greenland and Iceland into the North Atlantic.

Having made his decision Timm, hands clasped behind his back, went for a stroll on the upper deck. The forward part of the deck was the longest clear space onboard—exactly 50 steps from the tower to the bow and back again. This was Timm's only real chance to be alone with his thoughts. In 1944 the stress on a U-boat commander was extreme and could rapidly wear down any man. Over the next twelve months Timm would make the stroll as often as he could and his ruminations would become the topic of much speculation by the crew.

Now the men of *U 862* prepared to face the increased dangers of the north and central Atlantic. It was here that Allied defences were normally strongest and here where most of their compatriots had been dying. Notwithstanding the movement of many aircraft and escorts from the Atlantic to the Channel to support the D-Day operation, there could be no doubt that the U-boat hunters would still be on the offensive.[11] Timm ordered time on the surface reduced still further, sufficient only to change the air. With growing confidence in its capabilities, they used the *Schnorchel* whenever possible.

Though operating independently, *U 862* was not completely cut off from world news. Dönitz tried to ensure that his men were kept informed of important events at home. The German Armed Forces Report over Radio *Norddeich* provided the vital link. Even heavy censorship by the Nazi propaganda machine could not hide the significance of the Normandy landings. The war was clearly in a critical phase, bombings of the homeland were increasing, and the realisation that they were heading away from their loved ones played heavily on the crew's conscience. However, not all the news was bad. On 9 June *Obersteuermann* Kirchner was informed of the birth of his daughter, while a few days later the U-boat received reports of the launch of the first V2 rockets against England. If the Propaganda Ministry could be believed, Germany's secret weapons might still turn back the tide.

U 862, for her part, attempted to maintain radio silence. Respect for the sophisticated network of Allied D/F stations had been thoroughly drummed into all U-boat commanders. Not surprisingly, requests from *BdU* for weather reports were not welcomed and any transmissions made were as brief as possible and invariably followed by a major course alteration.

For the first few days in the North Atlantic the weather continued to assist *U 862*'s passage. Visibility remained bad, the sea rough, and no breaks appeared in the heavy cloud cover. Nevertheless, as the boat moved farther south conditions slowly began to improve. Though they were still surfacing only at night, the dress for those on the bridge became lighter. Unfortunately for the U-boat the onset of better weather also brought increased danger from the air. Nerves remained taut and lookouts strained to sight the slightest movement above the horizon.

On 17 June *U 862* reached the main transatlantic convoy routes. With the massive and ongoing logistic requirement in support of the European invasion there was no shortage of shipping. That night the *GHG* detected the first sound contacts. Timm ordered the U-boat to surface but he could see nothing. A few hours later the radar displayed seven echoes, but reception was poor and in accordance with his orders Timm took no action.

During the day there were further sound contacts and, perhaps unwisely, Timm let his curiosity get the better of him. The periscope sweep revealed nothing on the surface, but also failed to detect a patrolling escort aircraft. No sooner had the periscope come down than several explosions occurred close by. Timm ordered his crew to action stations and took the boat deep for safety. Several more detonations were heard, but they were not getting closer. The aircraft did not persevere, perhaps happy to ensure the U-boat was being kept down and away from the convoy. They may also have had other more urgent business to attend to, for that evening *U 862* intercepted a radio message from another U-boat reporting three ships torpedoed. By 23 June *U 862* had reached the warmer waters of the Gulf Stream. Though she was moving away from the principal sea routes, the danger from aircraft remained.

Only when clear of the Azores could Timm relax slightly. Before long it was possible to ventilate the boat more frequently during the night and for the bridge watch to enjoy a few minutes of early morning sunshine before diving. For those who normally remained below there would also be some relief from the noise and damp. From 27 June Timm allowed one additional man out on the bridge while the boat was on the surface—the first opportunity for most to get fresh air since leaving Narvik. The next night he felt confident enough to order bedding shaken out and briefly aired. Additional amenities appeared in the setting up of a toilet hanging over the *Wintergarten*, and a saltwater shower on the upper deck. If the boat passed through a suitable rain squall it was not uncommon for the bridge watch to unclothe and bring out the soap. However, the passage into the tropics soon overshadowed these small comforts. Before long the temperature had climbed to 30°C in the boat, and over 40° in the diesel compartment. The U-boats were not airconditioned and fans provided only limited relief. Internal humidity hovered between 85–90 per cent and sleep became increasingly difficult.

On 5 July Timm received news of his promotion to *Korvettenkapitän*. Though alcohol was not generally consumed at sea, exceptions were made on special occasions. To celebrate their commander's promotion a bottle of specially cooled champagne was found for the officers. The remainder of the crew each had a small glass of watered-down *Schnapps*. A week later *U 862* was approaching the main central Atlantic shipping lanes and Timm reinstated a full upper-deck lookout.

Shortly before dawn on 12 July the bridge watch sighted the first Allied ship of the voyage. Ahead to port, they could just make out a large tanker, alone and on a converging course. As the range closed it became clear that the ship was unloaded, but Timm estimated it was at least 10 000 GRT and, from its track, probably going from Freetown to the Caribbean. Without any form of escort the vessel would make a perfect target. As it would shortly be light, *U 862* dived to periscope depth. Timm decided to be cautious. For a time the U-boat remained submerged, though the men listened on the distress frequency to determine if she had been sighted. Nothing was heard. U-boat commanders were taught that 'surprise was a condition of success' and Timm wished to retain it until the last moment.[12]

Confident at last that they would be left undisturbed, Timm ordered his crew to begin their attack procedure. When the tanker was out of sight *U 862* surfaced and proceeded at full speed, following the plume of smoke from the vessel's funnel and paralleling her course. For the remainder of the day Timm tracked his target, using the radar whenever necessary. On the surface a U-boat usually had the advantage in speed over a merchant vessel. Her commander would try to manoeuvre into a suitable attack position ahead of the target; attempting all the while to remain just out of sight below the horizon. As night fell *U 862* altered course to bring the tanker into view again. Too late, Timm realised that his intended victim was also running at high speed. *U 862* had been gaining ground much too slowly. Moreover, for

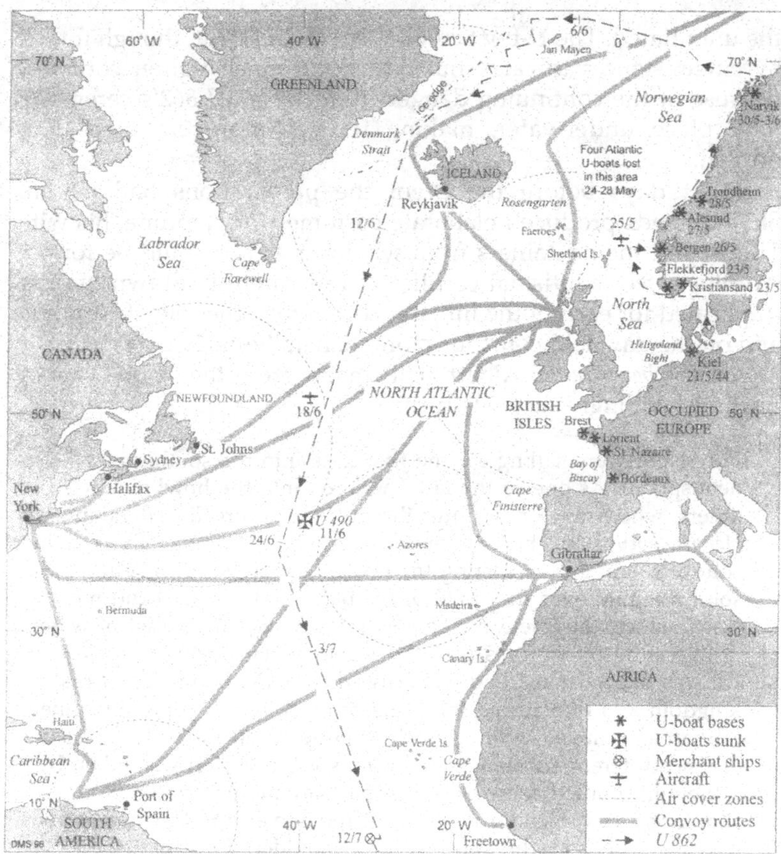

The North Atlantic, May–July 1944

half a day the U-boat had been heading away from her planned track, consuming precious fuel at an extravagant rate. To continue the chase would only further deplete her limited reserves. Timm made the difficult decision to turn back. The tanker would have been a fine prize, and its loss was a great disappointment to the crew. Nevertheless, the attempted attack had at least sharpened reactions after many days of inactivity.

Further diversion was offered the following day by a ceremony held to celebrate the crossing of the Equator. For most of the crew it was the first time they had left the northern hemisphere. The ritual initiation, or baptism, of these first-timers is a tradition common to all those who travel the world's oceans. Ceremonies seemingly vary only in the degree of humiliation inflicted upon the uninitiated. The U-boat crews were no different, though forced by circumstances to carry out the rite in much tighter confines. Because of the continuing danger from the air *U 862*'s ceremony took place underwater, making it even more cramped than normal.

Eight days before the event the preparations had begun. Skilled hands produced elaborate costumes for Neptune, his wife Thetis, and their retainers from whatever scraps could be found. An illustrated 'baptismal certificate' was carefully drawn up and duplicated for each of the initiates. Timm took the role of Neptune and on the day held court for more than an hour. Twenty-year-old *Maschinenobergefreiten* Albert Schirrmann, from the small town of Bochum, willingly took his turn:

> Fifty-eight were sailing for the first time into the southern hemisphere. As one of the last I was led into the howling circle of others, whom were now, after the procedure, already attendants of *Herrn Neptune* and behaved accordingly. I went ominously into the control room. For a greeting the end of a rope whacked into me, a solid flogging over the small of the back, and so that I did not lose balance, they held me against my stomach with a jet of water at five atmospheric pressures. Then the Sea God himself spoke. He was happy, that I had just crossed over the boundary of his kingdom and offered me this welcoming drink: diesel and engine oil, lovingly mixed, with a pinch of pepper and salt, a little castor oil and different substances from the spice chest. (I) was taken by a thought, pour this brew unseen past my mouth and over my shoulder, I did this and poured out the goblet into the face of an attendant who was looking over my shoulder. I was punished with ten blows with the end of a rope. Then I was funnelled through a trough between an enthusiastically howling band of sea-nymphs with powerful snapping jaws.[13]

On completion of the formal part of the ceremony the initiates received a glass of 'real liquor', and Timm went on to enthral his audience with tales of his previous voyages and his own 'baptism'.

The passage south continued uninterrupted for another six days. The Allied air base at Ascension Island—Timm's main cause for concern in the South Atlantic—was now left gradually behind. By 19 July Timm judged that he was sufficiently far away to allow *U 862* to remain surfaced throughout most of the day. Though a routine practice dive was still done at dawn, the change was welcomed by all. The simple matters of breathing and sleeping suddenly became much easier. A few days later Timm received a signal from *BdU* ordering him to proceed to the vicinity of Cape Town. There he was to operate with *U 861*, commanded by his classmate *Korvettenkapitän* Jürgen Oesten.[14] However, Timm was to receive another opportunity to score before reaching the area.

The morning of Tuesday 24 July brought the men of *U 862* into contact with their second steamship. The order allowing the watch on the bridge a final cigarette before diving had just been given when the port lookout shouted out, 'Smoke cloud in sight!' In seconds Timm appeared on the bridge and took a look through his glasses. Satisfied with the report's accuracy, he ordered the boat to action stations. Once again everyone closed up at their assigned positions. Timm ordered the course altered towards the smoke and the engines increased to full power. Soon the top of the target's masts became visible. It was almost certainly another freighter, alone and unprotected.

The *UZO* was manned by IWO Reiffenstuhl and kept trained on the target. A constant readout of bearings was passed down to the control room. There *Obersteuermann* Kirchner plotted the reports and calculated the ship's course, speed and range. Timm adjusted *U 862*'s movements to parallel the freighter's. For the remainder of the day the U-boat stalked the steamship, maintaining a position just out of sight.

By 1700 Timm had his boat in a textbook position ahead of the freighter. After a last check to ensure that the target's course and speed were unaltered and that there were no unwelcome aircraft above, *U 862* dived to periscope depth. In the conning tower above the control room, Timm and Reiffenstuhl took turns at watching the situation on the surface, maintaining the target in the attack periscope's cross-hairs. After ordering small corrections in course and speed, Timm gave the command to prepare Tubes 1 and 2 for a fan shot using two T-5 acoustic torpedoes. *Bootsmaat* Kurt Delfs, at the fire-control computer, entered the target's speed, range, length and inclination, and the torpedo speed and running depth. The torpedoes needed to lead the target, and relay motors transmitted the calculated departure angle to the tubes and automatically adjusted the torpedo settings after each alteration of the cross-hairs. A green check light lit up on the deflection calculator to indicate completion of all adjustments. With *Torpedoobermaat* Heinz Pfeifer's report that both torpedo tube doors were open and the tubes flooded, all was in readiness.

At 1748, with his eyes still glued to the periscope, Timm ordered the torpedoes fired. There was a slight shock as the first torpedo left the tube and a momentary increase in pressure as compressed air vented into the boat. Hugo Seggermann counter-trimmed the boat forward to make up for the sudden loss of one and a half tons of torpedo. Seconds later, a time switch automatically discharged the second torpedo. The T-5 had an adjustable arming run and when it reached the selected range the acoustic homing mechanism became active. In the control room everyone looked at the stopwatch. *Funkmaat* Kurt Möller passed a report from the hydrophone operator that the torpedo noise was becoming softer as the range opened, and that the freighter's propeller revolutions were steady.

The expected torpedo run time was over. Timm was still at the periscope and for a few moments nothing happened. Then came a disastrous message from Möller, 'Torpedo noise becoming louder!' Immediately Timm ordered depth increased to 40m, both engines stopped, and absolute quiet in the boat. With a noise resembling a circular saw, one of the torpedoes roared back over the U-boat. Three times it passed over as it continued to trace a wide circular path in search of a target. Finally, its power exhausted, the errant weapon exploded. On board *U 862* the shock of their narrow escape was evident in the ashen faces of the crew.[15]

Both weapons had missed, but despite the explosions the steamship remained oblivious to her danger and her speed remained steady. Timm determined to continue the attack. He brought *U 862* back to periscope depth and, after an all-round look, ordered her to surface. Again the diesels were brought to full power ahead. It took an hour before the target was regained and preparations for the attack recommenced. *U 862* approached from the east and stayed on the surface. This time there were no mistakes. At 0200 they fired a fan of three torpedoes, scoring at least two hits. Explosions were seen below the target's bridge and another behind the mast. Within ten minutes the freighter had sunk.

U 862's first success had been the US registered SS *Robin Goodfellow,* built in 1920. Loaded with ore and general cargo, the 6885 GRT vessel had been on a voyage from Cape Town to Brazil. *Robin Goodfellow*'s radio room managed to get off an SOS before the ship went down, but it was of little use to the men on board.[16] All 41 of the merchant crew and 19 Naval Armed Guard members were lost in their ship's final plunge. By the time *U 862* approached the scene there was nothing living left on the surface. Only crates and broken pieces of timber marked the site, while the smell of diesel oil hung in the air. The U-boat crew felt little inclination to express sympathy for their victims. They had been at sea for more than two months, constantly hunted and with no quarter expected. Now they had struck back and felt the elation that only success could bring. In high spirits, members of the off-duty watch crouched over the first victory pennant to be painted up on this voyage.

For the time being it would remain the only pennant. After this last high-speed chase, fuel conservation became even more important. The prevailing wind and sea, coming from directly ahead, did not help their progress. The U-boat continued into ever-worsening weather, her bow alternately pounding into the swell or racing skyward. Soon they were in the teeth of a gale and the bridge watch had long since fastened themselves to the hand rails with heavy leather belts. The restraints were uncomfortable but necessary—there had been stories from other boats of an entire watch lost overboard and not missed until their reliefs arrived to replace them. By 3 August *U 862* had reached the southernmost point of her journey. Writing that night in his journal, Reiffenstuhl vividly described the conditions:

> The heavy seas look enormous in the light of the full moon. Clear white light illuminates the foaming crests and rolling swell along the boat's hull! . . . The sea now comes from directly astern and sometimes rolls over the boat. When this happens the boat goes so deeply into the sea, that the front of the bridge hits it full on. It is good for once to become completely wet, that is what all sailors must learn, however, I frankly concede that I could gladly renounce this one time and rather lie in a warm bunk than to stand for two and a half hours on an unprotected bridge with filled boots and an icy wind. Incredible hunger in this cold.[17]

The seas were less than ideal for an attack on shipping, while the full moon made a surprise attack by aircraft that much easier. In the event, help from an unexpected quarter saved *U 862* from remaining off the Cape. *Oberleutnant zur See* Burkhard Heusinger von Waldegg, commander of *U 198*, had recently made a short report from the northern entrance of the Mozambique Channel, and as the *BdU* war diary recorded, 'Boat considers traffic situation in this area definitely auspicious. *U 861* and *U 862* therefore received orders not to remain in Cape Town area, but to proceed to the Gulf of Aden. Operations about . . . Mozambique Channel according to the traffic situation.'[18]

Continuing round the Cape and then keeping some 280 miles off the east coast of Africa, *U 862* made her way towards her new operations area. Progress was slow and uncomfortable and one night Reiffenstuhl dismally noted that 'these heavy seas have despatched our last china plate from the temporal world'.[19] Timm continued to worry about the deteriorating situation in Europe and his boat's fuel consumption. They had lost considerable ground and there would be no chance to refuel before Penang. He sat for hours pondering the charts, contemplating potential courses of action. In what had already become a common means of conserving fuel, Timm ordered one engine shut down and a change to a simultaneous combination of diesel and electric propulsion.[20]

In the meantime, Allied knowledge of *U 862*'s passage was being updated regularly. The British intelligence and cryptanalytical organisation at Colombo, known as the Far Eastern Combined Bureau (FECB), plotted the U-boat 'off the Cape' on 6 August.[21] On 10 August the CinC South Atlantic, Vice Admiral W.E.C. Tait—whose trade protection responsibilities extended around the Cape as far as Lourenço Marques in Mozambique—predicted that U-boat activity in the Mozambique Channel would soon necessitate the reintroduction of East African coastal convoys.[22] Tait added that his available air and surface strength was inadequate for maintaining an efficient escort, and requested that his forces be augmented by groups borrowed from the adjoining East Indies Station commanded by Admiral Sir James Somerville, CinC of the British Eastern Fleet. Unfortunately *U 198*'s depredations had already focused Somerville's attention much farther north. After von Waldegg's sinking of SS *Empire City* on 5 August, Somerville had given blunt orders to his primary hunter-killer group to 'operate as required to hunt U-boat'.[23]

On 10 August, the day of Tait's request for assistance, a carrier aircraft sighted and attacked *U 198* west of the Seychelles. Somerville signalled back to CinC South Atlantic, regretting 'that at present not possible to loan groups', and adding that, in view of the sighting, 'threat in Mozambique Channel area is unlikely to develop for about ten days'.[24] Von Waldegg had unwittingly provided Timm with vital breathing space.

It had taken longer than planned, but by 12 August 1944 *U 862* was positioned in the southern part of the Mozambique Channel, midway between Madagascar and Africa, ready, waiting, and if not completely unexpected, at least unlikely to be disturbed.

6 Paukenschlag

The Indian Ocean is quite large as oceans go; in fact it is 2½ times the size of the North Atlantic. It is studded with coral isles, sharks and photogenic native sailing craft. The weather is simple, you can either see 40 miles or you can't see your wing tips. Into this modest area emerge at regular intervals small wavelets of about five U-boats which immediately split up unsociably into individual units, and proceed to patrol the focal points for our shipping.

—*Coastal Command Review,* October 1944

After Germany's declaration of war against the United States on 11 December 1941, Karl Dönitz implemented plans to send a force of long-range U-boats to the east coast of North America. Dönitz hoped to strike hard and quickly, before the Americans had time to place their shipping on a wartime footing. He had originally intended to have twelve boats available, but restrictions imposed by the higher naval staff and delays in repairs reduced this number considerably. Eventually only five Type IXB and IXC U-boats began the offensive in January 1942, under the code name Operation *Paukenschlag* (Drumbeat). The results were nevertheless impressive. In the first two weeks of the campaign the U-boats sank 25 ships totalling 200 000 GRT. In the six months it took for the US to introduce effective anti-submarine measures, 360 ships of 2 250 000 GRT would be lost. For the Allies it was a major disaster. Within the *U-Bootswaffe,* however, the period became known as the second 'happy time' of the Battle of the Atlantic. More than two years later the '*Paukenschlag*' seemed a fond but very distant memory. The word itself, though, lived on in U-boat jargon as a synonym for success.

Sunday 13 August 1944 dawned as a perfect day in the Mozambique Channel—cloudless, still, not yet too hot. For those in *U 862* the calm was a welcome relief from the buffeting they had so recently received. Nevertheless, the lookouts needed to be particularly alert. The mirror-smooth sea could be deceiving, and every real or imagined smudge on the horizon required careful examination. Daylight also brought increased danger from the air, so at sunrise Timm ordered the boat down to 50m. The crew moved into their usual patrol routine. Those on watch went about their duties, monitoring gauges, adjusting and repairing equipment where necessary. Those off-watch tried to get some sleep before the increasingly stifling atmosphere prevented all such thoughts of rest. As always, an all-round listening watch began on the *GHG*. The boat was soon quiet, and the hydrophones provided the only contact with the outside world.

Not until mid-afternoon did an event intrude to disturb the mood. *Oberfunkmeister* Richard Baumgärtel, on watch in the listening room, gave the short report directly to Timm, 'Sound bearing!' The U-boat went immediately to action stations. After a quick periscope check, Timm brought *U 862* to the surface, and at full power proceeded in the direction indicated by the *GHG*.

Within a minute they sighted the tell-tale plume of smoke. After confirming that the new target was on its own, they began the now-familiar attack process. The near-perfect visibility continued to act in the U-boat's favour and for three hours—she stalked the steamship on a parallel course, just keeping the top of the target's mast visible.

Those onboard the British freighter SS *Radbury* (3614 GRT) must have been well aware of the danger. They had sailed from Lourenço Marques only three days before on charter to the Ministry of War Transport, carrying a 5000-ton cargo of coal to Mombassa.[1] Possible U-boat activity would have formed a significant portion of their pre-departure intelligence briefing. Nevertheless, given Admiral Somerville's benign threat assessment and both his and Vice Admiral Tait's claims that they had insufficient forces for a heavy escort program, it was not surprising that anti-submarine measures showed some significant gaps. Though traffic between South Africa and India, the Persian Gulf, and Aden was being routed outside Madagascar for safety, independent shipping between East African ports was for most practical purposes being left to fend for itself.

Built in 1910, *Radbury* was an old ship. She was also slow, but to provide some measure of protection the Master ordered his

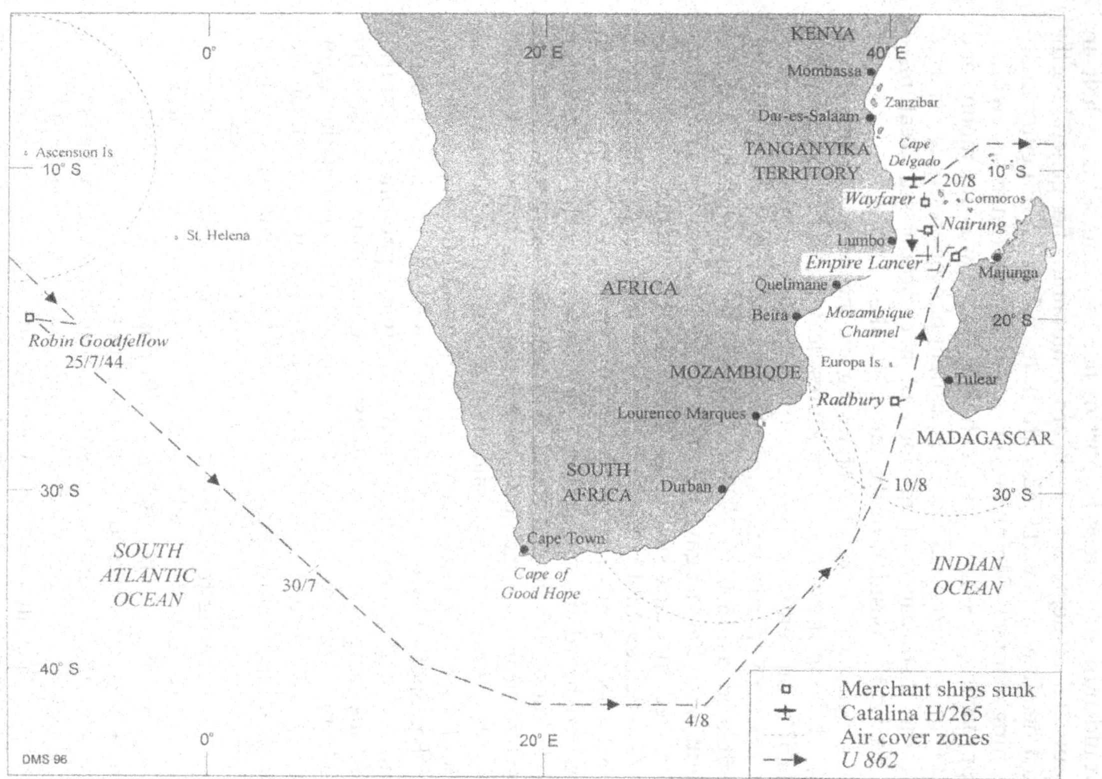

South Atlantic and Mozambique Channel, July–August 1944

vessel to steer a zig-zag course. Unfortunately, these alterations had lapsed into an unvarying routine. Every half hour the ship would turn 30 degrees to port of her base course, then half an hour later, 30 degrees to starboard, maintaining her general north-east heading at 7kts. *U 862*'s attack team had no difficulty maintaining contact. Timm began to close the range as twilight approached. Soon it was pitch-dark, there was no moon, and *Radbury* showed no lights. Only a slight phosphorescence—caused by the disturbance of millions of microscopic sea creatures—betrayed the position of the target's wake.

When the U-boat was attacking on the surface, Reiffenstuhl directed the fire control procedures, leaving Timm to command *U 862*'s movements. The complete darkness made the final manoeuvres particularly difficult. At a range that could only be estimated as 1500 to 3000m, Reiffenstuhl believed he had the solution and at last gave the order to fire. A fan of three torpedoes departed in quick succession from the bow tubes. None detonated. Reiffenstuhl cursed his aim, but it is possible that not all the torpedoes missed. At about this time those below deck in *Radbury* heard an unusual noise. It sounded to some as if the ship had struck a submerged object. A greaser nervously remarked that he had heard similar noises just before being torpedoed in the Mediterranean. He later said that he was sure a submarine was about. *Radbury*'s Master, however, took no additional precautions.[2]

For another two hours *U 862* followed the steamship, maintaining station some 5000m away. The silvery phosphorescent trail became brighter, and Reiffenstuhl could now also see the *Radbury*'s bow wave clearly illuminated. It was a fascinating sight, but created further risks for the U-boat. An alert watch on the target might in turn spot the evidence of *U 862*'s presence. Finally Timm moved in to attack from the freighter's starboard beam, this time closing the range to 1100m. Reiffenstuhl fired a narrow fan of two torpedoes, which crossed the short distance at 30kts. The men on the U-boat's bridge did not have to wait long to see the results. Both torpedoes appeared to hit in the forward part of the ship. For an instant the scene lit up, but *Radbury* herself had disappeared, enveloped in a gigantic black explosive cloud.

When the air cleared of coal dust and smoke, the steamship could just be made out listing badly to starboard, with the bow well down in the water. For a few minutes the ship hung on as tons of water flooded through her torn and twisted bulkheads. Then the stern rose high in the air and *Radbury* slid down and disappeared.

The freighter had only two lifeboats. One was damaged by the initial explosion and for those of the crew not already killed or knocked senseless, there was time to only half lower the remaining boat. As *Radbury* sank, the craft floated free. It was bottom up, but a few men managed to right it. Those in the boat set about picking up the other survivors. In all, 42 of the 55-man crew eventually reached the relative safety of this one lifeboat. Of the Master there was no sign.

Timm remained on the surface and ordered *U 862*'s signal projector swept over the scene. A few magnesium distress flares were burning, providing an additional eerie lighting that revealed a few struggling survivors and large amounts of floating wreckage. Using the signal projector, the U-boat directed some of those still swimming towards better refuge—a small humanitarian gesture in stark contrast to the hunting instincts that had so recently prevailed. Timm then manoeuvred *U 862* over to the lifeboat and demanded in English the name of the ship and cargo. The survivors, probably too shocked too care, passively provided the information, in return asking for cigarettes and the direction of the nearest coast. For most in the U-boat this had been their first time in close personal contact with their enemy. In his journal Reiffenstuhl later contemplated the survivors' quiet acceptance. Had it been, he wondered, because they had been torpedoed before, or because they had good prospects for being rescued? This was the limit of his concern. U-boats were not provisioned to provide aid to their victims, and by now Dönitz had specifically forbidden the offering of any assistance. Not wishing to remain in the area any longer than necessary, Timm ordered *U 862* to depart from the scene at high speed. The U-boat's crew had misheard the freighter's name and, unable to positively identify *Radbury* in the U-boat's recognition books, Timm estimated her size as 5500 GRT, which figure was duly painted on a second victory pennant.

For the *Radbury* survivors, their trial was just beginning. Seconds after the torpedoes hit, one of *Radbury*'s radio officers managed to get away a distress signal. *U 862* picked up the message, but not the British authorities. The ship was not reported overdue at Kilindi until 20 August, and her fate did not become known for over two months. Three days after the sinking, 39 survivors landed on Europa Island, three having died in the boat. Europa is a small island at the southern end of the Mozambique Channel. In 1944 it was uninhabited, but there were several goats and some hens and under the direction of the chief engineer the survivors built an evaporator to provide drinking water.[3] After a month, hopes of rescue were fading, and four of the survivors decided they would prefer to take their chances at sea in another attempt to reach the mainland. On 28 September they left the island on a raft made from hatch covers and the lifeboat's air tanks. It was to be a fatal error. Those who remained on the island had to wait until 26 October before a RAF Catalina flew over and spotted a distress flare, but two days later these survivors were picked up by the corvette HMS *Linaria*. Nothing more was heard of the raft until 14 November, when one of the party, chief cook Sing Kiang Yung, drifted ashore unconscious and almost dead, near Quelimane in Mozambique. His three companions had already perished from lack of water.

U 862 had meanwhile moved farther north into the Mozambique Channel. The weather remained calm and the routine of submerging at dawn and surfacing at sunset continued. The night after the sinking, Timm ordered some of the upper deck torpedoes moved from their compartments and into the boat. By the shaded light of torches, the seamen opened the forward hatch and erected a steel mast. Then each torpedo was manhandled out of its stowage and by means of block and tackle carefully lowered into position. It was back-breaking work, with the added danger that the U-boat was virtually unmanoeuvrable and easy prey if discovered.

U 862 continued north. For the next two days the passage was quiet. Nothing more was seen or heard and the clear tropical skies ensured accurate navigation. Over the loudspeakers the radio room played pieces by Wagner and Beethoven, Timm's favourite composers. Occasionally a more popular tune would slip onto the playlist and interrupt the serious music, but Timm let these incidents pass without comment.

A constant supply of open sandwiches and coffee passed from the galley to those on watch. The cook even created a new delicacy, and jellied pig's head in vinegar and oil, trimmed with onion rings, appeared on the menu. However, with temperatures inside the hull soaring to 50°C, appetites were minimal and quenching an ever-present thirst became the primary desire.

On the morning of 16 August, *Funkgefreiter* Werner Busch, nicknamed *'alter Specht'* (Old Woodpecker), closed up for the submerged listening watch. Shortly before 0900 he announced that he had detected the engine noise of another steamship. Again *U 862* surfaced and stalked the vessel until nightfall. The ship was the 7037 GRT SS *Empire Lancer*, like *Radbury* on charter to the

SS Empire Lancer *at anchor. In 1939 the Ministry of Shipping adopted a standard naming system and all merchant ships built in Britain to government account were thereafter given the prefix 'Empire'.* Empire Lancer *was a Y4 type standard cargo steamship launched in August 1942 and completed three months later. Of her complement of 71 crew and 8 naval gunners, 37 crew and 5 gunners were lost in* U 862*'s attack.* (National Maritime Museum, London P22352)

Ministry of War Transport. She was only two years old and sailing independently from Durban to Majunga in Madagascar carrying 2000 tons of copper and 1000 tons of military and general stores.[4]

Again it was a completely dark night. A heavy swell was running, but this did not upset the U-boat's approach. *Empire Lancer* was on a steady course, steaming at her maximum speed of 11kts. Timm completed his manoeuvres and set Reiffenstuhl up for an attack from the starboard side of the steamship. Just before 2000, *U 862* fired a fan of two torpedoes from the forward tubes. The first torpedo hit *Empire Lancer* in the engine room, immediately disabling the ship. The second torpedo hit in No. 2 hold. It exploded directly under the wheelhouse and, according to the senior survivor, chief engineer Wilkieson, probably killed the Master and all the deck officers.

From Timm's perspective *Empire Lancer* had stopped but did not appear to be immediately sinking. To ensure the kill he ordered the U-boat around for another attack. This time Reiffenstuhl fired a single torpedo from the stern tubes. The weapon hit in hold No. 5 and detonated the ammunition in the freighter's cargo. The explosion tore off the entire stern. With the sudden inrush of water the bow rose sharply and *Empire Lancer* sank within a minute.

The aftermath of the sinking presented a now well-known scene to the Germans. A few oil-covered men struggled to find safety amid the floating wreckage that was all that remained of their ship. Those of the U-boat's crew that could be spared came up on deck to survey the results of their attack. Many calls for help were heard, but they had to be ignored, though again Timm ordered the signal projector to deliberately sweep back and forth across the area. The survivors noted this action, but whether it helped any of them to reach safety is not recorded in their accounts.

Recovering his senses after the initial torpedo hit, chief engineer Wilkieson had found himself in the water on the port side of his ship. He was soon holding on to the side of a waterlogged lifeboat, and well placed to witness the subsequent events. Wilkieson noticed how large, fast and easily manoeuvred the submarine appeared to be. It eventually came right up alongside his lifeboat. He watched the submarine's crew smoking on the upper deck. To Wilkieson they looked like large individuals and most certainly German. From the tower Timm asked in English the name of the ship and its cargo. Someone by the lifeboat answered, '*Empire Lancer,*' and the chief engineer quickly added, 'No cargo.' Timm then regretfully told the survivors he could do nothing to help and sheered off. The reply from the British was poignant in its simplicity and, as Reiffenstuhl noted in his journal, 'These shipwrecked Englishmen have a remarkable attitude. One can only imagine what it is like to be floating in a small lifeboat in the Indian Ocean, having paid for this horrible war at sea with the loss of your ship, and yet still be of the opinion, "It's all right"!.'[5]

Such melancholy reflections, however, did nothing to dampen the enthusiasm onboard the U-boat. *Empire Lancer* was a fine prize. She was a big ship and despite Wilkieson's comments, obviously loaded. Timm credited himself with 8000 GRT for the sinking. Since *Empire Lancer* had been unable to broadcast a distress message, he felt safe to return to the vicinity of Juan de Nova Island and await the next target. As Reiffenstuhl commented, 'Besides, the cat does not leave the mouse.'[6]

Wilkieson's lifeboat had been narrowly missed by the U-boat as she headed off at high speed. For the next twelve hours the chief engineer stood in the submerged boat with 29 other survivors. Only after daylight did they find it possible to bale out the lifeboat and make it serviceable. A further seven crew were picked up from among the wreckage. There was no sign of any of the other lifeboats, or the four rafts that were aboard. Uncertain of his position and fearing that if he headed east he might miss Madagascar, Wilkieson instead headed west. The lifeboat reached the coast of Mozambique, about 60 miles from Lumbo, on 25 August. The survivors eventually met two natives who assisted them in reaching the Portuguese authorities.

On the morning of 18 August, *Funkgefreiter* Busch was once more on the hydrophones. At around 0900 he walked into the wardroom and reported to Walter Spieth, '*Herr Leutnant*, I believe I have another one.' Again the harsh ringing of the alarm and flashing light brought the crew to action stations. At periscope depth Timm could already see the plume of smoke. The target was heading towards the U-boat and, as it was already daylight, Timm decided to attempt a quick submerged attack. He missed with an electric torpedo and the ship passed by seemingly unaware. Once clear, Timm ordered *U 862* to the surface and recommenced the slow process of stalking at the limit of visual range.

This freighter was different from the previous two. She altered course irregularly and often, making tracking much more difficult. The U-boat's attack team wondered about the reasons. Had their target received warnings, had they been seen? But the radio room reported nothing on the distress frequency and Timm decided that she was simply being cautious.

As twilight approached the ship continued to zig-zag, making the final approach difficult. It needed all the U-boat crew's skill to maintain contact. Nevertheless, by 1900 they were moving into an attack position. The sea was mirror-smooth, the night pitch-black, but the bright starlight provided ample visibility. *Marineoberstabsarzt* Jobst Schäfer requested permission to come up to the bridge. Timm approved. With slight alterations of course, Timm manoeuvred the boat even closer. At 600m to go, the U-boat was just forward of the target's beam. At 500m, *Bootsmaat* Friedrich Peitel on watch at the rear of the bridge, could barely contain the target in his lens. Reiffenstuhl stood at the *UZO* and reported continuously that the enemy was in the cross-hairs. The torpedo men in the forward compartment reported the torpedoes ready to fire.

Timm then opened the range until the U-boat was at 1000m. At 1940 Reiffenstuhl fired a fan of two torpedoes. Peitel could see nothing in his sector, so he again stole a quick look at the attack. The bubbles left by the torpedoes stirred up the phosphorescence and allowed those watching to clearly follow the twin wakes. It was a nerve-racking period. To Peitel it looked as though they were going to miss astern. He was mistaken. After a 58-second run the first torpedo hit directly under the target's bridge.

There was a tremendous detonation. A yellowish-red wall more than 100m high stretched out before the U-boat. The steamship disintegrated into thousands of fragments. Within moments the hot pressure wave of the explosion hit the U-boat with a resounding crack. *U 862* was shaken throughout her length. Those on the bridge were knocked to the deck and left feeling concussed and disorientated. Those inside the hull were thrown violently against the bulkheads. The U-boat maintained her course, heading directly into the centre of the conflagration. Timm regained his senses only just in time and yelled for both engines to be put full astern.

The freighter's cargo continued to explode, gigantic flames stabbing into the air. Pieces of wreckage up to half-a-metre across flew over the U-boat's bridge and rattled on the casing. Reiffenstuhl lay beside the *UZO* support with another crewman on top of him. He struggled to his feet in time to see a gigantic red mushroom cloud and a heavy rain of explosive fragments and ship parts. It was a good minute before the holocaust subsided, leaving behind only a thick, black smoke cloud.

> The steamship had in one second literally been atomised. We went to the place where the wreckage was and found nothing but a large expanse of small pieces of wood. There was nothing living. Some 1000 metres away we found a demolished life raft, which was empty. In it was a badly dented container of provisions which for inexplicable reasons lay there loose and full, and which we got on board. There were besides a first-aid kit, chocolates, biscuits, milk, energy food and also a torch, everything was in waterproof packages. The items were distributed amongst the crew. Our engineers procured for themselves some copper wire, which was lying there, torn away. Remarkably, the only injury was sustained by the *Oberstabsarzt*, who hit his head when descending through the hatch. Our sailors, who were below deck during the torpedoing of the steamship, believed that we had received our own torpedo hit. *Matrose* Jukubeit thought, as those below were spun and crashed against the bulkheads, that the bridge had been torn away. Most frankly conceded that at that moment they had become as white as cheese.[7]

U 862's fourth victim had been the 5414 GRT ammunition ship SS *Nairung*, on her way from Durban to Bombay via Dar-es-Salaam. There were no survivors from the crew of 91 men, nor was there time for the U-boat to paint up an extra pennant. At

SS Nairung, *at a port in the United Kingdom. She was built in 1942 for the Asiatic Steam Navigation Company.* U 862 *sank her on 18 August 1944 with the loss of all hands.* (National Maritime Museum, London P23536)

about 0600 the following morning, five minutes after diving, '*der alte Specht*' made another report to Timm: 'At 340 degrees engine noise!' Timm replied, 'You are mad!' Whereupon *Funkgefreiter* Busch simply answered, 'Yes, mad!'

Extreme fatigue was affecting everyone's judgment. Neither Timm nor his crew had had sufficient rest for a week. For a few moments they struggled to grasp the implications of the report. It seemed incomprehensible that yet another unescorted steamer was entering their area. Obviously the British remained oblivious to the U-boat's presence.

An hour later the steamship was in sight. Timm endeavoured to make a quick end to the target with a submerged attack. But submerged, the U-boat was at a speed disadvantage, and he was soon forced to give up the attempt. Instead Timm ordered *U 862* to the surface and began the hunt anew. His target this time was the SS *Wayfarer*, of 5068 GRT. She had left Beira in Mozambique on 16 August, and was sailing for Aden and Port Sudan with a load of 3000 tons of copper and 2000 tons of coal.[8] *Wayfarer* was to prove one of the most difficult of *U 862*'s victims, for, like *Nairung*, she was making large and unpredictable alterations in her base course.

Some thirteen hours after first detecting the steamship, *U 862* began her attack. *Wayfarer* had ceased zig-zagging after sunset and was now apparently steaming on a steady northerly course at 10kts. It was dark but clear, with light airs and a smooth sea, perfect conditions for the U-boat. Once in position, Reiffenstuhl fired a fan of two torpedoes. Just as the weapons left their tubes, *Wayfarer* again changed course. The torpedoes passed well ahead of their target and sped on to explode harmlessly at the end of their run. Though they could not be seen, the explosions were not missed by *Wayfarer*, and were described as sounding like depth charges detonating a few miles away. The purser, R. B. Jones, who had been torpedoed before, remarked specifically on their violence. Nevertheless, like his unfortunate compatriot in *Radbury*, the Master, Captain J. Wales decided the incident was not worth raising an alarm over, and *Wayfarer* sailed on regardless.

Timm had meanwhile recommenced his attack. Ninety minutes after the first attempt he had regained position. At 2130 Reiffenstuhl fired again, this time using only a single torpedo. The weapon struck deep on the port side between Nos. 4 and 5 holds. From the U-boat the explosion looked quite small. On board *Wayfarer* there was no flash or smell, and no water was thrown up, but there was no doubting they had been hit. The bosun, Mr A. Apps—who was asleep in his cabin starboard side aft—was awoken by the terrific noise of the blast:

> All lights failed, and when I stepped on to the poop deck, some 40 seconds after the explosion, it was already awash with the ship sinking rapidly by the stern. I promptly jumped over the starboard side into the water, as there was obviously no time for any boats to be lowered. The crew was accommodated aft, under the poop, where many of the men must have been trapped, as the whole of the after end was under water in less than half a minute, so their quarters would be submerged. The ship slid under by the stern without any suction, there was a shower of red sparks from the ventilators and funnel, and within 1½ minutes of the explosion she had completely disappeared.[9]

All the ship's boats were lost in the sinking, and of the 61 men on board only ten managed to find their way to a single raft. These men watched the U-boat first approach an empty raft on which a flare was burning, then move off in the direction of some more of the crew, who were shouting in the water. This second group of men were not among the survivors, but there is no suggestion that *U 862* had any role in their disappearance. Before heading off at 0400 the next morning, the U-boat lay on the surface charging her batteries in full view of the occupied raft. Apps was the senior survivor and at daylight took stock of the situation. There was no sign of any other useful wreckage so he immediately rationed the meagre supplies of food and water they now possessed:

> I allowed 2 oz of water per man each morning, and 2 oz at night, with 2 biscuits and a ladle of pemmican each for breakfast, and 2 pieces of chocolate at night. I set watches, keeping two men on watch for an hour at a time, whilst the rest slept. During daytime we took turns at paddling the raft with the two oars but did not make much progress. We remained stationary with the sea anchor out throughout the 20th and 21st, as there was no wind, but on the 22nd the wind freshened, so I rigged one of the oars as a mast, cut up a sleeping bag for a sail, and set a westerly course, continuing on this course for 6 days. During the afternoon of the 25th we sighted land on our beam. We took down the sail, put out two oars, and pulled towards the beach but made very little progress. We lay to the sea anchor for the night, but the next day, the 26th, the wind was more in our favour so we hoisted the sail and steered for the land.[10]

Progress was slow and not until 30 August did the survivors reach the island they had sighted. It was uninhabited, but fortunately a native fishing dhow arrived two days later. The fishermen took all the survivors back to Lumbo, from where they eventually made their way back to British territory.

On the day he sank *Wayfarer* Timm received an order from *BdU* to proceed to the Gulf of Aden area, where he was given 'free manoeuvre according to traffic encountered'.[11] The men of *U 862* had no quarrels with this. Having achieved their own '*Paukenschläge*' they felt supremely confident. As Reiffenstuhl concluded, 'By ourselves we have frightened everyone away from this area.'[12] It was now only wise to move on.

During August, *U 859* and *U 861* had also achieved successes in the western Indian Ocean. Together with *U 198* and *U 862*, they sank eight British and one American ship and damaged a tanker, the heaviest Allied losses in any theatre for that month.[13] Viewed simply as a loss of shipping tonnage, the U-boat's achievements were unremarkable. However, from Dönitz's perspective the continued campaign could be seen in a rather different light.

Opposing the few *Monsun* U-boats in the Indian Ocean there were now at least 90 Allied escort vessels and five escort carriers.[14] The small escort vessels alone required some 9000 crew and a similar number of maintenance, base and administrative staff.[15] In addition, air cover was being provided by approximately fifteen Air Force squadrons dedicated to reconnaissance and escort duties.[16] Furthermore, though many merchant ships sailed independently, the Admiralty calculated in December 1943 that the Indian Ocean convoy system inflicted a decrease of about 20 per cent (equivalent to about 150 ships) on the available carrying capacity.[17]

The German presence also delivered direct strategic benefits to the Japanese. Allied escort forces in the Indian Ocean were always recognised as inadequate, and as destroyers arrived in the theatre they were invariably used for anti-submarine convoy duty.[18] As a result, through most of 1944—and despite considerable reinforcement—the British Eastern Fleet was immobilised by a lack of destroyers to screen it. Though strongly supported raids were carried out on Japanese-held territory in April (Sabang), May (Surabaya) and July (Sabang), the Eastern Fleet would not be ready to take a more active part in the war at sea until late in the year. But Dönitz was again deluding himself if he believed that tying down Allied forces in this area would make any difference to the war's outcome. Both the British and Americans regarded the Indian Ocean theatre as a holding war, with the Admiralty rating it only third in priority for resources after the Atlantic and Mediterranean theatres. By August, moreover, the success of the Allied breakout from Normandy meant that there were many on both sides who expected the European war to be over before the end of 1944.

Dönitz's distant operations would also continue to exact a high toll on his boats and men. Since mid-1944 a specialised submarine-hunting group had been available to Admiral Somerville for operations in the Indian Ocean. Designated Force 66, it consisted of the CVEs HMS *Begum* and *Shah*, the frigates HMS *Taff*, *Nadder*, *Findhorn*, and *Parrett*, and the Indian sloops HMIS *Godavari* and *Cauvery*. After the attacks by *U 198*, Force 66 received further reinforcement with the addition of HMS *Falmouth*, *Jasmine* and *Genista*, and Catalinas of No. 246 Wing RAF. Placed under the operational control of the Flag Officer East Africa, the group carried out an exhaustive search for the offending U-boat. After the first sighting by a Grumman Avenger aircraft from *Shah* on 10 August the hunt continued in what was later described by the Admiralty *Monthly Anti-Submarine Report* as a 'model anti-U-boat operation'.

The carrier aircraft searched by carrying out a visual sweep of a rectangular area ahead of the CVEs. The result was a swept lane 66 miles wide on either side of the advancing force. At 0700 on 12 August another of *Shah*'s Avengers found and made a brief attack on *U 198* in a position west of the Seychelles and only 53 miles east of *Begum* and *Shah*'s outer screen of escorts. The U-boat dived but, homed in by the aircraft, the four escorts in the extended screen increased to maximum speed and closed the datum. Based on the U-boat's estimated submerged speed of three knots, a slowly expanding circular search area was calculated. By 1022 the first pair of escorts had reached the 'furthest towards' position and carried straight on, sweeping towards the point of diving and through it to the 'furthest-on' position. The second pair of escorts followed 30 minutes later and searched in the same general direction, but keeping clear of the water swept by the first two vessels. Meanwhile, another two escorts from the close screen were detached and ordered to drop some deep depth charges as they approached with the object of 'encouraging the U-boat to proceed eastwards into the net'. The coordinated Asdic sweeps continued back and forth through the search area until 1725, when *Godavari* at last detected and confidently classified the U-boat. The Senior Officer of the escort group then:

> told GODAVARI to hold on to the contact at all costs, and this he most efficiently did, sticking like a leech to the U-boat's tail for fifty-three minutes. In accordance with Group policy, he also restrained his very natural desire, and that of his jubilant Ship's Company, to have a crack at the enemy himself before another Ship was in contact.
>
> By 1800 FINDHORN and PARRETT had closed and both obtained contact almost immediately. I told GODAVARI to take charge of the three ships and to carry on until I arrived, also advising him to use Hedgehog first to avoid causing disturbance in the water and any risk of losing the U-boat before killing him. This he most loyally did, even though it meant depriving his own Ship (which is not so fitted) from a chance of making the attack.
>
> As soon as the stage was set, he ordered FINDHORN to attack and her first Hedgehog pattern scored a bull's eye.
>
> Contact was held after this attack for about five minutes, during which time the detonation of the projectiles was followed by a series of explosions of varying intensity, culminating in a particularly heavy one after which contact faded. Subsequently nothing but wooly non-sub echoes could be obtained by any ship.[19]

The following day a patch of light diesel oil was found and a new search commenced for firm evidence of a kill. 'All escorts were now thoroughly enjoying themselves, nosing about like terriers round a good smell—as it undoubtedly was, being so strong and distinctive that it had been smelt by the Escorts some time before they sighted the patch. I understand even the aircraft crews obtained a few whiffs.' Human remains were the most conclusive and thus sought-after proof of a U-boat's destruction, and several ships reported sighting indeterminate objects resembling 'entrails' floating slightly below the surface. But in the prevailing choppy sea they were soon lost to sight and all attempts, both by boat and swimmer, to recover any trophies proved abortive. It was indeed a model operation, demonstrating both excellent teamwork and the difficulties a U-boat faced once localised. Not stated, but just as clear is that a tendency towards blood lust was not the sole prerogative of the German side.

An RAF summary of general reconnaissance (GR) operations for the period August–October 1944 reflects the Allies' optimism:

> Five German U-boats operated in the Indian Ocean during August, one of which was sunk by aircraft and escort vessels of Force 66 on the 12th. One was indicated by poor D/F bearings to be in the Bay of Bengal, but did not attack shipping. The other three operated off the African coast, one of them moving as far north as the Gulf of Aden.
>
> Six ships totalling 41 986 gross tons were sunk, four off East Africa, one off South Africa and one off Aden. In addition, a tanker was attacked and damaged off South Africa, but eventually reached port. The U-boats operated with extreme caution, and their achievements were almost negligible when compared with the amount of shipping in the Indian Ocean. As sinkings occurred between 1554N and 3058S and the U-boats in this part of the ocean only broke W/T silence on five occasions, the difficulty in locating them is obvious.
>
> GR aircraft failed to make any sightings, but the small success achieved by the enemy is a tribute to the sweeps and patrols which were flown.[20]

At the time this report was written some of the German successes were still unknown, but the final sentence was also not quite correct. On 19 August D/F fixes had twice been obtained on *U 862* in the Mozambique Channel as Timm attempted to pass news of his successes to *BdU*.[21] Force 66 was by this time returning to harbour for fuel and maintenance, but three RAF aircraft operating from Tulear in South Madagascar were recalled by the British to Pamanzi in the Comoro Islands, and this base was further reinforced with four aircraft from Mombassa. A 'stopper patrol' between the Comoros and Cape Delgado on the mainland was commenced immediately and in addition three warships were ordered to the area to carry out an anti-submarine sweep.[22]

These efforts soon brought results. Shortly after dawn on 20 August, Catalina FP 104 'H' of No. 265 Squadron RAF spotted

U 862 on the surface. One of the favourite sayings of the *U-Bootswaffe*, 'He who sights first has won,' was about to be tested.[23] The captain of the aircraft, Flight Lieutenant J.S. Lough RAF, ordered his radio operator to broadcast a 'SSS' submarine warning signal and took his Catalina down into a diving attack.

7 Flieger, Flieger!

No inflexible rule for the attacking of U-boats by aircraft can be laid down. It is stated, however, that a pilot cannot go far wrong if he makes for the sighted U-boat by the shortest route so as to get his release in before the sub has disappeared.

—Allied document, 'Submarines—method of attack by aircraft'

Aboard *U 862*, Günther Reiffenstuhl had the morning watch. Everyone was exhausted; a full week of constant effort lay behind them. The U-boat would be diving shortly and after a long night the four men on the bridge were looking forward to a good sleep at 80m. As the sun rose over the eastern horizon Reiffenstuhl ordered his lookouts to take out their sunglasses. Friedrich Peitel was petty officer of the watch and on this particular morning was responsible for the eastern sector, from right ahead through to the U-boat's starboard beam. He noticed his glasses were dirty and looked down to clean them. On looking up he saw something else. Diving out of the sun straight towards the U-boat was an aircraft. The range was already down to 4000m. For an instant Peitel stumbled over the words before managing to shout out a warning: '*Flieger, Flieger*!' Reiffenstuhl pressed the alarm and within seconds Timm had stormed onto the bridge.

The aircraft had been spotted too late for *U 862* to escape. Timm's orders specified that he should not dive unless a safe depth of 60–80m could be reached before the bombs began to fall.[1] To attempt to dive now would simply allow the aircraft to attack without interference. Timm had no choice but to remain on the surface and fight back.

The 3.7cm and the two twin 20mm automatic cannon were

already manned and ready. Peitel had assumed his station as commander of the 3.7cm weapon. Timm ordered full power. He needed only to alter course 20 degrees to ensure his full *Flak* armament could train on the attacker. Inside the U-boat, everyone was at action stations. They knew their chances were slim: after weeks of exposure to sea water there was a high probability that their weapons would fail at the crucial moment. The 3.7cm cannon in particular had a reputation for frequent disorders. Moreover, if the aircraft wished, it could simply circle them just out of range of their weapons and call for help.

However, there had been little excitement in No. 265 Squadron's war, and its patrols were generally long, hot, uncomfortable and uninteresting. The rare chance of a U-boat kill had evidently convinced Flight Lieutenant Lough that he should not wait for assistance. Probably believing he had surprise on his side, the pilot kept his Catalina diving directly towards *U 862*. At 1000m, the flying boat was down to an altitude of only 100m. Lough was determined not to miss with his stick of 250-pound depth charges. The aircraft was now well within effective range of the U-boat's armament and rapidly filling the ring sights. Peitel requested permission to engage. Timm held his nerve and remained silent. A few seconds later Peitel asked again and Timm ordered, *'Feuer frei!'*

With the aircraft now less than 500m from the U-boat, all three anti-aircraft weapons opened up simultaneously. The Catalina was a lumbering target and it flew straight into the bursts. Fulfilling the fears of many in the boat, after firing only seven rounds the 3.7cm cannon refused to function. The gun nevertheless scored hits on the aircraft. Wreckage could be seen falling away from the wing and the starboard engine began pouring out smoke. The four 20mm cannons, each with a rate of fire of more than 200 rounds per minute, were meanwhile directing a steady stream of shells into the aircraft's nose and cockpit. The Catalina continued to close despite the mortal damage.

Deliberate or not, the aircraft did not change its course. It seemed that the doomed pilot had determined to take the U-boat with him. Forced to shout over the noise of automatic fire, Timm ordered *U 862* into a hard starboard turn. Now proceeding at maximum speed, the U-boat heeled far over to one side. The huge flying boat dragged itself barely 10–15m over the water's surface. The men on the bridge instinctively ducked for cover. Scarcely missing the tower, the aircraft continued on for another 50m before hitting the sea and exploding off *U 862*'s bow. The

Thick smoke rises from the burning wreckage of RAF Catalina H/265 on the morning of 20 August 1944. The blurring of this photograph no doubt has something to do with the mixture of terror and elation so recently experienced by the photographer. (A. Schirrmann)

detonation of the fuel and weapon load sent a fountain of water high into the air. Seconds later the water showered over the U-boat and down through the open hatch into the control room.

For a moment after the blast there was comparative quiet. Then the *Zentraleobermaat*, Fritz Zimmermann, called out in his slow East Prussian manner, 'Comrades, everyone on deck, I think we are sinking.' Recovering from their shock, the crew burst into a spontaneous celebration. For several minutes shouts of joy and vigorous backslapping resounded through the hull. Special congratulations were offered to *Matrosenobergefreiten* Walter Loch, for it was he who had scored the majority of hits on the Catalina's cockpit.

What remained of the aircraft continued to burn and thick, dark smoke clouds billowed up from the crash site. Timm turned *U 862* back to investigate. Some wreckage remained on the surface. Part of a wing with the red, white and blue British roundel was readily identifiable, but there was no trace of Lough or the other twelve members of his crew. A solitary rubber dinghy was floating close by and Reiffenstuhl received Timm's permission to take a closer look. He jumped overboard and swam to the dinghy, retrieving Lough's logbook, a bundle of navigation charts and some clothing.

Having survived one close encounter, Timm had no wish to remain in the vicinity. After recovering Reiffenstuhl, he ordered *U 862* to dive to 100m and head directly east. For two hours they ran submerged at high speed, attempting to put as much distance as possible between themselves and the 'crime scene'. The logbook and charts provided some useful information on the proximity of British air bases, and since Timm could not be certain whether the Catalina had alerted other aircraft before its destruction, he determined to be cautious.

Timm was being eminently sensible. H/265's final 'SSS' message had been picked up by another of the squadron's Catalinas.[2] Though nothing further was heard from Lough's aircraft, his last position could be determined with reasonable accuracy. A combined Navy and Air Force search was immediately initiated, but though it continued for four days no trace of survivors or wreckage was found. As no further sightings or contacts had been obtained on the U-boat, the hunt was gradually moved to the northeast along the enemy's estimated track. By 31 August the Catalinas had flown over 750 operational hours in the search for *U 862*.[3] They again found nothing but their efforts did not go unnoticed by the Germans.

After sunset on 20 August Timm had brought *U 862* back to the surface. The Comoro Islands were ahead, the first land seen by the Germans for almost three months. There was no time to enjoy the novel sensation. Hardly had the U-boat surfaced when the *Wanze* detected an aircraft radar. His equipment was capable of showing only whether an aircraft was near, not its range or exact bearing. Without this information Timm could take no risks, so *U 862* crash-dived and then headed north for a few hours. Just before midnight Timm made another attempt to surface. Again the warning sounded and again the U-boat crash-dived. The succession of alarms continued into the early morning. It was a frustrating and frightening time, made worse by fatigue and stale air.

At last Timm consented to the release of the radar decoys known as *Aphrodite*. These were balloons some 80cm in diameter, each attached to a float and carrying three metal foil streamers. They were designed to reflect radar transmissions, producing false and confusing targets for the aircraft operator. Eventually the search moved on and the alerts ceased.

Aircraft, however, had been only part of the force allocated to the hunt. Just before dawn Timm observed in the distance the three British warships ordered to conduct an Asdic sweep. He kept his boat submerged and pondered his options. The batteries were dangerously low and his men exhausted. In the smooth conditions prevailing even using the *Schnorchel* would be dangerous. Timm had sunk four ships and shot down an aircraft in the space of a week. It was a performance far beyond anyone's hopes. He still had three torpedoes left, but his luck could not be expected to last. The forces arranged against him were simply too strong and he had little capacity for evasion. The British would probably be expecting him to continue towards the Gulf of Aden, so Timm decided it would be safer to alter course now towards Penang.

The crew greeted the decision to cease operations with relief. After a week of unrelenting stress there might now be an opportunity to calm frayed nerves. Within two days *U 862* had cleared the Comoro Islands and was heading directly east across the Indian Ocean. For the first time in weeks the crew could sleep easily and without fear. After another week Timm felt he was far enough from air patrols to allow the boat to remain on the surface during the day.

Timm's assessment of British expectations had been accurate. An Allied special intelligence report at the end of August listed *U 862* as heading for her operations area in the Arabian Sea and not expected to leave for an eastern port until the middle of October.[4] The report also gave the U-boat's estimated position as near the northern entrance to the Mozambique Channel.[5] Force 66 and another anti-U-boat carrier group, Force 65, centred on the CVE *Battler*, were operated against *U 862* until 30 August. But without information to assist localisation, offensive operations seldom achieved success. After finding nothing, the two groups proceeded to an area northeast of Socotra to hunt a further U-boat indicated by D/F in that vicinity.[6] At the time of the report *U 862* was in any case already almost 800 miles east of Madagascar. Timm had successfully escaped from the first net cast by Somerville's forces.

The crew had proved themselves efficient, but recent operations had tested the limits of their endurance. Now *U 862* was once more heading towards the equator and the temperatures and humidity inside the hull rose steadily. Outside, the sky was grey and for the first few days the tropical rain squalls seemed never ending. Feelings of relief at survival inevitably gave way to monotony. Only six days after the Catalina's destruction, Reiffenstuhl noted in his journal 'Boring passage. After the exciting days of the last week this week appears endlessly tedious. Hopefully we will soon have a steamship in sight again.'[7]

However, for the present nothing more was heard, and nothing more was seen. The crew settled down into their regular but artificial existence. For everyone but the *LI*, *Obersteuermann*, and commander, there was an unending 24-hour cycle of watchkeeping, eating and sleeping. With the internal lights permanently burning there was no sharp distinction between night and day and the normal rhythms of life were 'reduced to an even monotony'.[8] A U-boat man spent most of his spare time in his bunk and there could never be enough reading material. For the long-range U-boat crews, boredom was something palpable. It sat grinning and crouching in every corner. According to some, it was even more difficult to get rid of 'than a pack of destroyers'.[9] Morale was ultimately the responsibility of the commander and Timm attempted to add some variety to the routine.

A succession of competitions provided the principal diversion. The most popular games were chess, the ubiquitous card game *Skat*, and *Fang den Hut*, a simple board game played with dice. A cake was produced for the victor and, depending on supplies, perhaps a can of strawberries for second place and a can of plums for third. A ship's newspaper was published containing both '*BdU* News' and local news derived from events onboard. A daily 'coffee hour' was held. Instruction groups were formed, with the officers delivering lectures on subjects in which they were interested. After diving, a concert program would run over the internal loudspeakers, and Timm would provide detailed commentaries on the composers and the music. If someone had a birthday he received a cake and was able to choose his favourite recording. To enhance the sense of passing time, Sunday was set apart as a special day, with a particular concert program, freshly baked cakes or an extra course at dinner.

Still nothing appeared, no ships, not even any birds. The diesels hammered on incessantly and the days dragged by. The simplest things began to grate. The engineers monitored fuel consumption daily. Progress was good but the long ocean swells, blown up by the southeast trade winds, were from the beam. The boat developed a slow, regular roll that made every task a chore.

For days on end the crew could only continue to function by hanging on to fittings or bracing themselves against bulkheads.

Now that they were far from Allied bases, Timm allowed more men on the upper deck to exercise, get some sun, admire the deep blue tropical ocean and breathe the fresh salty air. Shorts and straw hats appeared from lockers. But after months of life in a twilight world, the crew were pale and bloated, their skin easily afflicted. Soon they added the stinging annoyance of sunburn to the discomforts of life below.

By 4 September *U 862* had travelled more than 2000 miles across the Indian Ocean. She was five days from Penang, and Timm found it necessary to warn the German naval base of his approach. The Penang wireless station set a continuous transmitting and receiving watch on the normal U-boat service known as '*Afrika 2*', but direct communication between Penang and the U-boats was forbidden. Instead Penang worked in the same way as U-boats, despatching its messages 'blind' to be picked up by the control station in Berlin and, if intended for another addressee, incorporated into the regular repetition plan.[10]

In his message Timm again reported his successes in the Mozambique Channel, but added further details, including the number of torpedoes used and quantity of fuel remaining. He completed his message with his expected time of arrival at the rendezvous point outside Penang.[11] The rendezvous and entry route had been promulgated before Timm sailed, but *BdU* had found it necessary to broadcast an alteration in July.[12]

The danger of Allied D/F was uppermost in Timm's mind, and he ordered speed increased to maximum. But before U 862 had cleared the transmission area, a piston in one of the diesels jammed, the engine overheated, and the packages and letters imprudently stored in the compartment began to burn. The fire was soon out, but the diesel was now damaged, while much of the mail had either been burned or turned into pulp by the extinguishers. Before repair work on the diesel could begin it would be necessary for the engineers to clear away the mess—no easy task in the confined space and at the temperatures inside the compartment. It was another fourteen hours before *Dieselobermaschinist* Seppl Edelhäuser could report that the diesel was ready again. The delay put Timm well behind schedule for his rendezvous. *U 862* maintained maximum speed to make up for lost time.

The weather offered no assistance. The southeast trade winds had gone and the heavens were again always dark grey, allowing

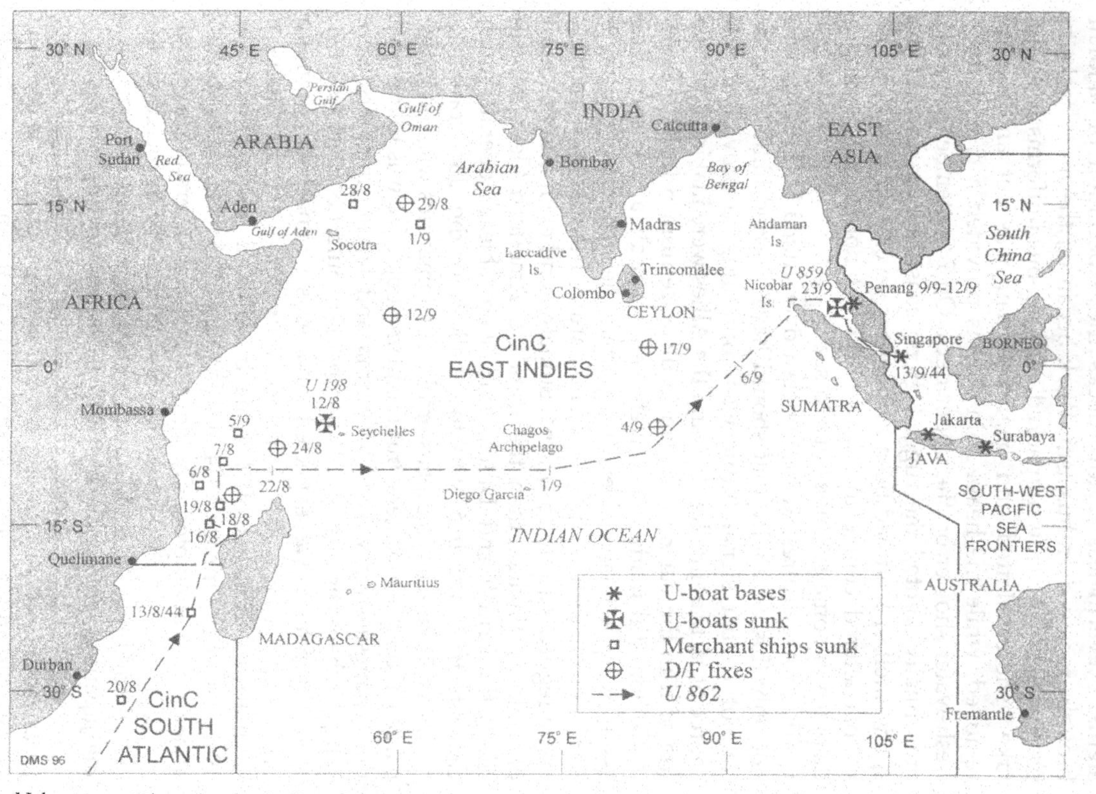

U-boat operations in the Indian Ocean, August–September 1944

the Germans no opportunity to fix their position with sun or star sights. Nevertheless, below decks the expectation of landfall brought renewed enthusiasm. Work began on the many tasks in preparation. The crew unpacked walking-out uniforms ready to take ashore. Matted and begrimed hair was cut and beards removed, while the heavy rain storms provided a chance for a fresh-water shower on the upper deck. On 7 September the look-outs finally sighted the rugged green coast of Sumatra, yet the spicy smell of land had been evident for several days before. The U-boat altered course to follow the coast north, maintaining a distance of some six miles out to sea.

Timm had expressed his concern over Allied D/F, but it was not only this capability that should have worried him.[13] Decryption of U-boat signal traffic was continuing to provide a rich source of tactical intelligence, and the Allies were making effective use of it in the Far East. Penang's distance from British air bases in Ceylon still made it relatively safe from air attack, but other assets were available. Deploying from the major naval base at Trincomalee, British and Dutch submarines from the Eastern Fleet made regular patrols off Burma, Sumatra, and even into the Strait of Malacca. Smaller than the standard American 'fleet' submarines, the British and Dutch boats were able to operate much closer to the coast, in waters too shallow for the USN craft.

Most of the attacks by Eastern Fleet submarines were on junks, barges and small coasters, but the prime objective was to interdict the Japanese supply lines to Burma and larger freighters were sought whenever possible. Warships too could be attacked when their movement was expected, and Axis submarines became a particular priority. The first success was against the Japanese submarine *I-34*, sunk off Penang by HMS *Taurus* in November 1943. Between January 1944 and January 1945 at least another 21 attacks were attempted. Though many attacks were unsuccessful, before *U 862*'s arrival those in the Malacca Strait included: the ex-Italian U-boat *UIT 23*, sunk by HMS *Tally Ho* in February, and the Japanese *I-166*, sunk by HMS *Telemachus* in July.

Timm had been briefed on the danger. The ineffectiveness of Japanese air and surface anti-submarine capabilities was common knowledge and proved a constant source of concern to *BdU*. The German naval staff in Penang could do little on their own, their only organic assets being two Arado 196 single-engine floatplanes, that had both been landed by the raider *Michel* before she was sunk. On 6 September the Penang base passed *U 862* a welcoming message and warned, 'No Japanese surface forces, convoys or

U 862 displays her victory pennants on the attack periscope during the entry to Penang. (A. Schirrmann)

Japanese submarines on the entrance route. Reckon everywhere with enemy submarines.'[14] The following day another message provided more detail, noting that between 2 and 6 September enemy submarines had been detected four times in positions stretching from the Nicobar Islands to the waters surrounding Penang.[15] As ordered, Timm elected to spend the last day of the passage submerged. The extreme humidity made for an uncomfortable time. The crew stripped off whatever they could, but the air soon grew heavy and they were never free from perspiration. The cook produced a salad and the men tried to ignore their surroundings and play *Skat*. Despite the conditions, the Germans' spirits remained high. After more than three months at sea they would soon be stepping ashore.

On the morning of 9 September *U 862* surfaced at the rendezvous position approximately 80 miles north of Penang. Timm had been lucky. Though intercepted by the Allies, his message of 4 September appears to have taken at least five days to decrypt.[16]

The British submarines *Statesman*, patrolling off the Nicobars and Andamans, *Sirdar* off Sumatra, *Strongbow* off Thailand, and in particular *Tantalus* in the Malacca Strait, were given no opportunity to arrange an ambush.[17]

Instead of an enemy the men of *U 862* found a small Japanese torpedo boat ready to greet them, while an Arado circled above. Once the Japanese craft was alongside, a German officer from the base staff came aboard to brief Timm on the procedure for the entry. The pilot brought with him fresh lemonade and several baskets of bananas and other local fruit. These offerings were rapidly passed below and distributed eagerly among the U-boat's crew. For most it would be the first tropical fruit they had seen for over five years.

U 862 fell in astern of her escort and in grand style glided towards the welcoming, palm-covered coast. Eight hours later Timm ordered everything made ready for a ceremonial entry into Penang harbour. Those members of the crew not required below proudly lined the upper deck. They had shaved and washed as best they could and turned out in brand-new tropical uniforms. From the attack periscope flew the five victory pennants marking the tonnage sunk and, despite the loss of much of the mail, *U 862* also flew a small *'Deutsche Reichspost'* pennant.

The German base commander in Penang, *Korvettenkapitän* Wilhelm Dommes, sailed out in a pinnace to meet the U-boat at the harbour entrance. Thirty-seven years old, Dommes was another merchant marine officer and had entered the *Kriegsmarine* the year ahead of Timm. Though he was the first of the U-boat commanders to arrive in Penang, a diagnosis of nervous exhaustion had forced Dommes to give up his boat soon after arrival. Several months recuperation followed, until in March 1944 he was made the commander of the Penang base, or *'Stützpunkt Siegfried'*, as it was more commonly known.

Dommes had arranged a substantial reception. As soon as the U-boat appeared an Indian military band struck up with 'Lili Marlen', 'Horst Wessel' and other German songs. Immediately apparent on the wharf was a group of more than twenty senior Japanese naval officers, formally dressed in full white uniforms, wearing gloves and carrying swords. Behind them stood a large squad of Japanese sailors in khaki. To the right, also formed up in ranks, was the entire German base staff. To the left, the crew of a large Japanese submarine waited on the bow of their vessel ready to salute the new arrival.

Once *U 862* was alongside, the band played the German and

U 862 *makes her final approach to Swettenham Pier in Penang. The Japanese submarine* I-8 *is on the left. A large group of Japanese naval officers stand ready to greet the latest German arrival.* (A. Schirrmann)

Japanese national anthems while everyone stood stiffly at attention. Then Timm assembled *U 862*'s crew on the upper deck to hear some words of welcome from Vice Admiral Jisaku Uozumi, the commander of the local Japanese submarine squadron. It was a long speech that apparently praised them as heroes for having conquered 'such a dangerous adversary of the U-boats' and being 'up to now the most successful U-boat in East Asia'.[18] Unfortunately no one on *U 862* understood a word of Japanese, but as ordered they were all enthusiastic and applauded on cue.

Dommes had several cars ready, and those not on duty were soon motored out to their accommodation. The officers moved into a large two-storey house in the former English residential district. It served as both living quarters and German Naval Headquarters. The ratings were sent to a requisitioned hotel. The members of the *U-Bootswaffe* were used to privileged treatment, but the men of *U 862* found that Dommes' organisation had surpassed even their wildest expectations. For each man there was a large, soft, bed enclosed in a personal mosquito net, and on each bed lay new underwear, snow-white shirts and trousers. After a hot bath assisted by 'charming helpers', the crew prepared themselves for the first of a succession of social engagements.

That evening the Japanese held an official reception for all ranks. 'A large cold buffet offered wonderful foods and drinks. Only the best of the best. Fish, meat, a table of unknown east

German submariners were not the only ones to celebrate their victories. Here the crew of HMS Trenchant *display their 'Jolly Roger', flown as they entered port after a successful patrol. In addition to the swastika signifying the sinking of* U 859*, the flag commemorates several gun actions against junks, minelaying and 'special' operations, and the sinking of the Japanese heavy cruiser* Ashigara. *Between July 1944 and July 1945* Trenchant *made seven patrols in the Far East.* (Western Australian Maritime Museum, MA 4533/18)

Asian fruit, Nambuko-whisky, rice beer and wine in any quantity. We ate and drank like starved prisoners. Many empty trays and casks remained after this evening.'[19]

At the end of his first day in Penang, *Obermaschinenmaat* Rudolf Herrmann simply recorded, 'We live very well!'[20] For others, however, the contrast between life ashore and their recent time at sea would take longer to accept. From strained nerves in a hot steel tube to relaxation in luxurious surroundings was a change too great to absorb in a mere 24 hours. Günther Reiffenstuhl probably reflected a more common experience when he wrote, 'We feel we are dreaming.'[21]

In many ways the experience of Timm and his crew was unreal, for the last few hours of a patrol were often the most dangerous. Only two weeks after *U 862*'s arrival another U-boat attempted to enter Penang. *U 859*, commanded by *Kapitänleutnant*

Johann Jebsen, had left Kiel the month before *U 862* and by 5 July had reached the waters south of Madagascar. Like Timm, Jebsen had been caught on the surface by a Catalina and attempted to fight back. However, damp or defective ammunition took its toll and two of *U 859*'s weapons failed after only a few rounds had been fired. The Catalina was able to complete its bombing run, and though it only achieved a near miss with one depth charge, the damage to the U-boat was considerable. One fuel tank was holed, the *Schnorchel*-elevating machinery was smashed, all lighting went off, the seating for the diesels was loosened and the batteries short-circuited. Casualties included one seaman killed by machine-gun fire and another three crew wounded. *U 859* nevertheless escaped and managed to sink two ships in the Gulf of Aden area in late August. Lack of fuel then forced her to break off operations and head for Penang. After exchanging signals with Dommes, Jebsen was expected to arrive at the rendezvous point during the forenoon of 23 September.

Heavy cloud and tropical rain squalls reduced the prevailing visibility, and *U 859* failed to meet either the Japanese escort or the German Arado. Her commander instead decided to continue independently towards Penang on the surface. Although warned that two Allied submarines were operating in the area, Jebsen seemed satisfied that he had passed through the danger zone. He took no special precautions and around midday on 23 September, while her officers were at lunch, *U 859* was attacked by HMS *Trenchant* some 25 miles northwest of Penang.[22] A torpedo hit the U-boat below the conning tower, instantly killing the five men on bridge watch and blowing several others on deck, into the water. *U 859* sank rapidly in 40m of water and there were less than 20 survivors. By the time the loss of *U 859* became known to the Germans, however, *U 862* had already moved on to Singapore.

8 Penang und Shonan

Crews should be generously provided with clothing. Intercourse with such sharp-eyed comrades as the Japanese requires more than mere U-boat tropical outfit.

—*Kapitänleutnant* Siegfried Lüdden, commander of *U 188*, 6 May 1944

In September 1944 Penang was still the principal operations base for U-boats in the Far East. Of the other bases, Singapore, known to the Japanese as Shonan, was exclusively for major repairs, while Jakarta was primarily used for loading raw materials. A well-equipped repair base at Surabaya, on the north-eastern corner of Java—a former main naval base of the Dutch—had been opened in July 1944 to relieve the overcrowded conditions in Singapore.

Under British colonial administration the island of Penang had been the capital and commercial centre of the Straits Settlements, but it had no history as a naval base and technical facilities were in most cases inadequate. In the face of the Japanese invasion of the Malay peninsula, Penang had been abandoned by the European population on 15 December 1941, and three days later Japanese troops entered the town unopposed. The Japanese proclaimed that they came as liberators of the oppressed peoples of Asia, but soon all the street names were in Japanese, the biggest shop was the Daimaru Department Store, and the former premises of the Chartered Bank had been occupied by the Bank of Japan.

The Japanese readily appreciated the strategic advantages of Penang's island position at the northern approaches to the Malacca Strait. They promptly began developing the port facilities and their 8th Submarine Squadron first sortied from Penang into the Indian Ocean at the end of April 1942. Electric cranes and workshops were available and the Japanese allowed the Germans their own warehouse space. Other facilities were shared, including the torpedo-adjusting station, a barely adequate situation which the Germans, with their passion for security, found difficult.

But Penang was not yet able to cope with major repair work, and had trouble meeting the maintenance demands of a U-boat after a lengthy voyage. Though the Japanese were able to supply some basic equipment, most spare parts had to be brought out from Germany and were invariably in short supply. There was also a dearth of experienced manpower and although the German base staff—approximately 200 spread between the four bases—did what they could to help, there would often be six or more U-boats requiring work simultaneously. Thus, the bulk of maintenance work inevitably fell on the U-boat crews themselves. Everything was done in 40–50°C heat with the humidity often over 90 per cent. That the crews were usually exhausted after an arduous patrol did nothing to assist matters.

Though in Europe the period a U-boat spent in harbour between patrols was anything between 20 days and six weeks, in Far East ports the average was 70 days.[1] Much of this time would be spent awaiting dry-docking in the overworked Japanese yards in Singapore or dealing with the interminable delays of Japanese bureaucracy. The great disparity in rank between the German base commanders and the senior Japanese naval officers exacerbated the situation, and working from an inferior position and through an interpreter often meant delays and complications. The slow turnaround ensured that for much of the time the number of German boats available for operations was well below the nominal strength in the region. Nevertheless, U-boat commanders were generally happy with the Penang organisation and contemporary references note the good quality of work completed.

While Japanese civilian officials and the Army were often found to be obstinately difficult, the Japanese Navy, on the surface at least, appears to have made every effort to make the Germans' stay as pleasant as possible.[2] Official relations between German and Japanese officers were normally warm and cordial, and there were occasional invitations to the Japanese Navy Club for drinks, a meal or to watch the horseraces. The Germans could also invite Japanese officers to their mess, but these relationships seldom grew into friendship. Privately, there was little love lost between the *Kriegsmarine* and the Imperial Japanese Navy, the two services normally mixing no more than common courtesy and operations liaison demanded. Many Germans, brought up to believe in the superiority of the 'Aryan' races, were quite open about their intense dislike for the Japanese. The interrogation report of one German officer, captured after the sinking of his U-boat, cheerfully noted, 'After hesitating at first about giving information of any kind, he later decided to tell anything he knew about the Japanese, as he felt no patriotic responsibility toward Japan.'[3]

The Japanese had similar difficulties. The IIWO of *U 181* later described the Japanese attitude to the Germans as 'cautiously friendly. It was tolerant, occasionally arrogant, and loosened by liquor it could become aggressive.'[4] The Germans gained the impression that for the Japanese, the war was a matter of the 'yellow race against the white races' and that any Europeans were viewed with a 'deep-seated suspicion'.[5] Only those Japanese officers in direct contact with the Germans seemed to understand why Europeans should still be permitted the use of Japanese territory. The 'simple Japanese soldier' knew how to respect rank and uniform, but apparently often 'wondered why there were still white men in a position of command'. Used to the obsequiousness of the local population, many ordinary Japanese were also unprepared for the less subservient German attitude. In Jakarta, one German *Obermaat*, in civilian clothes, 'was slapped in the face by a drunken Japanese civilian while visiting a house of ill repute. The German beat up the Japanese and delivered him directly to the *Kempetai* [Japanese secret police] HQ.'[6]

The Japanese maintained their separation at the operational level and never made attempts to coordinate their submarine deployments with the U-boats. Specific Japanese operations and successes were kept very secret, and only occasionally would any mention of the subject be made. The Germans soon recognised that the Japanese were 'keen observers' and generally felt that they provided much more information than they received themselves. Many of the U-boat commanders issued explicit instructions forbidding Japanese personnel from ever examining the inside of their U-boats. *U 862*, though, was the first submarine the Japanese had seen with a *Schnorchel* and was therefore an object of particular interest. Two days after their arrival *U 862*'s officers played host to Vice Admiral Uozumi and a group of officers from *I-8*, the Japanese submarine berthed immediately ahead of them.

The commander of *I-8* was 40-year-old Commander Tatsunosuké Ariizumi, a short stocky man with a Hitler moustache and one of the few Japanese officers in Penang to be on familiar terms with the Germans. On at least one occasion he arranged a successful tiger-hunting party in the jungles of Thailand, inviting Dommes and several other senior U-boat officers to accompany him. Between July and December 1943, *I-8* had gone from the Far East to Europe and back, the only Japanese submarine ever to make the return journey safely. Ariizumi took command shortly thereafter and between March and July 1944 he accounted for four Allied ships sunk in the Indian Ocean, making him a 'submarine ace' in Japanese terms. However, outside the Imperial Navy his successes had brought him a different level of notoriety. After two particular displays of barbarity against the survivors of his torpedo attacks, Ariizumi became known as 'the butcher' to the Allies.[7] One German officer who met Ariizumi described him as 'a quick-witted, slightly imperious officer with harsh manners'[8] while another thought him 'very reserved and conceited'.[9] Reiffenstuhl, who acted as guide for the visit to *U 862*, had his own views:

> Purest Japanese espionage. Officers are very suspicious they note down everything. They ask if she has a *Schnorchel*. Disagreeable people! The Japanese have an inferiority complex when facing us. Their commander gives us two bottles of Japanese saki. He said he was ashamed to be facing us after having sunk so few in such a long time, never lose face![10]

The Germans were quite aware that Japanese submarines had at times attempted to exterminate the crews of their victims, but whatever their private thoughts, relations continued to be affable. That afternoon *U 862*'s officers accepted Ariizumi's hospitality and made a return visit to *I-8*.

Like all sailors, the U-boat men lived life to the fullest when they were ashore, and having come to terms with their new surroundings *U 862*'s crew did their best to enjoy themselves. On arrival half of the men were immediately driven to the mountains for a short period of recuperation in the more moderate climate. Exceeding the standards of even the U-boat rest camps in France, the recreational facilities at Penang Hill allowed swimming, fishing, golf and tennis. Surrounded by lush tropical vegetation and breathtaking scenery, the U-boat men could easily forget the war. The remaining crew members stayed behind to conduct essential work on the U-boat. The two groups swapped roles halfway through the visit, but even those who stayed in Penang were able to savour the sights, sounds and smells of an exotic city. Cigarettes, ample pay in 'banana dollars', and personal comfort items had been issued on arrival, and outside duty hours the Germans were free to wander around the town shopping and drinking until the 2300 curfew. After that time only German and Japanese officers were allowed on the streets. The Germans wore civilian clothes, usually only white shirt and shorts, with a black–white–red cockade on their chest to signify nationality. They soon found that as Europeans they received many friendly smiles, and felt—perhaps naively—that the local people trusted them more than they did the overbearing Japanese.

With the crew fully engaged, *U 862*'s officers managed to do their own recuperating. The well-appointed officers' mess was situated on the bottom floor of the Naval Headquarters building, and the presence of good German cooks encouraged the U-boat officers to dine there almost exclusively. There was also a plentiful supply of Malay stewards, and *U 862*'s officers were allotted their own 'boy': a mixer of excellent cocktails named Osram. The Germans were not slow to rechristen him '*Sohn einer Glühbirne*' (son of a light globe).

Dommes had provided two American-make cars with Malay chauffeurs for the duration of *U 862*'s stay. One was exclusively for Timm and the other was shared by the remaining officers. The daily routine, though markedly different from their time at sea, was still somewhat exhausting. Reiffenstuhl recorded in his journal that on his first full day in Penang he played badminton and tennis in the morning and went for a sightseeing drive around the island in the afternoon. After a swim in a waterfall he returned to the villa for coffee, then dined at the Shanghai Hotel—the all-ranks German naval club—and in the evening visited an amusement park. The Sakura amusement park was probably the most popular place of entertainment in Penang. Here there was music and dancing, and young and beautiful Eurasian women 'who had been health checked' were also available. These were not prostitutes but could be hired at little cost to act as drinking partners. Here also were more exotic diversions including a ball-and-target game involving women that Reiffenstuhl, at least, found 'incredible for European minds'.[11]

U 862's time in Penang was all too short, and during the early evening of 12 September she sailed for Singapore for docking. An Arado provided an initial anti-submarine search and brief escort, but the Germans hoped that the gathering darkness would cloak the U-boat's departure from Allied eyes and allow *U 862* to pass through shallower waters during daylight. Before leaving, the U-boat had been loaded with fresh fruit and vegetables grown by

An Arado floatplane photographed from U 862 *(note the Japanese markings and small underwing bombs). The two German aircraft in East Asia were clearly inadequate to provide effective anti-submarine patrols and in October 1944 the* Bachstelzen *from* U 862 *and* U 196 *were exchanged for a Japanese* Reishiki *floatplane. In December 1944 all aircraft were transferred from Penang to Jakarta.* (A. Schirrmann)

the base staff and, in a benevolent farewell gesture, Dommes had opened a bottle of champagne and proposed a toast. Because the Strait of Malacca was navigationally difficult, a German pilot named Charly Militzer was embarked for the passage.

Though lying within Japanese-occupied territory, the Strait was a dangerous place. Militzer was more than happy to confirm the hazards to Timm, for he had been torpedoed while travelling in a Japanese merchant ship just three weeks before. With the Strait's unfamiliar waters, poor landmarks and shifting sandbanks, the U-boat could not risk a submerged passage. However, with no need to move far from the safe channels, a hostile submarine could patrol at periscope depth, awaiting the opportunity to ambush.

Such was the fear of sudden attack by British submarines that *U 862* went fully on to the defensive. The bridge watch was strengthened, while all those who could be spared donned lifejackets and remained on the upper deck. If torpedoed they had orders to jump. Despite the risks, many found the balmy tropical night refreshingly peaceful and were soon dozing wherever they could find a space.

The following day the waters were calm and the sky cloudless. In other circumstances the passage south could have been a

U 862's *crew crowd the rear of the bridge during their passage through the Strait of Malacca. From left* Zentraleheizer *Günter Weise,* Dieselheizer *Albert Schirrmann and, with binoculars,* Seemänn *Josef 'Seppl' Schwenk.* (A. Schirrmann)

pleasure cruise. For the men of *U 862*, though, it must have seemed strange to be running in fear from another hunter like themselves. They nevertheless made the most of the unusual transit. Shirtless, those not on watch perched on the guardrails surrounding the conning tower, chatting, smoking and generally enjoying the fresh breeze and sunshine. With nothing else to do, most relaxed or slept and got badly sunburnt.

Around noon Dommes arrived overhead in an Arado and completed a circle of honour around the U-boat before flying on to Singapore. Timm had spent much of the day in his bunk with a high fever, but during the afternoon he got up and ordered the 10.5cm gun's crew closed up for a practice shoot. Several shots were fired at a small uninhabited island. In a break from procedure and perhaps to give vent to feelings of helplessness, Timm directed this evolution himself. Later the rumour grew in Singapore that *U 862* had driven away a hostile submarine with the fire.[12]

The passage through the Strait of Malacca took 29 hours, and by the time *U 862* secured in Singapore on 13 September it was almost midnight. A pilot boat had met the U-boat outside the entrance, but there was no large official reception as there had been in Penang. Only Dommes and the Singapore base commander, *Korvettenkapitän* Erhardt, were there to welcome them. *U 862* was directed into a basin on the side of the harbour which, along with warehouses, had been placed by the Japanese at the Germans' disposal. A minimum watch again remained onboard, while cars and buses took the remainder of the men to Pasir Panjang on the eastern side of the island. There they were accommodated in bungalows built on stilts directly over the shallow waters of the Johore Strait. The Germans awoke the next morning to a setting remembered by Albert Schirrmann as

> a beautiful park with palm trees and banana palms, farm houses and other dwellings round about. The kitchen spoiled us with delicious things which in this paradise were offered in abundance. Chinese and Malaysians predominantly prepared poultry, Indonesian rice dishes and different salads. Many other foods came from a captured English ship. She had enough food on board to have sufficed for a medium size city for half a year.[13]

While staying in the Pasir Panjang camp, *U 862*'s crew did not want for comforts. There were male and female Malay servants who every day provided them with fresh bed linen and twice daily with fresh underwear. Separate accommodation was again offered to the officers. They were billeted at the Haw Par Villa, originally erected by a rich Chinese businessman and now run by a Japanese manager and known as the Tiger Club.[14] Here bands provided entertainment in a central hall and Eurasian girls could be hired to dance for the evening. Despite the apparent quality of the arrangements, Reiffenstuhl complained that they did not live as well as they had in Penang: there was no running water and the cars provided were not reliable. However, the Japanese Navy continued its efforts to make the Germans feel welcome, and the local Admiral held a well-received reception on the third night after arrival: 'Japanese food eaten with chopsticks. The wife of the manager of the Tiger—a very pretty Japanese—appears in a splendid kimono; she is an excellent piano player and recites German pieces. A Jap Commander performs a national dance on the table.'[15]

Dönitz had been kept informed of *U 862*'s achievements and on 19 September Timm received word from Germany that he had been awarded the *Ritterkreuz*. The medal—which could be awarded for both acts of bravery and outstanding service—acknowledged Timm as one of the leading U-boat commanders of the period, certainly one of the very few who were still at sea and achieving results.[16] His crew were not forgotten, and another fourteen Iron Crosses First Class and 36 Iron Crosses Second Class were distributed among officers and men. The awards warranted a big celebration. According to Reiffenstuhl, the evening was marked by 'a crazy party, that spread through several houses. A water battle at the end was very funny.'[17]

A few days after arriving in Singapore *U 862* was moved into a vacant dry dock. Here the keel plates were removed, revealing hundreds of small steel flasks of mercury, stowed horizontally in layers. The flasks, which the U-boat had by now hauled more than 17 000 miles, were removed and passed over to the base staff for eventual use in the Japanese war effort.[18] Before the keel was resealed, the ballast was replaced. The cargo for Europe included molybdenum and tungsten, needed by the Germans for the production of high-grade steel. The raw materials were put into thick-walled tin canisters and sealed with similar plates of tin.

Dockyard meetings were held in the morning, and Timm ensured that work pressed along according to a prepared schedule. The diesel engines were overhauled, and the compressors, fresh-water evaporator, electric motors and batteries were all examined, serviced, and repaired where needed. Of all the crew the engineers kept particularly busy, but a party of non-technical sailors was put at Hugo Seggermann's disposal to labour as cleaners. Not trusted to work in the U-boat's interior, the local coolies were employed cleaning sea growth from the outside of the hull. *U 862* then received a new coat of protective paint, mainly below the waterline. Using two shifts, the maintenance plan was soon finished. Much of the credit for this was due to the German interpreter, who spoke Malaysian as well as Japanese. He liaised constantly between *U 862*'s officers and the Japanese dockyard personnel to ensure that the work met the Germans' requirements. Engine parts in particular had to be acquired from Japanese sources, and without agreement it would have been an impossible task.

In view of the extremely hot and humid conditions, those of the crew not actually on duty worked only between 0900 and 1200. Smeared with dirt and oil, the men would then return to the main camp. Many would spend the time until the evening meal sleeping or swimming, but not always. Though it was not unknown for some of the Malaysian women in Pasir Panjang to

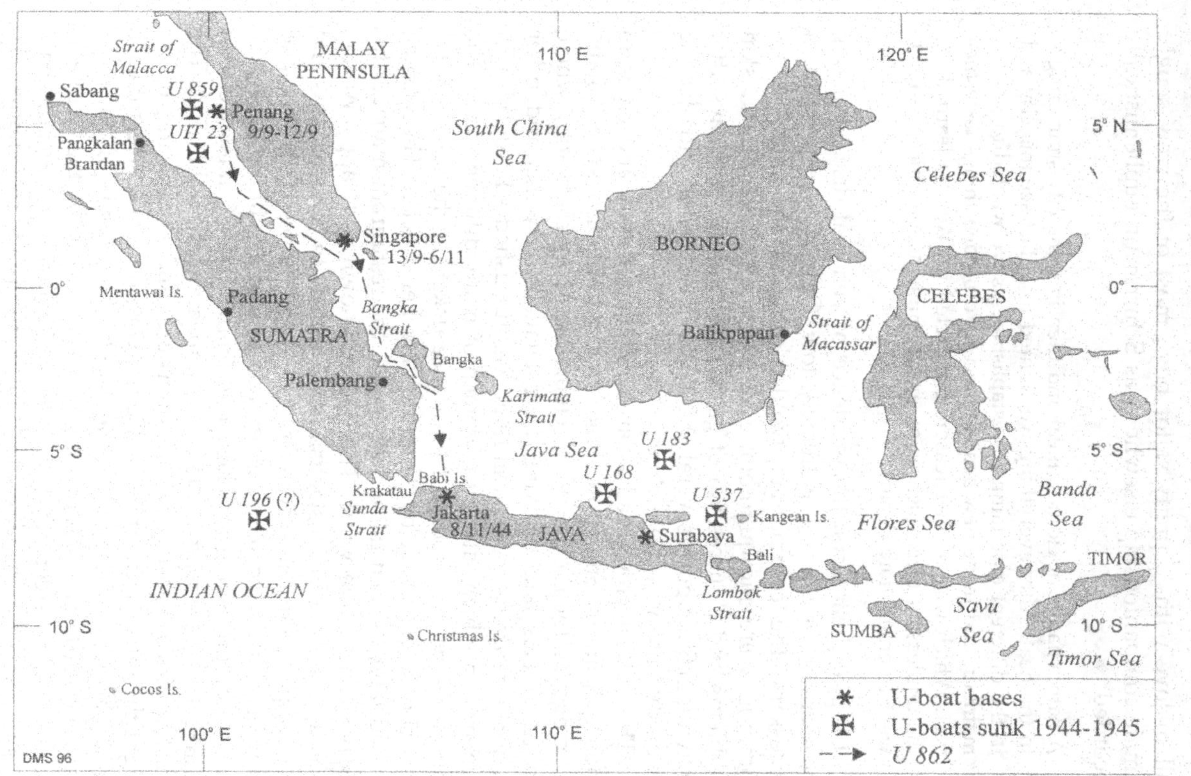

German bases in Malaya and the Netherlands East Indies, 1944–45

fall in love with 'a pretty sailor boy', most of the crew sought female companionship elsewhere, as Schirrmann euphemistically recorded:

> A bath, change of clothes, meal and then into the city simmering in the heat. After everything we wanted to at last see this city and in the different entertainment establishments we wanted to maintain and make new acquaintances. Forbidden things taste the best. Which was another reason it attracted us. We also learned the unpleasant consequences of such excursions, of which I do not want to enter more details.[19]

Despite their fears, the incidence of venereal disease among the German crews was extremely low. Only the doctor and, if necessary, the commander would know of the case.[20] More common were mosquito-borne diseases such as malaria, skin problems and a succession of gastric complaints. Two days after arriving in Singapore, several of *U 862*'s sailors fell ill with dengue fever, dysentery and diarrhoea.

The U-boat crews had a large number of bars and clubs to choose from in Singapore. The men would also spend many evenings at their own naval club, the *Mannschaftshaus*, where dances, meals and drinking were available. At this and other dance restaurants the central floor was furnished all around with benches on which sat young women of many different races. The sailors would buy books of ten dance tickets at the cash register and choose a partner by simply giving her a ticket. The women would later redeem these tickets with the restaurant manager for 50 per cent of the value. The casino, known as 'Happy World', was another popular establishment, both with the Germans and the locals. Here there were long rows of tables with dice and domino games and many other varieties of gambling. Bets were also made on boxing matches, and *Zentraleheizer* Günter Weise of *U 862* was one who made some appearances in the ring. The gaming house closed towards morning, and after being up all night the most stalwart of the Germans would stroll straight back to the boat, ready again for their daily three hours of duty. The casino recorded a monthly turnover of $30 000 from the Germans, unremarkable except that only some $10 000 was officially paid to the crews. A thriving black market existed, and among the many commodities the sailors found to sell, bunk sheets were the most coveted. The distinctive imprint '*Deutscher Lloyd Bremen*' was apparently not uncommon on the white head coverings worn by Malaysian women.

Despite or perhaps because of the relative luxury they enjoyed, the U-boat men still found they could not simply ignore the oppression, poverty, ill-health and hunger that dominated the lives of most inhabitants of Penang and Singapore. Reiffenstuhl was quite ready to comment in his journal on how strictly the Japanese disciplined the Malays, noting in passing how one 'boy' who worked in the officer's mess 'was beaten by them because the garden grass was too long'.[21] However, the U-boat crews also found that the local populace seemed quietly and patiently resigned to their fate. The Germans observed, but as guests were not about to interfere with the Japanese administration. In consequence the only thing they did of a positive nature was for other Europeans:

> The Japanese had set up a camp for English prisoners close to our accommodation. Daily these prisoners marched past. Poor soldiers! Chalky-white, sick with Beri Beri, they all suffered from deficiency diseases. There was no variation in their diet, rice, rice and rice again. Before they reached our home the English began to whistle. The tune was the Siegfried Line. Then we knew, that they were coming. Canned foods, cigarettes and medicines were positioned in some places. The English set up a *Pinkelpause* there and so could take the items and smuggle them into camp.[22]

Writing after his own postwar experiences as a prisoner of war in the hands of the British, Albert Schirrmann added somewhat bitterly, 'We should not have done it for nothing!'

9 Die Australien Operation

History has many examples of precarious and even seemingly hopeless situations being mastered by a strong leadership. It is such leadership that we have today. By contrast, our situation is full of possibilities. The Navy in particular may be proud in its consciousness of the fact that, while Germany is fighting off the enemy who is storming in from all sides, it is reserved for the Navy one day to thrust out from the narrowed room into the wide spaces and again to attack and get at the enemy's throat.

—CinC *Kriegsmarine*'s short situation report, 26 September 1944

After completion of the overhaul and replacement of her keel ballast, it might have been expected that *U 862* would attempt the return passage to Europe, perhaps delaying for a brief period of operations off Africa *en route*. However, while still in Penang Timm had sought permission from *BdU* to carry out a subsidiary operation off southwest Australia. The exact text of the message has not survived, but Timm apparently pointed out the time he had saved at sea and the good condition of his crew, boat and batteries.[1] The motives behind Timm's request are not entirely clear. On first glance the proposed operation would hardly be an effective utilisation of scarce resources. *U 862* was again carrying raw materials, and with Germany cut off from most sources of supply there was a pressing need to return them to the Fatherland. If Timm wanted to achieve further success he need look no further than the Indian Ocean, where targets were still plentiful. Australia was not only in the opposite direction, but operations there could in no way assist Germany's European war.

Even in the Pacific theatre, the island continent could hardly be classified as a target of prime importance. Though a vital staging area for Allied troops and matériel in 1942, since mid-1943 and General Douglas MacArthur's drive north along the New Guinea coast, Australia had been largely superseded as an operating base. However, in light of Dönitz's aim of tying down Allied forces, Timm's proposal did have a certain logic. The sudden appearance of a U-boat in Australian waters might demonstrate to the Allies that they could not afford to lower their guard even in the remotest areas. It would certainly prove that Germany could still reach out and strike deep within enemy territory. Far from the current theatres of war the Germans may have also assumed that Australian defences would be both weak and poorly trained, making the possibility of an easy success that much greater. This would certainly have been in keeping with Dönitz's normal pattern of U-boat deployment.

Timm had not been alone in making his request. *Kapitänleutnant* Helmuth Pich, commander of the Type IXC U-boat *U 168*, had sought permission to accompany Timm's boat. Though *U 168* was in Jakarta, the feasibility of an Australian operation must have received some general discussion before the mission was suggested to *BdU*. Unfortunately, *U 168*'s batteries were at low capacity and she was already programmed to undergo a basic overhaul and battery renewal in Kobe. That Pich would suggest another operation before the overhaul adds further weight to the assessment that the Germans did not have a high regard for Australia's anti-submarine defences.

Serious consideration of U-boat operations in the Australian area was a relatively new phenomenon. Certainly, before the acquisition of the Penang base, extending operations to include the eastern Indian Ocean or Pacific would have posed insurmountable difficulties. Not until May 1944 does the first official record of such a proposal appear. In that month *U 188*, a member of the first *Monsun* Group, returned to France. Her commander, *Kapitänleutnant* Siegfried Lüdden, produced a detailed report on the prospects for operations in the broader Indian Ocean and suggested that:

> Preliminary reconnaissance in the sea area South and West of Australia would be advantageous as this would mean that alternative areas would already be explored, so that if it is intended to make a surprise attack with a larger group of boats, the group will not first have to feel its way, but will be able to operate with a sound knowledge of traffic and defence conditions.[2]

U-boat numbers, losses and sinking rates 1944–45

	U-boats in Commission	*Operational U-boats*	*Average no. of U-boats at sea*	*Actual losses*	*Tonnage sunk in '000 of GRT*	*Average daily sinkings in GRT per U-boat at sea*
May 1944	454	162	43	7	17	13
Jun	446	178	47	23	51	39
Jul	429	177	34	13	56	53
Aug	418	158	51	17	86	79
Sep	402	146	68	12	29	14
Oct	394	131	45	3	–	–
Nov	395	130	41	4	27	21
Dec	409	135	51	5	59	38
Jan 1945	423	139	39	6	57	47
Feb	455	156	47	13	51	39
Mar	459	165	56	16	56	32
Apr	429	166	54	33	71	47
May	–	–	45	25	10	–

Source: Hessler, vol. III, diagrams 29, 30, 31.

The Germans took no immediate action on Lüdden's recommendation. Resources to conduct a reconnaissance were in short supply and other missions at first retained priority. Though Dommes may have seen value in an Australian operation, he could not authorise such a mission on his own initiative. Nevertheless, the situation in the Atlantic was continuing to worsen. In August 1944, U-boat Command had been forced to evacuate the northern Biscay U-boat bases of Brest, Lorient and St Nazaire in the face of advancing Allied armies. In September, with many U-boats still in transit to Norway, sinkings per boat were well down while U-boat losses remained high. By eliminating the French bases and by forcing the U-boats to rely on *Schnorchel* during passage, the Allies had succeeded in severely limiting the operational range of the U-boat fleet. With unexpected problems in completion and training of the new Type XXI and XXIII electro-boats delaying their introduction into service, and hopes of success fading except in inshore waters, Dönitz apparently felt ready to risk another far-flung operation. Perhaps he even believed Australian waters would fulfil Lüdden's somewhat optimistic prediction of a 'grand opportunity of being at last able to conduct a U-boat offensive again . . . bridging the time until a new offensive in Home Waters can be undertaken'.[3]

On 14 September *BdU* sent the following message to the Penang base:

1 Agree to Pich and Timm operating in Australia area. Departure on obtaining war readiness. Send proposals regarding operational area. Make use of Japanese knowledge of traffic and defence situation.
2 Pich is to undergo another capacity test prior to departure. Report result.
3 The Naval Attache is to report as soon as possible when Pich can (call at) Japan to change batteries. Decision will then be made whether Pich is to proceed to Japan or Penang after his operation.[4]

In noting concurrence with Timm's suggestion, the *BdU* war diary included a comment that *U 862*'s commander had sailed the route before as a merchant navy officer. However, there was yet another factor influencing *BdU*'s decision that does not seem to have been recorded. As Timm and Pich pressed to extend U-boat operations farther than ever before, the Japanese were exerting similar pressure for their own purposes.

Japan had begun 1944 with some 75 operational submarines, more boats than she possessed in December 1941. Her submarine arm, though, could in no way be counted as an effective force. While the IJN as a whole was slowly rebuilding—for yet another quixotic quest for the final decisive battle against the US Fleet—the submarine arm was being squandered on strategically pointless tasks. Pressure from the Japanese Army had meant the expenditure of as much as 25 per cent of active submarine strength on supplying men and matérial to outlying and cut-off bases.[5] Furthermore, with the more general loss of initiative to the Allies most of the other boats were restricted to static patrols, vainly watching for the direction of the next USN carrier strike. These submarines would then be rushed from the expected to actual points of attack, usually arriving too late to take action. With the positions of their patrol areas and planned movements often revealed through Sigint, and undeniably outclassed by the anti-submarine forces ranged against them, Japanese submarine losses increased dramatically. Between January and August 1944 the Japanese lost 43 submarines, with monthly losses peaking at ten sunk in June. During the same period the Japanese could manage only fifteen enemy ships sunk in the Indian Ocean and one in the Pacific. The Japanese campaign against Allied sea communications, never seriously pursued, was now most definitely moribund. By September 1944 Allied intelligence was routinely

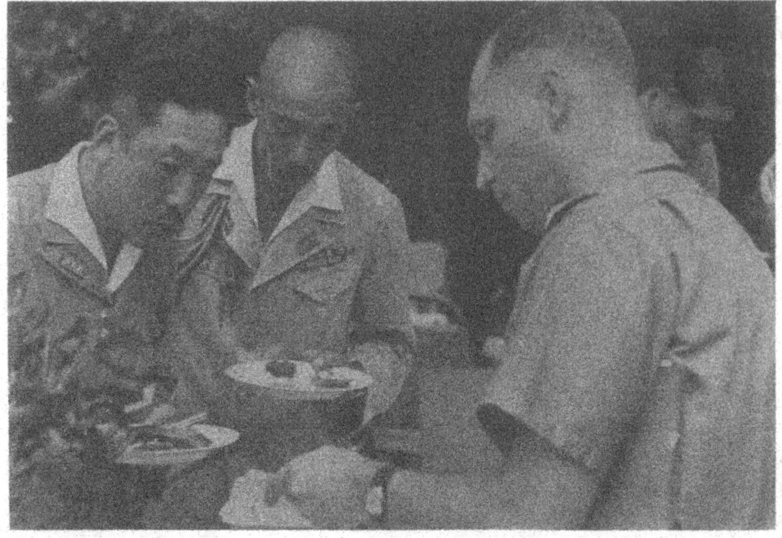

Marineoberstabsarzt *Dr Jobst Schäfer makes a point with two Japanese army officers during a reception held in Singapore. The Germans found the Japanese mentality difficult to understand. According to one U-boat officer, 'They were either smiling or stonefaced—no middle ground'.* (U-boat Archive, Cuxhaven)

noting the complete absence of offensive efforts by Japanese submarines.[6]

Rather than revise their submarine warfare doctrine, the Japanese turned instead to the Germans for relief. On 7 September Tokyo asked its naval mission in Berlin to request from Dönitz an increase in the number of German U-boats deployed to the Far Eastern theatre.[7] It is not certain whether the Japanese also suggested extending the operations of these U-boats into Australian waters, but any benefits to be gained from such operations would clearly be of primary benefit to them.

Heading the Berlin mission was Vice Admiral Katsuo Abe,[8] and on 26 September, having conferred with Dönitz and Chief of Naval Staff *Admiral* Wilhelm Meisel, he reported to Tokyo:

> (A) Up to date 12 German submarines have been sent to the Indian Ocean, of which 2 are for transport duties between Japan and Singapore area. A further 6 German submarines are detailed for the Indian Ocean and have already sailed. Three of these are to operate in the Australia area.
>
> In addition a new type of submarine with high submerged speed

and long cruising range will be sent at a future date, but the number of these craft and dates cannot yet be given.

(B) To our suggestion that it might be advantageous to send the old-type converted craft (which are dangerous in the Atlantic) to East Asia as they are replaced by new-type submarines, he [Dönitz] replied as follows:

The old-type converted submarines have not shown any weakness so far. The English coast is not too far distant, and submarine fuelling depots are installed in such places as Kiel, Hamburg, Bremen, Bergen and Trondheim, and there is little cause for uneasiness in regard to their defence. It is therefore worthwhile to employ the old types fully in the Atlantic.

(C) I strongly recommend that we adopt a policy of rendering every possible assistance in the friendliest manner to the Germans. Officials here are constantly requesting the co-operation of the Japanese Navy. In particular, they request adequate security measures in regard to arrivals and departures from ports. Today a report was received to the effect that another German submarine was sunk off Penang . . . The frequent occurrences of such events discourages sending additional submarines, Admiral Doenitz stated . . . I answered that for joint operations we were desirous of increasing submarine warfare as much as possible in the Greater East Asia area . . . [I]n the interests of Japanese–German co-operation, we should maintain strict security in our ports as regards arrival and departures. Further, . . . I urge the provision of better facilities for repairs and supplies, better recreational facilities for crews, and all possible assistance in special fields in which the Germans are outstanding. For the present, I will take every opportunity to press for more submarines being sent to the Greater East Asia area.[9]

Dönitz's concerns after the loss of *U 859* were real enough, and to add further weight to his words he ordered *Vizeadmiral* Wenneker to relay the same message to his IJN contacts in Tokyo. *BdU* noted specifically 'that a strengthening of A/S activities off the ports of entry is absolutely necessary in the interests of the exchange of commodities important to both countries, and for the continuation of U-boat warfare in the Indian Ocean and along the Australian coast'.[10] The *Großadmiral* was also serious in his plans for increasing the size of the offensive in Australian waters. The third U-boat to be allocated was the Type IXC/40 *U 537*, commanded by *Kapitänleutnant* Peter Schrewe. But how far Dönitz really intended to assist his Asian ally is an open question.

In October 1944 Wenneker told the Japanese that a further 30 U-boats would be in the Far East by the middle of 1945.[11] However, by December, in answer to another request from Abe for increased use of German U-boats in 'foreign areas', Dönitz was much less confident. He now responded apologetically that the rate of construction of new-type submarines had been delayed by enemy bombings, but that they should be sent by next spring.[12] In the meantime the Japanese could still expect one transport submarine which had left Germany in early December, another which would leave for East Asia at the end of January, one in March and one or two each month from April onwards (either Type IXD or XB), up to a total of seven.[13] The Japanese, attempting to sustain German interest, even briefly raised the possibility of establishing a combined submarine command under Vice Admiral Naokuni Nomura, '. . . a man well thought of by the Germans when he was the special representative of the Japanese Navy in Berlin'.[14] The Germans, however, were quick to reject this proposal.

At the beginning of October the U-boat construction program still aimed to produce 312 Type XXI electro-boats during 1945.[15] Had this production rate been achieved it was certainly intended to use some of these more modern boats as transports to and from East Asia. But a serious attempt to recommence offensive operations in the Indian and Pacific Oceans was another matter entirely. At a fundamental level German plans were rapidly disintegrating and the war situation essentially demanded the retention in Europe of all submarines already there. After *U 862*'s departure only eight U-boats actually left Europe for the Far East and at least six of these were on pure cargo-transport missions. In September 1944, however, these developments were still in the future and confidence between the Axis partners could still be espoused. The focus of Japanese–German cooperation thus remained on the offensive deployment to the Australian area.

The arrangements required to prepare the three selected U-boats were considerable. They received priority for spares and equipment, but the lack of resources in the Far East placed practical limits on fitting them out fully. Torpedoes, always in short supply, were a particular problem. Timm requested a full outfit for his boat, however *BdU* ordered the three U-boats be equipped with only fourteen torpedoes each.[16] Though Timm later managed to increase his allocation to fifteen, it was still far short of U 862's carrying capacity but perhaps a rational compromise, considering that only about 50 torpedoes were left in the Penang storage depot.[17]

The first U-boat ready to depart for the operation was Helmuth Pich's *U 168*. After completing final preparations in Jakarta, she undertook a one-day passage to Surabaya to conduct battery trials before heading for Australian waters. The particulars of *U 168*'s voyage were as a matter of routine passed to the local Japanese authorities who then, to ensure the U-boat's safety, transmitted them to remote units in the vicinity of her planned track. Details provided included departure and arrival times, position at midnight, and intended speed. The message specifically noted that the U-boat would remain on the surface throughout her passage.[18] *U 168* sailed from Jakarta at 0900 on 5 October, and as far as Pich was concerned it was a routine transit.

At 31 years old, Pich was slightly younger than Timm, but still one of the most experienced U-boat commanders in the Far East. He was a regular naval officer and came from an East Prussian military family. After entering the *Reichsmarine* in 1934 he had transferred to the *U-Bootswaffe* in 1941 at his own request. Pich commissioned *U 168* in September 1942 and after one patrol in the North Atlantic between March and May 1943, was ordered to take the boat to Penang as part of the first *Monsun* Group. Pich was known as a courteous man, cool and quiet even when under stress. Though Dönitz had initially expressed doubts about his suitability to the task, Pich had since shown himself to be a self-reliant and capable officer, very well liked by his crew.[19]

Unfortunately Pich, like many other U-boat commanders, had underestimated the extent of the threat in Japanese waters. Dommes, writing many years after the war, was to recall, 'As a matter of fact, it was my greatest problem to convince the captains of our boats of the size of the danger of hostile subs. When they reached the South they simply believed they had entered a paradise after all the stress behind them.'[20] Dommes, however, mistakenly believed that the main danger came when U-boats approached a prominent point of land to obtain a reliable fix. Allied submarines, he felt, must stand waiting in just such positions. Even after the public admission of Ultra's existence in the 1970s, Dommes was sure that losses had not been due to signal intercepts, noting that for at least one U-boat, 'You could not know of this commission, as we avoided to send a wireless about it!' Dommes was obviously still unaware of the degree to which the Allies had penetrated Japanese communications as well.

U 168's passage details appeared in Allied special intelligence summaries on 5 October. The Dutch submarine *Hr.Ms. Zwaardvisch* (Swordfish), part of the British 8th Submarine Flotilla based in Fremantle, was already in the U-boat's area. Commanded by Lieutenant Commander H. Goossens RNN, *Zwaardvisch* had left Australia for her second patrol in Far Eastern waters on 26

Hr. Ms. Zwaardvisch *(ex-HMS* Talent*) in the United Kingdom on 6 December 1943, the day of her commissioning into the Royal Netherlands Navy. She made five patrols off Sumatra and Java between August 1944 and April 1945 and is credited with the destruction of* U 168, *two Japanese minelayers and eight junks or coasters.* Zwaardvisch *was extensively modernised after the war and eventually stricken in 1963.* (Netherlands Institute for Maritime History)

September 1944 and passed through the Lombok Strait into the Java Sea six days later. Alerted to *U 168*'s precise movements, Goossens found it all too easy to intercept her.

Shortly after dawn on 6 October, with *Zwaardvisch* at periscope depth off the approaches to Surabaya, her commander sighted *U 168* as predicted and only 'five minutes late'.[21] Also as expected, the U-boat was on the surface on a steady easterly course at 14kts, and not even zigzagging. Eleven minutes after the first sighting Goossens fired a full salvo of six torpedoes from a range of only 900 yards.

On the upper deck of *U 168* a seaman saw the torpedoes approaching. He shouted a warning, but it was too late. One torpedo struck the U-boat in the forward torpedo room and exploded. The occupants of the forward part of the hull and many men on the upper deck were instantly killed by the blast. Moments later, a second torpedo pierced the pressure hull near the control room but did not detonate. A third hit also failed to explode. It made little difference, as the first blow had been mortal. The chief engineer, who had been drinking coffee in the control room, shouted for the watertight doors to be shut, but the U-boat was already settling quickly as water flooded the fore part of the boat. Many men were swept into the water as the bow sank. More died as they struggled to ascend to the deck through the conning-tower hatch. Pich, the *LI*, the medical officer and a few ratings found themselves trapped in the control room. They could do nothing as the U-boat sank slowly to the bottom in 40m of water. However, once at that depth the pressure in the control room had built up sufficiently to allow the reopening of the conning-tower hatch. As soon as it was released the resulting air bubble blew them out of the hull and up to the surface. Despite the lack of escape apparatus they all lived.[22]

Zwaardvisch surfaced ten minutes later and picked up 27 men swimming in the water. Twenty-three had gone down with the U-boat and the survivors offered no resistance. Pich, the IIWO, *LI*, medical officer and a wounded rating were kept on board the Dutch submarine for return to Australia and interrogation. The remaining survivors were placed in a nearby native fishing vessel and allowed to return to Japanese territory. Reports of the torpedoing reached Surabaya the same day, and two Japanese sub chasers were ordered to proceed to the area. They found nothing. Though the next day the Japanese told the Germans that the enemy submarine had been attacked by their aircraft 'and very probably sunk', *Zwaardvisch* returned safely to Fremantle on 26 October, having herself sunk another four enemy vessels.[23] Goossens' efforts received due recognition, being described by the Fremantle base commander, Rear Admiral Ralph W. Christie USN, as 'an admirably aggressive and splendidly conducted patrol'.[24]

For the Germans in the Far East, the loss of *U 168*, coming less than two weeks after the loss of *U 859*, was a severe blow. Dönitz was again ready to lay much of the blame on the failure of Japanese defences, but the U-boats themselves had hardly been acting with reasonable caution. Pich later admitted to interrogators that he had taken no countermeasures against an attack and offered no excuses. A fellow survivor, though, had no doubts where the fault lay, claiming that the Japanese '. . . never started anti-submarine air searches before 1100!'[25] In an attempt to reduce the danger during passage to and between bases, *BdU* sent detailed instructions to Penang and all East Asia U-boats to redouble their security efforts, urging better intelligence liaison with the Japanese, avoidance of busy areas and when surfaced passage was unavoidable, frequent zig-zagging and speed changes.[26]

The Australian operation remained the principal offensive mission planned for the East Asia area and, despite the loss of Pich, obviously remained important both as a means of offering practical support to the Japanese and as a demonstration that the *U-Bootswaffe* was not yet a spent force. In early November *BdU* ordered another Type IXD2 U-boat, *Oberleutnant zur See* Werner Striegler's *U 196*, to southwest Australia as a replacement for *U 168*.[27]

In the meantime Timm had not been idle. While *U 862* remained in dry dock in Singapore, he had acted upon *BdU*'s suggestion and flown to Jakarta and Surabaya in an attempt to elicit information from the Japanese. Timm later recalled, 'I learned nothing from the fleet there. The Japanese do not tell anything gladly. They smile. They were exceedingly friendly, but they were silent. And then there was Captain Fudjy, with a beard like Wilhelm II, he was terribly nice. He invited us for a beer and then we had to pay the whole bill afterwards'.[28]

The Japanese probably did not have much to tell in any case. They had not operated submarines off Australia for more than a year, while operations off the southwest coast had not been attempted since January 1943. Disappointed, Timm returned to his U-boat and stood by while final repairs were completed on an exhaust valve. Berlin had originally scheduled *U 862* to sail for Australia on 20 October but work was progressing slowly. It was not until 5 November, a month after the loss of *U 168*, that *U 862* was finally ready to sail for Jakarta. Even then things did not quite go according to plan:

> Put to sea from Shonang on course for Djakarta with the M-boat '*Quito*' as escort.[29] We departed via the east exit, however, we very soon had to turn back because the starboard drive shaft was banging so much that the whole electro switchboard was shaking. Major breakdown, return to port, everywhere astonished faces and laughter. Damage soon repaired (coupling), in the afternoon engine test, in the evening at the Tiger again.[30]

The attempt to sail the following day was more successful, and after final farewells from *Korvettenkapitän* Erhardt, *U 862* was soon crossing the equator for the third time as she headed south towards the Bangka Strait. In accordance with *BdU*'s instructions the U-boat steered a zig-zag course, but navigational hazards again forced her to remain on the surface. The crew were still required to remain on the upper deck, but the weather was perfect, the sea glassy, and Reiffenstuhl for one set up a hammock and made the most of the opportunity to catch up on sleep.

Though blissfully unaware at the time, the crew may have been extremely fortunate that their departure plan had changed suddenly and unexpectedly. On 6 November another Allied daily intelligence summary noted:

> Singapore Base Force's 041943 gives following programme for 1 'friendly' (?German) submarine in company with 1 merchant ship—
> 5th at 1200—east entrance to Singapore Strait.
> am 6th—north entrance Bangka Strait.
> am 7th—arrive Batavia.[31]

However, Timm's luck had not deserted him and no unwelcome intrusions disturbed his boat's short passage.[32] *U 862* safely entered Jakarta on the morning of 8 November, one day late. She was met by the base commander, *Korvettenkapitän* Kandler, who piloted her in for the long journey to the main port from the outer harbour of Tanjong Priok.

After the squalor of Singapore the Germans found Java a very cultivated country in the European style. Jakarta itself boasted many restaurants, where meals were excellent in both quality and quantity. Though drinks were scarce and expensive there were also many bars, often run by European neutrals. There were not many German civilians remaining, but some had been left by the Japanese in charge of the plantations they had managed under previous Dutch ownership. The U-boat men were even able to see the occasional German woman, the first since leaving Europe.

Jakarta, however, was a city both at war and under foreign occupation. As in Penang a curfew existed, and a 'brownout' was the normal condition at night. Though in 1944 air raids were still rare, shelters and ditches were common throughout the city and efficient Indonesian police ensured that all air-raid measures were strictly enforced. To secure popular acceptance of their rule the Japanese used many Indonesians in their administration, promised self-government and armed volunteer 'puppet troops'. These, the Germans noticed, were spirited and enthusiastic and usually acclaimed by the native population wherever they marched.[33] The locals nevertheless lived in constant fear of the Japanese secret police, and whenever a group of *Kempetai* officials entered a restaurant, general silence would follow. The Japanese had also put up loudspeakers in parks and various street intersections, and only the Germans were not required to stop and listen to the propaganda broadcasts. The U-boat men soon found that as long as they could prove their identity they faced no undue restrictions, but though they were never openly shadowed, they knew they were always being watched.

On arrival, trucks took half of *U 862*'s crew into the mountains of Java. Eighty kilometres from Jakarta the Germans had acquired a 4400-acre tea plantation known as Tjikobo, and were cultivating it with the assistance of Javanese workers. There they grew vegetables and produced a variety of preserved foods, including bread, which were packed and sealed in containers of pure tin. *U 862* reprovisioned with as much as she could, but in what would later be regarded as a dubious decision, also embarked some tinned meat and mushrooms from Japanese stocks.

On the plantation the U-boat men could go for long walks in the countryside, relax and forget their worries. *Dieselobermaat* Rudolf Herrmann, who shared a room with *Zentraleobermaat* Fritz Zimmermann and *Funkmaat* Kurt Möller, was part of the first group to go to the plantation. He spent only three days at Tjikobo, but recalled them as a 'wonderful' time which 'none of us will ever forget!'.[34] On the final evening they must have found it hard to board the bus that would take them back to *U 862*. It would be a long time before they would experience such peace of mind again. Their second *Feindfahrt* was about to begin.

10 U 537 und U 196

Why the U-boat war? Every member of the Navy must tell himself with pride that his service and his efforts are at least as important for the outcome of this war as those of the best tank trooper or people's grenadier on distant fronts. Yes, who knows, perhaps after all the final issue will be decided by the U-boat war that is now gathering way.

—CinC *Kriegsmarine*'s special short situation report, 23 October 1944

The Allied intelligence network continued to maintain a close watch on all German U-boat operations and the preparations for the offensive in Australian waters were no exception. Joining with FECB in Colombo, and performing the bulk of naval work in the Pacific theatre, were the purely USN radio unit in Hawaii (Fleet Radio Unit Pacific or FRUPAC), and the joint Royal Australian Navy (RAN)/USN unit in Melbourne (Fleet Radio Unit Melbourne or FRUMEL). Information and problems were constantly passed between these units and the principal Allied intelligence centres in the capitals of London, Washington and Ottawa. Depending on its operational priority, recovered information could be either passed directly between the radio units for forwarding to the relevant local commander or included as part of routine special intelligence summaries. Because of its sensitivity, Ultra intelligence was normally divulged only to the highest levels of command. It could only be distributed further if the source was disguised.

The text of *BdU*'s message of 14 September, granting approval for the Australian operation by Timm and Pich, seems to have been decrypted by the Admiralty on the day following its transmission.[1] The full text was first broadcast to American authorities in the British Eastern Fleet's Intelligence Bulletin of 17 September, and the information appeared in the FRUMEL daily summary on 18 September.[2] Thereafter the boats destined for Australia were regularly reported as they moved between ports. Not only were the individual U-boats' positions accurately plotted, but the Allies could also closely follow the difficulties Dommes and *BdU* experienced as they tried to match resources to boats, and from this make deductions regarding German intentions and operational capability.

Though the Allies did not know the specific area of intended operations, the position of German bases in the Netherlands East Indies made deployments off southwest Australia seem most probable. Also missing from the intelligence appreciations was the exact nature of the mission, but the presence of Rear Admiral Christie's ten British and Dutch, and 41 American submarines suggested the Fremantle base as a logical, though difficult target. A submariner himself, Christie had assumed command of US submarine forces in theatre in early 1943 and, by his superior's account, 'did an extremely fine job . . . His operations were well-planned, sound and highly successful'.[3] Fully aware of what his submarines had achieved in operations against the Japanese, Christie was not comforted by the thought of two experienced U-boats lying in wait off Fremantle or moving in to lay minefields in the approach channels.

While Christie, as Commander Task Force 71 (CTF 71) and Commander Submarines Seventh Fleet, was the submarine operating authority, responsibility for the security of Australian waters remained with the Australian Commonwealth Naval Board (ACNB) under the guidance of the First Naval Member and Chief of Naval Staff (CNS), Admiral Sir Guy Royle. An officer of the Royal Navy on loan to the RAN, Royle had taken up his appointment as professional head of the Australian Navy in July 1941. Though still ultimately responsible to the federal government for Australia's maritime defence, Royle, like Christie, was also a subordinate commander within General MacArthur's larger South-West Pacific Area (SWPA). In this latter role Royle was designated Commander South-West Pacific Sea Frontiers (CSWPSF) and, though senior in rank, worked under the authority of MacArthur's naval commander, Vice Admiral Thomas C. Kinkaid USN. Notwithstanding MacArthur's high opinion of Royle's professional ability, there is some evidence of discord between the two. The British admiral was a particular critic of MacArthur's

Vice Admiral (later Admiral) Sir Guy Royle, KCB, CMG, photographed soon after his arrival in Australia in 1941. Royle came to Australia at the age of 56 after an appointment as the British Fifth Sea Lord and Chief of Naval Air Services. As the Australian Chief of Naval Staff he soon adapted to local conditions and in 1942 found himself working as a subordinate commander within General MacArthur's South-West Pacific Area (SWPA). Royle always felt that MacArthur failed to appreciate the importance that 'control of the sea' had in SWPA campaigns. (AWM 057215)

exhibitionism, and had in the past expressed his 'considerable concern' over the lack of recognition given by the SWPA's publicity machine to the work of Royle's ships and men.[4] MacArthur for his part believed that the admiral was also critical of the existing command arrangements and strongly objected to Royle's habit of communicating directly with the British Admiralty on operational matters. In 1943, when Royle's appointment as CNS was under review, the general had gone so far as to note that had he been consulted, he would have urged that Royle's term not be extended.[5]

As CSWPSF, Royle had originally been charged only with the safe conduct and routing of all merchant shipping and routine shipping in support of military operations.[6] However, as a succession of Allied offensives moved the focus of attention north and

South West Pacific Sea Frontiers, 1944

farther away from Australia, Royle gradually regained operational control of all escort and minesweeping vessels otherwise assigned to him. After all, there seemed little residual threat in local waters, and by late 1944 MacArthur was so engrossed in the Philippines that he had virtually no further interest in Australia. Quite naturally, Kinkaid too had had much broader concerns and, as he once wrote to his wife, 'I am interested only in the Allied Naval Forces when they are in contact with the enemy.'[7]

Royle discharged his defence-of-trade task using a series of Port Directors, District Naval Officers and Naval Officers-in-Charge (NOIC) of areas. It was the NOICs who dealt directly with the allocated escort vessels and dispersed them to the various ports as directed by CSWPSF. Since 1943, NOIC Fremantle had been Commodore Cuthbert J. Pope, RAN. Aged 57 and later described as 'tall and ascetic . . . (and) reticent to the point of shyness', Pope was nevertheless a highly professional officer and had already spent a year as NOIC Darwin, arriving in that town only a matter of hours after the first and most destructive Japanese air raid in February 1942.[8] Having moved to Fremantle, Pope now had little direct interaction with enemy activity, but still had a major administrative role to play in meeting the requirements of passing Allied warship and merchant traffic.

Both Royle and Christie had access to Sigint information on a daily basis. Royle, however, normally dealt only with the special intelligence summaries, while Christie received a much greater range of current operational material, the success of the American submarine fleet owing much to the cuing provided by Ultra. With the close relationship established between the intelligence community and the submarine operating authority it is hardly surprising that it was Christie who first acted upon the information unwittingly provided by *BdU*. At a meeting he convened on the morning of 18 September, Christie informed Pope and the Air Officer Commanding Western Area (AOCWA), Air Commodore R.J. Brownell, of the intelligence. He also said he believed that the threat was directed more against submarines operating from Fremantle than against merchant shipping and added that 'any increase in aircraft for seaward patrols could not be expected from American sources and that an increase of American anti-submarine surface craft could not be expected for at least a month, even if any were forthcoming at all'.[9]

Whether the local Australian naval and air commanders were cleared for access to Sigint is not known, but Christie had evidently divulged more than enough detail to make the source clear.

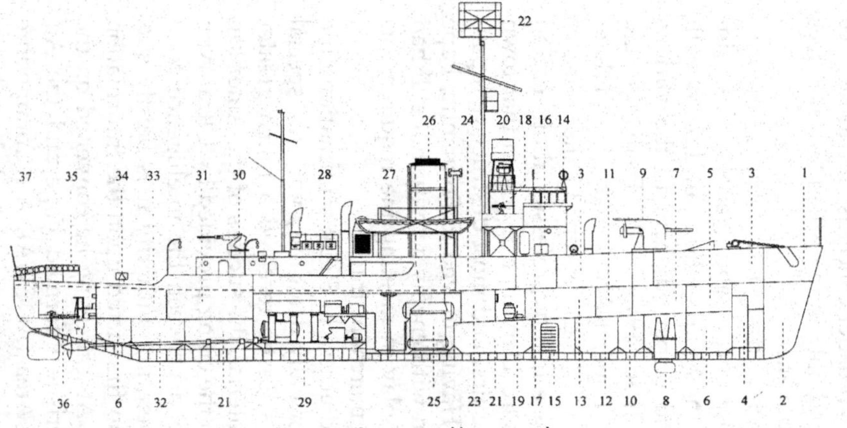

Bathurst class Australian minesweeper

Displacement	815 tons
Length	56.7 m
Beam	9.5 m
Draught	2.6 m
Fuel Capacity	153 tons
Speed	15.5 kts
Range	2640 nm at 10 kts
Armament (typical)	
guns	1 × 4-in
	1 × 40-mm
	2 × 20-mm
depth charges	20–60
Crew	70–90

1 Paint store
2 Fore peak
3 Crew space
4 Chain locker
5 Gunners store (port)
6 Trimming tank
7 PO's mess (starboard)
8 Asdic dome
9 4-in gun
10 Provision store
11 Victualling office (starboard)
12 Fresh water tank
13 CPO's mess
14 D/F loop
15 Magazine
16 Captain's cabin
17 W/T office
18 20-mm Oerlikon
19 Gyro compass room
20 A272 surface warning radar
21 Oil fuel tank
22 A286 air/surface warning radar
23 Naval store
24 Galley
25 Boiler room
26 Funnel
27 27-ft whaler
28 Engine room ventilation
29 Engine room
30 40-mm Bofors gun
31 Wardroom (port)
32 Small arms magazine
33 Minesweeping/depth charge store
34 Depth charge thrower
35 Depth charge rails
36 After steering compartment
37 Officer's baggage

In a remarkably candid message, Pope set out his problems and asked Royle for assistance:

> CTF 71 has received reliable information indicating two U-boats whose numbers are known are leaving Singapore and Batavia respectively for operations on west coast with Fremantle as most likely focal area. In view of shortage of A/S ships and removal of Catalina[s] suggest CINCEF be asked to consider retention here of *Ipswich* and *Tamworth* at least until situation is clear. Can any other AMS be released from other areas for reinforcements? Have ordered *Dubbo* return Fremantle with *ML 815*.[10]

HMA Ships *Ipswich, Tamworth* and *Dubbo,* were *Bathurst* class Australian minesweepers (AMS). More commonly known as corvettes, they were the RAN's 'maids of all work', employed in all theatres on tasks as diverse as search and rescue, shore bombardment and troop transport. Relatively small and uncomfortable for their crews, the *Bathursts* tended to behave unpredictably in anything other than fine weather. 'As stomach pumps they were hard to beat' was one ex-corvette officer's considered opinion.[11] The *Bathurst*'s top speed was barely 15kts, they had only a 4-inch gun for main armament, and their plotting facilities were inadequate. However, they were fitted with Asdic in a retractable dome and, carrying up to 40 depth charges, they provided Australia's primary anti-submarine patrol and escort capability.

Dubbo was under Pope's operational control and currently on detached duties to Onslow on the northwest coast. *Ipswich* and *Tamworth,* however, were attached to the British Eastern Fleet and only in Fremantle for refitting. Nevertheless, in response to Pope's request the two vessels were lent to the ACNB when their dockyard work was done.[12] Royle also ordered NOIC Darwin to transfer three, and NOIC Sydney one, AMS to the temporary operational control of NOIC Fremantle and sail these at best speed as soon as they were ready.[13] These reinforcements eventually arrived, but it was questionable whether they could be classified as 'ready'. As Pope's war diary was later to protest, 'one had no dome or gun, two others had defective A/S [equipment] and all required boiler cleaning'.[14]

In the meantime Christie, Pope and Brownell had been in consultation, placing port defences on alert and ensuring the movements of Allied ships and submarines carefully safeguarded. This was by no means routine, as there was no clear-cut delineation of responsibility between the three local commanders and any coordination was ultimately dependent upon their individual priorities. Complicating the provision of an effective defence, the prolonged absence of enemy submarine activity had caused a deliberate reduction in anti-submarine measures. Pope did what he could with the few assets he had left. Effective immediately, he placed all escort vessels on short notice for steam and allocated at least one escort to all vessels leaving port. Submarines exercising were also escorted to and from their areas, and Christie agreed that none should be permitted in the exercise areas after sunset. The harbour itself was already protected by magnetic indicator loops laid on the seabed, and patrols outside these were established with a few 75-ton Fairmile B Motor Launches (ML) and coastal minesweepers (YMS). The patrols were intended to give early warning of a submarine's approach and to increase the range at which the submarine attempting to attack shipping at anchor would have to fire torpedoes.

For offensive operations Pope formed the three Australian corvettes already in Fremantle, together with the USS *Chanticleer* and USS *Isabel*, into a 'hunter-killer' group under his direct operational orders. The inclusion of *Chanticleer*, a submarine tender most nearly resembling a large tug, and *Isabel*, a small submarine training ship, clearly illustrates the *ad hoc* nature of the measures Pope was forced to adopt.[15] As more corvettes arrived, Pope planned that they would be used to establish a distant patrol 130 miles from Fremantle. Here, he thought, they would be in a favourable position to attack a submarine surfacing to make a run in during darkness, and also able to render prompt assistance to merchant ships. The AMS and YMS vessels likewise carried out 'LL' electric pulse sweeps to keep the approaches to Fremantle clear of magnetic mines.

Brownell was similarly hampered by a lack of assets. Through the first months of 1944, Royal Australian Air Force (RAAF) squadrons had been ordered to successively reduce anti-submarine patrols and since April close escort had only been given along shipping routes between Darwin and Thursday Island in northern Australia.[16] The worst blow, however, came in mid-1944 when the USN withdrew Patrol Wing 10 and its Catalinas from their base near Perth. This left the huge RAAF Western Area, with a coastline stretching from the South Australian border to just north of Derby, without a capable anti-submarine aircraft. For patrols AOCWA now had only the eighteen Beaufort aircraft of No. 14 Squadron RAAF. These were based at Pearce and only fifteen were considered serviceable. The Beaufort was a light bomber rather than a reconnaissance aircraft, but owing to the lack of anything more

A Bristol Beaufort Mk VI of No. 1 Bombing and Gunnery School, East Sale. As the RAAF's workhorse in the Pacific war, more than 700 Beauforts were built in Australia between 1939 and 1944. They were designed as a general purpose light bomber and in Australian service were used extensively for reconnaissance and the protection of coastal shipping. With a 2000 lb bomb-load, the Beaufort had a range of 1060 miles. (RAAF)

suitable, it was widely used in the patrol role by the RAAF during the war. From 19 September No. 14 Squadron began carrying out what were termed 'anti-submarine patrols of a special nature'. Flown twice daily at dawn and dusk, the patrols covered an arc of 150 miles radius centred on Fremantle. They required approximately 22 hours flying each day and the squadron found it necessary to withdraw detachments from other areas to complete the assignment. Brownell held three of the Beauforts in reserve as a striking force. There were also a few American Dauntless aircraft available, and these were used to patrol directly over the exercise area. The 'Special Submarine Patrol Western Area' was to remain in operation until May 1945.[17]

Though the primary threat was thought to be directed against Fremantle, measures for the wider protection of merchant shipping were also implemented. As of 19 September, Royle ordered all shipping bound west for Indian Ocean ports to follow well dispersed routes so as not to pass less than 250 miles south of the coast between Albany and Cape Leeuwin. Ships bound for Western Australian ports were to arrive only during the three hours before sunset and no navigation lights were to be burned west of 130°E.[18] In consultation with Pope, Royle also considered the introduction of coastal convoys between Fremantle and Albany, but owing to the shortage of escorts they decided to wait until the need developed.

The acute alert maintained throughout the remainder of September and October ensured that any possible sighting was taken seriously. The presence of a suspected Asdic contact or periscope sighting off Rottnest Island more than once resulted in all available anti-submarine vessels and aircraft being called out to search, while the shipping control network either diverted merchant ships away from the area or delayed sailings.[19] On each occasion all exercises with Christie's submarines were cancelled and aircraft were authorised to attack any submarines sighted. These restrictions not only disrupted submarine training but also increased pressure on aircraft maintenance. Complete air coverage of the threatened area called for approximately 80 hours additional flying each month, and the 'Western Area Tactical Appreciation' for October noted the adverse effect on available engine hours if these operations were to continue.[20]

Despite the lack of suitable resources, the evident cooperation and integrated anti-submarine measures brought into force off Fremantle provide an interesting contrast with the lack of corresponding action taken by the Japanese. Yet the extra patrols and evasive routing of shipping were still only a secondary line of defence. *U 168*'s interception and sinking had clearly demonstrated that Christie intended to deal with the threat with pre-emptive action whenever practicable.

U 537 was to be the next German boat to depart for the Australian offensive. Though not successful in terms of tonnage sunk, *Kapitänleutnant* Schrewe was an experienced U-boat officer and this next operation would be his third war patrol in command. *BdU* had expected Schrewe's U-boat to be ready for sea by 17 October, but maintenance problems forced a three-week delay. Not until 4 November did the Japanese Surabaya Guard Force send out the following program for the U-boat:

> 9th 1700—leave Surabaya
> 10th 0030—in 6–42S 114–00E
> 0700—in 7–12S 115–17E where diving test will be carried out for 10 miles on course 156 degrees.
> 1000—proceed on surface course 161 degrees.
> 1500—2 miles off Tanjung Iboes (Bali) and thence along 100 fathom line to eastward of Bali.
> 1800—in 8–48S 115–22E then proceed south.[21]

This text is taken from the FRUMEL periodic summary of 10 November, but the message had already been decrypted in sufficient time for decisive action to be taken. The orders that would seal *U 537*'s fate were hurriedly drafted by CTF 71 and forwarded to Darwin.[22]

The US submarines *Flounder*, *Guavina* and *Bashaw* arrived together in Darwin from Brisbane on 5 November 1944. The three large 'fleet boats' were all products of the massive wartime building program that saw 195 submarines of almost identical configuration launched by the Americans between 1941 and 1945. Designed for long range and endurance on station, they were broadly comparable to the German Type IXD2, but slightly longer, faster, with a greater displacement—and far more habitable.

Once in Darwin the three boats secured to the *Chanticleer*, which had moved up from Fremantle in October, while they replenished fuel, lube oil and fresh water and made voyage repairs. However, their stay in Darwin was to be shorter than expected. As soon as they arrived the boats received their new patrol orders. They were to be organised into a 'coordinated search and attack group', with *Flounder*'s commanding officer, Commander James E. Stevens USN, as group commander. For Stevens, already a veteran of seven war patrols, this would be his third patrol in command of *Flounder* and his most successful assignment of the war. Immediately after receipt of the orders a conference of commanding officers was held and an officer from Christie's staff provided a briefing on the mission and expected target.

Flounder and *Guavina* sailed from Darwin during the early afternoon of 6 November. *Bashaw* departed later following a different route. With little time to spare if he was to complete the intercept, Stevens took his group north, passing east of Timor on the evening of the following day. Once in the Banda Sea the two submarines altered course to the west and remained on the surface to facilitate a quick crossing. No Japanese ships or aircraft were seen and though there were many native 'sailboats', the two submarines altered course as necessary to avoid being sighted. *Guavina* parted company on the evening of 8 November to patrol her allocated area, and *Flounder* continued on alone to her prime objective. At 0503 on 10 November she was in position south of the Kangean Islands and Stevens ordered her to dive. *Flounder*'s subsequent patrol report provides a detailed description of events as they then unfolded (times are one hour ahead of the 'Tokyo time' used by the Japanese and Germans in East Asia):

USS Flounder *in 1945. A typical USN 'fleet boat' of the* Gato *class,* Flounder *had a standard displacement of 1526 tons and was launched in August 1943. She made six war patrols and, in addition to* U 537, *was credited with sinking one and a half Japanese merchant ships totalling 5533 GRT. The submarine was stricken in 1960.* (Naval Historical Center 83207)

> 0524 Picked up pinging on sound gear.
> 0557 Sighted an escort vessel. Closed to see if he was escorting anything. He was alone and seemed to be making an anti-submarine sweep. Decided not to attack him as he might be clearing the way for something more worthwhile. Avoided him at periscope depth.

As already noted, knowledge of Sigint was strictly controlled and Stevens could not refer in his report to the intelligence source that allowed him to make such an accurate forecast. Moreover, his seeming disregard for Japanese anti-submarine forces was not uncommon and indicates the extent of the problem faced by the Germans in relying on their ally's protective measures. *Flounder* was now in position and Stevens began his patient wait. Two hours later he sighted something approaching, its position recorded in *Flounder*'s log as 7°13'S 115°17'E. *U 537* was on her way as scheduled.

> 0754 Officer of the deck sighted what appeared to be a small sailboat bearing 347° (T), distance about 9000 yards.
> 0800 Sail turned out to be the conning tower of a submarine, angle on the bow about 30° starboard. Went to battle stations submerged and came to normal approach course.
> 0809 Target was identified as a German submarine making 12 knots.
> 0817 Target zigged towards, so swung around so as to be able to

shoot electric torpedoes from the stern tubes. Was very glad he did this because electric fish are ideal for a target of this kind.
0826 Fired four stern tubes. Track angle 90° starboard, range 1000 yards, gyro angles very small. Torpedoes were set to run at 8 feet.
0827 Observed hit about forty feet inside the bow. There was a tremendous explosion and the whole target was obscured by smoke and flame . . . felt another timed hit. Ran up other scope twenty seconds after first hit but nothing could be seen but smoke well above water.
0833 Another explosion.
0836 Another explosion. These were violent and seemed close and were thought to be aerial depth bombs, so we went to 150 feet and cleared the area. Subsequent consideration and information from the sound operators indicates that these were probably explosions inside the sinking sub because the sound operator reports that they were accompanied by breaking up noises and hissing.
0905 Returned to periscope depth all clear.

The electric torpedoes worked beautifully. The target seemed to have no idea that anything was coming toward him, he did not change course one degree before he was hit.

This fellow was painted a light grey with a dark horizontal stripe near the top of his conning tower. There was no doubt from his silhouette that he was German. His size seemed to correspond to a 750 tonner. He was flying colours, but they were too small to identify.[23]

Stevens had shown quick thinking in his attack. Though *U 537*'s last-minute zig had simply been a routine alteration to take her through Lombok Strait, *Flounder*'s shift from bow to stern tubes had allowed her to remain in an ideal firing position. The use of electric rather than steam torpedoes had also demonstrated good judgment. The electric weapons left virtually no wake and ensured the U-boat received no warning. For Schrewe and the other 57 officers and men aboard his boat the end was swift. As Christie later noted in his endorsement to *Flounder*'s patrol report, 'Twenty seconds after the first hit the U-boat had completed her last, and probably fastest dive. There were no survivors.'[24] Yet again the East Asia U-boats had allowed themselves to be surprised.

Neither *BdU* nor the Penang base expected to hear from *U 537* until near the end of her mission. On the evening of the U-boat's loss, Dommes signalled best wishes for good hunting to Schrewe, and messages would continue to be sent to the sunken U-boat until late January.[25] This lack of information was not so applicable to the Australians, yet Admiral Royle still appears to have had difficulty maintaining an accurate appreciation of the situation. In particular, it was not clear whether the three 'Australian U-boats' mentioned by Vice Admiral Abe in his message of 26 September included the two previously scheduled to operate in the west.[26] So although Royle had certain knowledge of the losses of *U 168* and *U 537*, as late as 29 November he still informed NOICs Darwin and Fremantle that 'there are indications that two German U-boats may be operating on the West or North West coasts of Australia'.[27] Twenty-four hours later he added that 'a third German U-boat is expected to operate off the southwest coast of Australia from early December'.[28] Air patrols off Fremantle, reduced since early November to a single aircraft search at dusk, were now doubled. CTF 71's submarines were again put on the alert and surface warships put renewed effort into anti-submarine patrols.

U 862 was one of the 'two German U-boats' mentioned by Royle, and the third was presumably Striegler's *U 196*. She had departed Jakarta on 30 November and after passing through the Sunda Strait was due first to head west into the Indian Ocean to act as a refuelling stop for the homeward-bound *U 510*. *U 196* was then to operate off southwest Australia for one month before proceeding to Japan to have her batteries renewed. Serious leaks in her exhaust tubes forced *U 510* to return to Jakarta, and the refuelling operation was cancelled on the day of *U 196*'s departure. Penang sent a recall order six times, and a hastener on 15 December, but despite repeated requests for a position report, Striegler failed to respond.[29] On 22 December *BdU* informed all East Asia U-boats that *U 196* was presumed to have been sunk by a submarine shortly after leaving Jakarta, and drew their attention again 'to the great danger from submarines, especially off narrow channels and harbours. The greatest caution is necessary.'[30] No claims were actually made by either British or American submarines and the Allies were just as baffled, though obviously grateful for the U-boat's disappearance. The cause of *U 196*'s loss remains a mystery. Though a Dutch submarine did lay minefields on the outward route through Sunda Strait, this occurred several weeks afterwards and the most likely explanation is that Striegler suffered a marine accident.[31]

Of the four U-boats allocated to the Australian operation, only *U 862* now remained unaccounted for. Given the ease with which two U-boats had already been dispatched, it must have seemed to Royle that Timm's own chances of survival were slight. However, by the time FRUMEL informed CSWPSF of *U 196*'s disappearance, Timm had already made his own dramatic entry into Royle's area, and in waters far from the southwest coast of Australia.

11 Zweite Feindfahrt

The submarine as a gunnery vessel is in itself a contradiction in terms. Being incapable of offering powerful resistance, and because of its low and unstable gunnery and controlling platforms, which are directly exposed to the action of the sea, it cannot be said to be built for artillery combat.

—*The U-Boat Commander's Handbook,* 1943 edition

U *862* sailed from Jakarta's harbour at midday on 18 November, passing on the same evening through the Sunda Strait and into the open sea. Unusually, there is only one record of a radio intercept that reveals *U 862*'s exact departure date. This appears more than two weeks later as a brief note in an American intelligence summary dated 4 December.[1] Neither the date nor text of the original source, nor whether it was a German or Japanese transmission, is included. Prior to this record the only apparent clue for Allied intelligence that *U 862* had sailed was a signal from Dommes on 24 November ordering Timm and Schrewe to include a report on 'southern area heavy diesel oil' next time they transmitted by radio. The following day there was another message allocating the two U-boats new call-sign series.[2] Timm's direct departure may have made an interception difficult, but it appears that either a lack of detailed information or a delay in decryption saved *U 862* from the fate of her two predecessors. Rear Admiral Christie was certainly not short of assets for an attack. During October–November 1944, there were 46 Allied submarine patrols originating from Fremantle.[3]

When Timm set out, it was with the expectation not only that he would be the second boat to reach Australian waters, but also that the appearance of the U-boats would be a complete surprise. Since Schrewe was due to operate in the southwest off Fremantle, Timm decided to try his luck further to the south of the continent. However, without accurate or current intelligence, the success of the mission would rely very much on Timm's own knowledge and experience. Before departure he had taken on board as many relevant charts as he could find, and he and his officers pored over these and the pilotage manuals to plan their patrol area.

Ahead of *U 862* stretched a passage of more than 1500 miles due south. Timm intended to pass about 450 miles off the Western Australian coast before finally turning southeast to round Cape Leeuwin. By keeping well out to sea, he hoped to avoid any routine air surveillance and thus allow *U 862* to stay on the surface and maintain a high speed. Moreover, Timm had no desire either to alert the Australians to his approach or to invite action before he had his boat and crew properly prepared. Two months of exotic living had taken their toll. It would be a few days before they had shaken off the lethargic effects of mountain air and unfamiliar food. Reiffenstuhl's experience was typical: 'Inhumanly hot in the boat. Sleep impossible. All have bad headaches. I have bad diarrhoea, have not eaten for 4 days.'[4]

Despite rough seas and freshening winds, the U-boat made good progress and after five days Timm altered course to close the Australian coast. Thereafter *U 862* would spend the daylight hours submerged. On 25 November the well-known high-pitched buzz of the Tunis equipment showed that at least some aircraft were up and searching. On 26 November Timm informed his men that they were within striking distance of Cape Leeuwin. He expected that this would be a fruitful area, for shipping traffic in both directions would tend to cut the corner, passing within a few miles of the coast and creating a local concentration of targets. They increased speed again overnight so that by morning they would be in position close off the cape.

The weather continued to worsen. The temperature dropped to an uncomfortable level. Rain storms lashed the boat and reduced visibility. Conditions, though, were apparently not bad enough to prevent flying operations. Early the next morning one of the lookouts sighted an aircraft in the distance. The watch officer sounded the alarm and Timm kept his U-boat down for the next eighteen hours. The Germans had not, in fact, been seen, but RAAF Western Area's 'special anti-submarine patrols' were achieving at least part of their aim.

The air patrols in this area were obviously more intense than

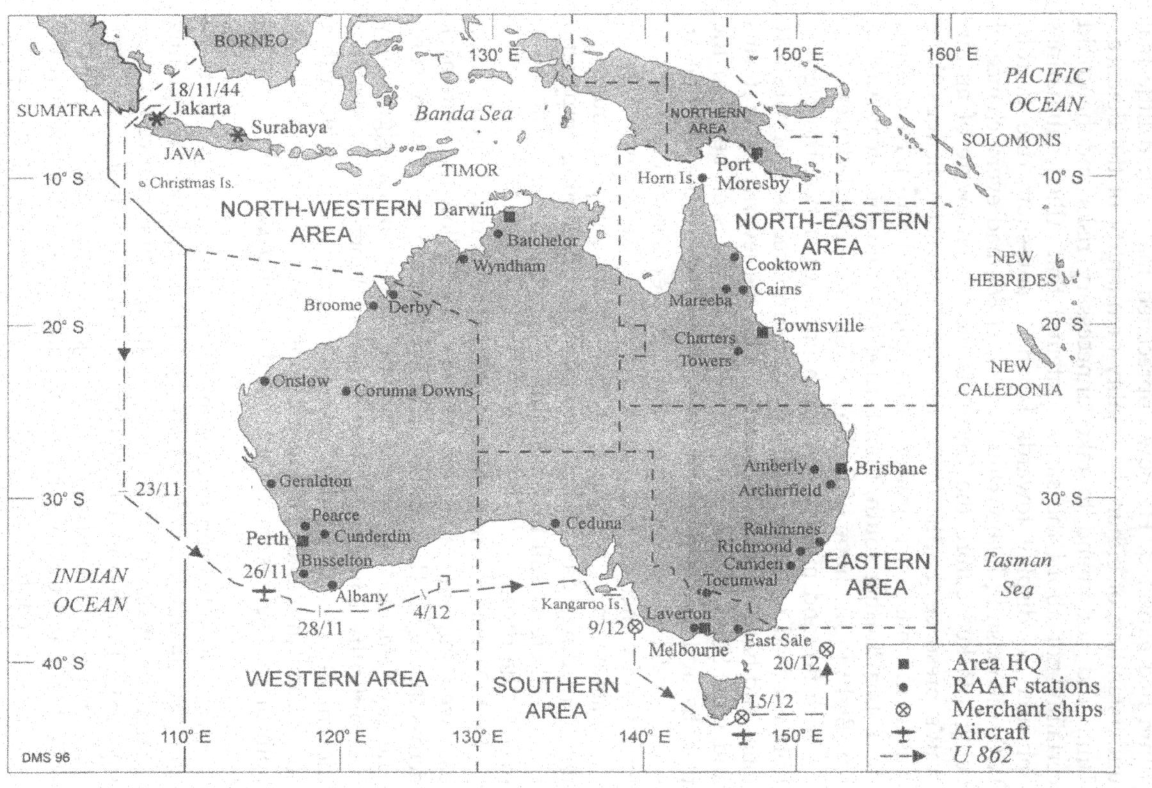

RAAF Command, November–December 1944

Timm had expected. He now appreciated that he had little real understanding of either the quality or quantity of the defences. Timm did not intend to take unnecessary risks and he could certainly not afford the same contempt that Allied submarines appeared to display towards Japanese anti-submarine patrols. With the existing heavy cloud cover, *U 862* had every chance of being attacked before the Germans were even aware of an aircraft's presence. Furthermore, despite Timm's predictions there was no obvious concentration of shipping in the area. He ordered the U-boat further south, then turned east into the Great Australian Bight in the hope of finding a less well-defended area.

With no land mass to the south until Antarctica, the Bight is fully exposed to the fury of the Southern Ocean's southwesterly gales and has always been notorious for the severity of its storms and seas. Soon *U 862* was 'playing hide and seek between the troughs and peaks of the waves'.[5] Buffeted by the long ocean swells and lost between grey sky and grey sea, it did not take long for the men to fall prey to boredom: 'We are now closing the coast again to try and find the primary shipping route . . . much reading, days rather monotonous. Becoming impatient, because there is still no steamship in sight—how gigantic, however, is the ocean . . .'[6]

By 1 December Timm calculated that they must be on the main east–west shipping lanes and turned east to follow the route back across the Bight. The barometer showed a sharp drop in pressure. The sky remained overcast and without sun or star sights they had difficulty confirming their position. When on 3 December they finally obtained a fix, Timm found they were much farther south than intended. He altered course to the north and, using both diesel engines, increased speed to get back to the shipping lanes.

It had already been three weeks since they had left Jakarta. In all that time they had neither seen nor heard anything resembling a target. Probably even more frustrating, Timm received a message from Penang on 4 December that at last contained concrete intelligence from the Japanese: 'a major British Fleet Unit coming from India and Ceylon arrived at Perth 22/11. Presume that the unit proceeded to East Australian ports at end of November, probably to support Philippine action. Transport traffic in West Australian ports in November was double that of October.'[7]

The Allies were not the only ones to appreciate the value of radio intelligence, but this would appear to be one of the very few instances in which the two Axis partners accomplished an effective exchange of information.[8] Whether the intelligence was obtained from D/F or decryption is not clear, but if not strictly inaccurate, the message was still rather misleading. The destroyer HMS *Queenborough* was the only British unit to arrive in Fremantle at this time, she could hardly be classified as a major unit and she had come from Addu Atoll rather than Trincomalee, but she did indeed continue east, to reach Sydney on 28 November.[9]

The presumed presence of major fleet units provided Timm with a likely explanation for the level of air patrols, but the absence of any signs of increased 'transport traffic' was more problematic. Still battling rough seas, *U 862* pressed stubbornly on across the Bight. Writing on 5 December, Reiffenstuhl described the bafflement felt on board:

> Searching north and south for the steamship route. Great debates, where are the hostile ships sailing: along the great circle route?(no), under the coast? Has Schrewe already taken a steamship? They are certainly not sailing on the peacetime shipping routes; I assume, that steamship traffic is being steered very far to the north and under the coast. Otherwise, perhaps there is little traffic on this route, since the ships from W-Australia evidently go up to the Gulf of Aden and from SE-Australia up to the Philippines, where war material is urgently needed. We become somewhat impatient, no one has sighted a steamship and debate goes on for hours.

In December 1944, the Germans were managing to keep an average of 51 U-boats at sea each day. Nevertheless, with boats forced to proceed almost entirely underwater, the days of coordinated wolf packs were long past and the chances of a single boat detecting a target in the open sea extremely limited. In fact *BdU* could only classify some fourteen U-boats as being in an 'operations area'. These were *Schnorchel*-fitted boats operating 'in enemy territorial waters where concentrations of enemy traffic are to be found'. However, in these circumstances *BdU* was no longer able to exert the same level of centralised control that it had in the mid-Atlantic convoy battles.[10] On 6 December *BdU* addressed Current Order No. 45 to all operating U-boats:

> In the assignment of operational areas, headquarters does not always have complete information regarding focal points, routes and times of shipping so that sometimes only general guidance can be transmitted to the boats.
>
> Therefore it sometimes happens that in spite of long waiting off the enemy coast, enemy traffic is not encountered. Hence in case of

> sparse traffic or movements by night there is no opportunity for a shot.
>
> In such cases captains are to strike out and leave areas without promise, trusting to a sixth sense and hunting instincts to bring them success. Change of area, such as moving closer to the coast or going farther into the bays, is also necessary. It is not necessary to report such movements to headquarters.
>
> All action along these lines which leads to better chances for wiping out the enemy will be approved in every case by headquarters.[11]

The message presumably referred to inshore operations in the Atlantic theatre, but it was just as relevant to Australian waters and *U 862* was certainly already moving in line with its intent.[12] Timm was confident in his knowledge of the normal shipping routes in the Southern Ocean and strongly voiced his opinion that traffic had been deliberately diverted. He decided to close the coast, in particular to move in towards the Spencer Gulf and the western approaches to Adelaide. There, in a natural focal area, there would be less possibility of rerouting shipping.

By the early morning hours of 6 December a rocky coastline could already be discerned through the periscope. Visibility was improving and *U 862* spent the next day near the Neptune Islands, some 40 miles from the mainland. Finding nothing, the Germans proceeded south of Kangaroo Island and continued farther along the coast. By the evening of 8 December they were only a short distance from Cape Jaffa on the southeast corner of South Australia. Those on watch on the U-boat's bridge were surprised to see the sweeping beam of a lighthouse. The possibility remained that the Australians were after all still unaware that a German U-boat was stalking off their southern coast, restlessly waiting for the opportunity to strike. In an almost unreal intrusion of sentiment, Reiffenstuhl received birthday congratulations from his parents on the other side of the world.

Saturday 9 December dawned bleak and grey. The wind had increased in strength overnight and rain threatened. Large waves had begun to form and the white foam crests were being blown as spray over the sea's surface. It was too rough for *U 862* to remain close to shore, so she dived and moved back out to sea. At around 1000 came the report they had all waited so long to hear: 'piston engine noise 345 degrees'.[13] The vessel was closing their position, but the heavy seas had meant a late sound detection and by the time Timm could see the steamship it was already almost on his beam. Though the target was only making 9 or 10kts, it was already too late to manoeuvre for a submerged attack. Still, after coming this far and waiting so long Timm did not intend to let it get away. He decided to engage the ship with his deck gun.

Reiffenstuhl was aghast and tried desperately to dissuade his commander. The sea was too rough, the IWO argued. Once on the surface, accurate fire would be impossible and the gun's crew would be at risk of being swept over the side. Moreover, their intended victim had its own gun platform fitted at the stern. A merchant ship was very difficult to sink with gunfire alone, yet in contrast it would only take one hit on *U 862*'s pressure hull to prevent her from diving. Timm remained unmoved by his second in command's reasoning. He answered that they would delay the gun attack until the U-boat's *Flak* weapons were within range, 'For as soon as our rapid-fire flies past his ears he will not attempt to approach his gun.'[14]

U 862 surfaced and began to close the steamship from astern. The gun crews appeared on deck and opened the containers of ready-use ammunition, being careful not to make preparations too obvious. As gunnery officer, Karl Steinhauser positioned himself behind the 10.5cm deck gun ready to direct the firing. It was daylight and the Germans were still close enough to see the coast. At any moment their prey could sound the alarm, bringing down an unknown number of Australian aircraft and warships. Timm was under pressure. In the tight confines of a U-boat everyone would have been aware that Reiffenstuhl had disagreed with him. It seemed to be taking forever to close the range. His patience at an end, Timm gave Steinhauser permission to fire. At the same moment a large wave rolled over the bow. The gun's crew were strapped to their weapon but Steinhauser was not and he nearly went overboard. The round went wide.

On passage to Port Melbourne, *U 862*'s intended victim was the 4724 GRT Greek cargo ship *Ilissos*. Reiffenstuhl recorded her size as only 2000 GRT, a significant underestimation of her worth that may have been influenced by subsequent developments. *Ilissos*' chief engineer, Peter Kypriatas, was the first to see the U-boat. Just before midday it had surfaced a little over a mile away on the starboard quarter:

> I was outside . . . looking at the open sea and I saw something like a little boat. I was surprised because the sea was very heavy and I was wondering why the little boat was in such a heavy sea. While I was still looking at the boat it was coming up out of the water and looked like a small American craft. After a little while, I saw the forepart. It was very long from the conning tower.[15]

Convinced it must be a friendly submarine, Kypriatas went to the bridge to find out if the watch was aware of their unexpected escort. The second officer was incredulous. He first laughed, then at Kypriatas' urging went to see for himself. No alarm was sounded and both men were looking at the submarine when they saw a flash and the shelling began. The first round splashed 100m from *Ilissos'* starboard side. Hearing the scream of the second shell passing over the ship, Kypriatas did not wait to see where it fell, 'After that I went to my cabin to get my life-belt'.

Captain Evangelos Svokos, master of *Ilissos*, was sitting in the saloon when he heard the first report of *U 862*'s gun. He instantly ran up to the bridge:

> when I got there I just heard the 2nd shot coming over the ship. I took the glasses from the 2nd Officer. The Chief Engineer was coming up to the bridge and I gave him 'Full speed ahead, hard aport' and I rang the alarm bell and the 2nd Officer was instructed to muster the crew and clear lifeboats. By that time the gunners were on the gun platform.
>
> We were just turning and the 3rd round I saw falling near the poop of this ship on the starboard side. By that time the 'Ilissos' started to fire. The first shot fell short, the 2nd was short but nearer the 3rd fell very near with waves covering the submarine from splash. The submarine then started submerging. We fired a 4th round which fell on the same position as the submarine submerged.[16]

It was an ignominious defeat for *U 862*. Timm realised the folly of his impatience as soon as he saw his opponent's first shot. Having opened fire while still outside the range of his small-calibre weapons, Timm had found himself engaged in the very gun duel he wished to avoid. He was probably fortunate that the crash-dive prevented his seeing how close the following rounds had come to his U-boat.

Ilissos' saviours had been her four-man team of naval gunners. They were known as DEMS (Defensively Equipped Merchant Ship) ratings, trained to man the quick-firing 4-inch gun in just this type of situation. Nevertheless, after months of absolute boredom it must have come as a rude shock to be needed in such an unexpected locality. Though the crew had conducted a practice firing less than an hour before the U-boat appeared, the weapon had then been covered and, against regulations, the normal gun watch had retired below deck for shelter. Hearing *U 862*'s first shot, they had managed to get from 'down on the mess deck having a cup of tea' to gun uncovered, loaded and first round fired, in only two and a half minutes.[17]

With the Greek firemen managing to produce an additional 2kts over her usual top speed, *Ilissos* ran for the coast. One lifeboat was swung out and the remainder of the crew stood by, ready to abandon ship if necessary. There was no panic. Svokos planned to approach as close inshore as he dared, then turn and run along the coast to the southeast. Ten minutes after exchanging the last shot heavy rain started to fall, further assisting the freighter's escape. If Timm had stayed to watch he would have seen the visibility close down to less than a mile and *Ilissos* rapidly disappear in the downpour.

Timm, however, had already elected to remain dived and likewise leave the area as fast as he could. *U 862*'s radio room had been keeping watch on the distress frequency and had picked up *Ilissos'* plain-language broadcast reporting an attack by an unidentified submarine. It would not be long now before the U-boat became the hunted once more. That night Reiffenstuhl poured out his frustration in his journal:

> I am annoyed with the Brass (angry) because of this senseless enterprise. Now we have alarmed the whole coast to our presence, certainly over the next few days no more steamships will be sailing past. We must move our operating area, without having sunk the steamship. We have only betrayed ourselves. Because of this nonsense we have destroyed all our chances here. Nothing has been proved.[18]

The hunt began as soon as *Ilissos'* cry for help was received. Ordered out through the Air Operations Room Southern Area, the first two Australian aircraft arrived over the freighter two and a half hours after the incident. These were rocket-equipped Bristol Beaufighters from Laverton, each with two 250-pound bombs. They had been briefed to carry out a search and strike mission but failed to locate any sign of the enemy. Relief aircraft soon took over and the requirement to perform searches of probability areas and provide air cover for important shipping continued for the remainder of the month. RAAF Southern Area eventually mounted an additional 373 sorties and of the 1180 hours flown, almost half the effort fell on the Avro Ansons of No. 67 (Reserve) Squadron based at Laverton.[19]

Unfortunately, the forces allocated to Southern Area to meet these increased operational commitments proved inadequate in terms of both numbers and capability. As a tactical appreciation later admitted, the effort was only possible through the allocation of some aircraft from Eastern Area and the borrowing of others

A Consolidated B-24L Liberator of No. 7 Operational Training Unit (OTU) at RAAF Tocumwal. Though normally used as a heavy bomber in RAAF service, in December 1944 three Liberators from this unit were ordered by HQ Southern Area to stand by as a striking force during the search for U 862 *by Ansons of No. 67 (Reserve) Squadron and Beauforts of No. 1 OTU operating from Mount Gambier, Laverton and East Sale.* (RAAF)

from No. 4 (Maintenance) and No. 1 (Training) Groups. Even then the lack of suitable operational aircraft had made a hunt to exhaustion impossible. The Ansons in particular were soon found to be unsuited to night operations, despite the fitting of ASV. Night searches were thereafter only carried out using three Beauforts borrowed from East Sale.[20]

NOIC Port Melbourne, Acting Commander F.W. Heriot RAN, was the responsible naval authority and had also been active. The corvettes HMA Ships *Burnie, Lismore* and *Maryborough* of the 21st Minesweeping Flotilla were *en route* from Fremantle to Melbourne and only 90 miles southeast of the position given by *Ilissos*. At 1300 they received the simply stated instructions 'to search and attack'.[21] An hour after her initial report, *Ilissos* sent an amplifying signal stating that the submarine had submerged after the Greek ship had fired back, and Heriot instructed her to continue her voyage to Melbourne. *Lismore* had already been forced back to Melbourne with engine defects, but the other two corvettes intercepted *Ilissos* about six hours later off Cape Northumberland. Finding that neither the steamship nor the aircraft now escorting her had anything more to report, *Burnie* and *Maryborough* continued on with their search. Weather conditions were exceptionally bad and both had to house their Asdic domes to prevent damage. Unsurprisingly, the two warships found nothing that night. The search continued until the early evening of the following day. The corvettes then set course for Melbourne, where they arrived on the evening of 11 December. *Ilissos* had already reached the port and after interrogating several members of the crew Heriot graded the submarine sighting 'A1'.[22]

Despite the succession of warnings received since September, the sudden appearance of Timm's U-boat off South Australia was still very much a surprise to Admiral Royle.[23] As recently as 6 December the Naval Board had dismissed as unlikely an American tanker's report of a probable periscope sighted some 200 miles south of Kangaroo Island.[24] Moreover, despite his apparent failure on this occasion, the German commander still had the initiative and the Australians could not be sure where *U 862* would now go. The Japanese had certainly never conducted serious submarine operations so far south, and the Naval Board had little previous experience to call upon. If the U-boat continued east the most likely area of operations would presumably be Bass Strait. Here at least was another focal area through which all east- and west-bound traffic would normally pass. Two US military transport ships were immediately diverted from Melbourne to Sydney; all merchant shipping except local traffic was routed south of Tasmania; and ships were ordered to darken at night when west of 150°E, to zig-zag in southern Australian waters, to stream paravanes when within the 200-fathom line, and to maintain radio silence.[25]

The exploits of enemy surface raiders in both world wars had demonstrated that the shipping routes through Bass Strait were areas favoured by the Germans for mining. Though there was nothing in the earlier intelligence reports to suggest that Timm planned a mining operation, or even that *U 862* was carrying mines, Heriot ordered *Lismore* and *Maryborough* to sail first thing on Tuesday 12 December to carry out a searching double Oropesa sweep of the shipping routes in Bass Strait. The western approaches to Port Phillip Bay were made the first priority, then the through route. Heriot scheduled *Burnie* (which was undergoing repairs) to assist in the search from 14 December, while another four corvettes from the 21st Minesweeping Flotilla, HMA Ships *Ballarat, Kalgoorlie, Goulburn* and *Whyalla,* were sailed from Sydney and ordered to join in by 16 December. With this not inconsiderable effort, Heriot expected the route between Wilsons Promontory and Cape Otway to be swept to at least 50 per cent

The Australian Minesweeper (AMS) HMAS Maryborough. *In a remarkable wartime effort, 60 AMS were constructed in Australian shipyards between 1940 and 1944, and 56 were commissioned into the RAN. Though built in 1940 for the Admiralty and serving in 1944–45 as part of the British Pacific Fleet's 21st Minesweeping Flotilla.* Maryborough *was fully Australian manned. She was sold in 1947 and served her commercial owners as the* Isobel Queen *until finally broken up in 1953.* (RAN)

by the evening of 19 December. Bad weather delayed completion and sweeping finally finished on 21 December. The seven corvettes then returned to Port Melbourne, though Heriot retained *Ballarat*, *Goulburn* and *Kalgoorlie* at four hours notice as a striking and searching force.[26]

In fact, the crews of *Burnie* and *Maryborough* would never be so close to the U-boat as they had been on the first night following Timm's attack. Despite the appalling weather, *U 862* had detected the two corvettes searching and Timm had even surfaced in a brief attempt to identify them. In the driving rain he could not see his pursuers—not that he could have attempted a torpedo attack in the prevailing conditions—but their presence nevertheless helped to determine his next course of action. Having no mines aboard and still attempting to reduce risks, Timm was well aware where the Australians would concentrate their defences. Instead he decided to go farther south and take the route around the bottom of Tasmania.

For the next few days the seas remained rough and the temperature continued to drop. Even at 50m depth the U-boat could feel the motion. To make matters worse, the provisions loaded in Jakarta had turned out to be of very poor quality, and the cook found it necessary to ditch many of the jars of preserved fruits. Timm soon allowed *U 862* back on the surface during the twilight, but the grey sunless skies only matched the miserable mood on board. They had come so far yet achieved nothing. For now there was little more to do except sleep and read and think. Thinking, however, only made matters worse. There was hardly any real news in the radio broadcasts, and the men could form no accurate idea of how the situation at home was developing. Though the approach of Christmas increased feelings of homesickness, it did at least provide some other diversions. Two days after the attack on *Ilissos* the U-boat's galley began baking the first of the festive foods.

The weather was also becoming calmer, and during the late afternoon of 14 December the bridge lookouts sighted the mountains of southern Tasmania. That evening they rounded South Cape and surprise was again expressed at the assistance provided by the lighthouse to the U-boat's navigation. Nor were the authorities diverting traffic away from their area, and the next day Reiffenstuhl recorded that *U 862* was offered another chance at success:

> We are now positioned outside the entrance to Hobart. Around 1645 sound bearing on the starboard beam! Quickly get on the periscope. I cannot believe my eyes: starboard beam, at a range of about 5 miles a large, fully laden tanker, a rare sight! He is on a course for the northern tip of New Zealand . . . Our hydrophones hear his screws loudly making 180 revolutions per minute. The bearing is slowly moving ahead, he moves more quickly than we do under water . . . For two hours before darkness falls we remain south of the tanker. On the port beam the coast of Tasmania can be seen. As soon as it becomes sufficiently dark, surfaced and at emergency speed followed the tanker. His masttops, however, can no longer be seen. We have therefore surfaced a few minutes too late. Still the fever of the hunt has gripped us tightly again. After an hour of pursuit we weakly see smoke . . . If our calculations of the tanker's course and speed are correct we will be abeam of him at around 2200. It would be annoying, if this large tanker (about 8000 GRT) slipped through our fingers.
>
> Suddenly, just after 2200, an aircraft flew around us 500m away and alternately flashed white and green, which means that we should send our recognition signal. He had thought that we were the tanker

> which he was to escort. If he only knew! Because of the very bright phosphorescence we were evidently easy to see from the aircraft. We immediately go deep. As we dived the battery cells slid due to the rapid change in angle; my hair stood on end since, shortly before, the batteries were being charged and it could have led to a gas explosion. There, a loud roaring screw noise on the starboard beam! That has to be the tanker, he can only be a few hundred metres away from us. Damned shit, that we have been forced by the aircraft to submerge. Because of the extremely bad visibility we could not see this gigantic ship at such short range before diving—and now we sit in the cellar and know we cannot surface. We had all expected, however, that the aircraft would bomb us so we still have some luck.
>
> The aircraft must have immediately informed the tanker that a U-boat was in close proximity, for the tanker sped off and began to wildly alter course . . . Within the boat you could hear with the naked ear the revolutions of the screws, as it went over us! . . . *Verdammt*, we have had bad luck today. Yet we were also lucky that the aircraft left us alone. Churchill has saved a tanker; it would have been a small battle won, if we could have sunk this ship. We continue our passage under water . . . . Now we run again towards the Australian coast and on to Sydney Harbour. That certainly won't be a pleasure cruise, however, after we have drawn attention to ourselves out here.[27]

Reiffenstuhl was mistaken. The aircraft that had caused them so much grief had not seen them and the unknown tanker was also unaware of their presence. *U 862*'s passage remained undetected by the Australians. Nevertheless, for three days after the incident the U-boat sailed east to open up the distance from the Tasmanian coast and shake off any possible pursuit. Timm then turned his vessel north and by 19 December, while the RAN vainly searched for mines in the west, *U 862* approached Bass Strait from the opposite direction. Though they may have experienced some ill fortune so far, Timm assured his crew that shipping traffic would be heavier off eastern Australia. They would still have an opportunity to strike a blow for the Fatherland.

On 20 December Timm informed his men that they were positioned on the shipping route between Melbourne and Wellington, New Zealand, and just after diving the Germans were rewarded by a new sound bearing to the southeast. For a U-boat commander the image in the periscope was magnificent, 'a very beautiful big steamship, in particular very long'.[28] Timm estimated the size of his target as approximately 8000 GRT. They were already too close for an attack so he dived deeper and waited for the vessel to pass overhead. It was now well after dawn, but the seas were still rough and visibility poor so Timm decided to risk an approach on the surface. Unfortunately the ship was proceeding at something more than 16kts. The U-boat, already struggling in the prevailing sea conditions, soon found that the range was opening rather than closing. Timm had lost his third steamship of the voyage.

However, no sooner had *U 862* dived than the listening room reported another sound bearing in the west. The U-boat surfaced and followed the bearing for an hour at full speed. Seeing nothing, Timm dived, and ten minutes later the *GHG* operator again heard the clear beat of a diesel engine. This time they chased the bearing for three hours but still found nothing. The crew cursed their luck again and placed the blame squarely on the targets, noting that 'almost all the ships are fairly large, of new construction and sail at high speed'.[29] However, *U 862*'s search for a suitable victim among a surfeit of prey was also hampered by the worsening weather. Ships might be heard, but if they could not be seen there would be no chance of attack. On 23 December the storm reached its peak and Reiffenstuhl recorded, 'Heavy rain squalls. It blows up to wind intensity 10; the saucepans in the galley are flying all over the place, the cool room looks like it hasn't been cleaned for a week, everything is in confusion. Very heavy sea. We dive for lunch, otherwise it would not be possible to have the meal.'[30]

For his part, Timm included the lack of support as a factor contributing to their difficulties. As a single U-boat he could do nothing against a fast target and, even if Schrewe's operational area had extended to the east coast, *U 537*'s current whereabouts were unknown and in conditions of radio silence a coordinated attack was out of the question. What made these missed opportunities particularly galling, however, was the lack of any obvious surface or air patrol. After detecting yet another group of ships near Cape Howe, Timm wrote in his war diary, 'If we could only have had more boats it would have led to a *Paukenschlag* like that off the coast of America.'[31] Yet, though there would be many more disappointments for Timm, the U-boat's run of bad luck was at last drawing to an end.

12 Sechste Kriegsweinacht

My U-boat men!
Those at the front and at home celebrate our sixth Christmas at war with firm resolve and in unconditional devotion to our Fatherland and with a fanatical belief in our Führer.
Today my thoughts are especially with you, my old and young U-boat men, who are fighting far from home during this very old German festival.

—*Großadmiral* Karl Dönitz, 24 December 1944

After spending more than a month at sea, sailing some 4000 miles, and yet achieving virtually nothing, it is not surprising that the men in *U 862* were feeling somewhat jaded. While they languished in the Tasman Sea, the eyes of the world were on Europe. There a surprise German counteroffensive in the Ardennes Forest threatened to throw the Allied advance into confusion, separating the British and Canadian armies in the north from the Americans in the south. At the same time the older U-boats were showing more activity and, against the recent trend, survival rates were going up as crews grew more confident with their new equipment and gained more experience in inshore operations. Of all the German arms only the *U-Bootswaffe* threatened real growth in fighting potential, and Allied intelligence began making dire predictions of a renewed U-boat offensive once the revolutionary Type XXI boats began operations in strength.[1]

The war in Europe was entering its final phase, yet *U 862* could not have been farther away. It no doubt seemed to some on board that their homeland's effort would gain little from their mission. Nevertheless, there could be no doubt of their complete loyalty to their commander. Dönitz had often said that he would never abandon one of his U-boats and despite their remote location the men of *U 862* were confident they would not be forgotten.

On Christmas Eve, notwithstanding their proximity to an enemy coast they were looking forward to an evening of celebration. A large selection of cakes and pastries had by now accumulated in the wardroom. Fruit juice and some bottles of liquor had been chilled, and the engineers had produced a 'very beautiful Christmas tree' from broom handles and salvaged copper wire. Torn-up strips of canvas were painted green to represent needles, and torch bulbs provided illumination. Standing in the bow compartment, the tree provided a welcome reminder of home. However, quiet reflections were soon pushed aside by the grim realities of war. Fortune had decided to deliver the men of *U 862* a Christmas gift.

> 24 December: Christmas at sea, calm sea, good visibility. As we surface at dusk a smoke cloud is sighted on the horizon! We push on in that direction. Suddenly yet another steamship with four masts, funnel and bridge is sighted in the distance! Since he appears to be large we turn our attentions to him. Carefully approach, darkness quickly closes in, the moon is in the first quarter. Around 2130 the Lion (*Großadmiral* Dönitz) speaks about the shining results achieved by the boats fighting in the East Asia area—therefore about us. We also receive a radio telegram from Headquarters: 'Parents, wives, children, relations and fiancées send all soldiers cordial greetings for the Christmas season and best wishes for a happy 1945'.
>
> At about this time we dived for a submerged attack. We get several different sound bearings, so it can be safely assumed that several steamships are here. Surfaced . . . Due to the deteriorating visibility, however, the steamship is now out of sight. Full speed afterwards. He runs parallel to the coast and evidently plans to enter Sydney tomorrow morning. He is proceeding at 12kts and we are on an intercepting course. We sail blindly behind him. Around midnight I suddenly see the steamship as a large shadow, we are about 2000m away. Luckily visibility is still so bad that I can pass unseen at this range. One hour ago he sent a radio message to Sydney notifying his time of arrival. Over there on the darkened steamship, Christmas is apparently being celebrated, for I can often see a light appear through an open scuttle. We attack. At a range of 600m I fire two torpedoes. Hits under the bridge and at the stern.[2]

Thus the American Liberty ship SS *Robert J. Walker*, on a voyage from Fremantle in ballast, began her agony as the sixth victim of *U 862*'s career. Though Timm was unlikely to be concerning himself with such thoughts, the 7176 GRT Liberty ships

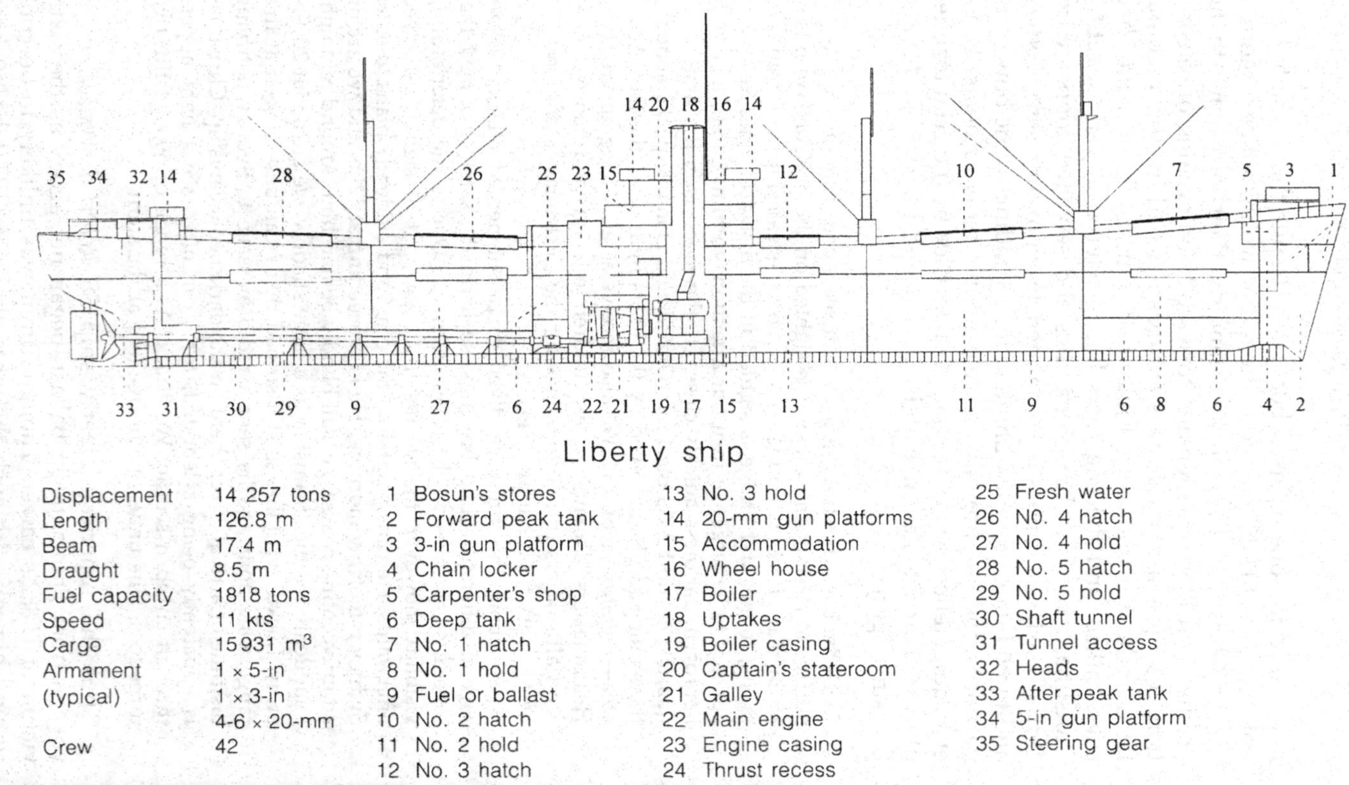

Liberty ship

Displacement	14 257 tons
Length	126.8 m
Beam	17.4 m
Draught	8.5 m
Fuel capacity	1818 tons
Speed	11 kts
Cargo	15 931 m^3
Armament (typical)	1 × 5-in 1 × 3-in 4-6 × 20-mm
Crew	42

1 Bosun's stores
2 Forward peak tank
3 3-in gun platform
4 Chain locker
5 Carpenter's shop
6 Deep tank
7 No. 1 hatch
8 No. 1 hold
9 Fuel or ballast
10 No. 2 hatch
11 No. 2 hold
12 No. 3 hatch
13 No. 3 hold
14 20-mm gun platforms
15 Accommodation
16 Wheel house
17 Boiler
18 Uptakes
19 Boiler casing
20 Captain's stateroom
21 Galley
22 Main engine
23 Engine casing
24 Thrust recess
25 Fresh water
26 N0. 4 hatch
27 No. 4 hold
28 No. 5 hatch
29 No. 5 hold
30 Shaft tunnel
31 Tunnel access
32 Heads
33 After peak tank
34 5-in gun platform
35 Steering gear

represented the unpalatable reality of Allied production capability and the ultimate futility of Dönitz's campaign on tonnage. In total more than 2000 Liberty ships were mass produced after America's entry to the war, most under the guidance of the innovative Henry J. Kaiser.[3] The ships were welded together from prefabricated sections and the German Propaganda Ministry christened them *Kaisersarg* (Kaiser's coffins), maintaining they would simply break apart at sea. *U 862* would soon discover that they were rather more durable.

The attack on *Robert J. Walker* took place about 160 miles southeast of Sydney, almost at the end of the freighter's voyage. Standing watch on the bridge was the second mate, Edwin Barthelman. At 0230 he heard a dull explosion on the starboard side just aft of his position and felt the whole ship vibrate. Barthelman turned to look astern and ten seconds later heard the second explosion. It was not as loud as the first, but he saw the flash and felt the hot blast. Most of the crew were asleep, but the master, Captain Murdoch D. MacRae, appeared immediately on the bridge and took charge, calling General Quarters about a minute after the detonations. According to MacRae, the explosions were initially 'a little bit of a mystery'.[4] He had received no specific warnings of submarine activity and, since he was far from the front he was neither zig-zagging nor taking any other special precautions. In fact MacRae at first thought the propeller might have struck a floating mine.

Only the second explosion appeared to have done serious damage. There was a sudden loss of steering and MacRae received reports of steam coming out of the doors to the after steering engine room. After waiting for the steam to clear, the chief engineer, Otho Anderson, entered the compartment and found the rudder blown off, the propeller shaft bent and a jagged 1m-by-2m hole on the starboard side of the counter above the waterline. The steering engine itself had been torn out and thrown against the bulkhead. Anderson observed that the torpedo appeared to have detonated on hitting the rudder.

The propeller shaft tunnel had flooded at once, and a little water was now coming under the door into the engine room. Nevertheless, the main engines could still turn slowly and the ship had already turned of its own accord and started heading back south. MacRae briefly considered continuing at slow speed, but Anderson now reported that there was a heavy jar in the shaft and that the bearings were starting to smoke. Besides, MacRae reasoned, if a submarine had indeed been the culprit, it might yet lose contact if his ship remained silent. He ordered the engines stopped and *Robert J. Walker* began drifting. Simultaneously he sent an urgent message to Melbourne for CSWPSF: 'Emergency SOS. 36.05S 150.43E torpedoed or struck mine air cover and immediate assistance requested.'[5] There was no panic in the Liberty ship. The vessel was no longer taking in water and everyone remained calm, waiting to see what would happen next.

Aboard *U 862*, the Germans were also waiting. Timm had assumed that the two hits would sink the target, but when he saw it was still afloat he allowed Reiffenstuhl to attempt another shot. The third torpedo missed, apparently because *Robert J. Walker* was still moving. Since the batteries were by now quite low, Timm then ordered the U-boat to turn away from her victim and begin circling while they recharged. For almost two hours *U 862* remained in the area while Timm discussed the situation in the wardroom. With only a few torpedoes on board, Timm wanted to use them sparingly. Now he had used up three, yet his victim showed no sign of sinking. Adding to her commander's concerns, the U-boat's radio room had intercepted the Liberty ship's distress messages and their acknowledgment from the authorities ashore. Not only could Timm be certain that Australian aircraft and warships would be on their way shortly, but MacRae in his latest message had requested a tug to tow him in.[6] After weighing up the risks Timm decided that if he wanted to be certain of a kill he would need to complete the attack.

To the Australian authorities *Robert J. Walker*'s reference to a mine was simply confusing.[7] The water in the area was more than 5000m deep—much too deep for a minefield. For the Germans, however, MacRae's uncertainty was a source of some amusement. As Timm climbed past the helmsman on his way back to the bridge he retorted, 'Now we will make a point of showing them what a mine is, don't you think?' '*Jawohl, Herr Kapitän,*' was the answer. *U 862* dived for the final approach, getting in close to ensure that the weapon would not miss. Timm fired the fourth torpedo at 0420.

Hot summer winds and bushfires had created a terrific dust haze that morning. It extended far out to sea and from *Robert J. Walker* the visibility looked to be only about one and a half miles. Everyone MacRae could muster was on deck peering anxiously into the gloom. Despite the choppy conditions, they sighted the torpedo just after firing, coming from less than half a mile out and approaching from the starboard quarter. Strangely, the weapon seemed to be running almost on the surface, its propeller spurting water all the way. Nevertheless, the Liberty ship was not completely defenceless. On board was an Armed Guard Unit of 25 men commanded by Ensign Edwin Turk USNR. The American equivalent of *Ilissos'* DEMS ratings, Turk's men manned the single 3-inch gun forward, the 5-inch gun aft, and the four 20mm guns, two each lining the port and starboard sides. Spotting the incoming torpedo himself and without waiting for orders, Seaman 1st Class Harold Stone USNR turned his 20mm gun on the weapon and 'after about the tenth shot there was a loud explosion. A geyser of water shot up about 50 feet accompanied by some dark smoke.'[8] The torpedo had detonated only 100m from the ship. With his confidence reinforced, Turk ordered smoke floats thrown over the side to shield the ship from further attacks. Only three ignited but they made a fairly good screen. Moreover, to prevent the submarine gaining an accurate sight Turk had all his gunners maintain a periodic fire in the general direction of their unseen attacker.

Misled by the explosion, Timm and his crew were easily convinced that their fourth torpedo had hit, making the refusal of their victim to sink all the more infuriating. Reiffenstuhl reflected the prevailing opinion in his journal: '*Donnerwetter*, it is well built, three eels in the stomach and still on the surface.'[9] The Germans would obviously need to expend yet another precious weapon to deliver a finishing shot, but perhaps took heart from another of Dönitz's basic principles, 'Better a few ships destroyed than many damaged.'[10] The intermittent gunfire from their target made no difference to the U-boat, but the smokescreen was a different matter. To Timm and Reiffenstuhl, who were each looking through one of *U 862*'s periscopes, it appeared that the smoke floats had been dropped by an aircraft. The approach of daylight simply added further weight to Timm's caution.

> Very, very carefully approach and send yet another eel . . . at the steamer. The steamship is lying there dead in the water and sees the torpedo track coming towards it. It shoots further distress signals and fires its guns at the torpedo track. The eel, however, continues on to hit and we immediately dive deep. Large roar and explosion.[11]

It had taken almost an hour and 40 minutes for *U 862* to make her last approach. Daylight had come and as Timm moved in to attack, MacRae was wondering why help was taking so long to arrive. Just before 0600 and without warning, John Mahoy, his third mate, cried out from the flying bridge, 'Here she comes!'

The torpedo's wake, visible as a thin streak, had been sighted 2000–3000m out. This weapon was running slowly, so slowly that most witnesses estimated it took more than four minutes to close, but against a stationary ship this hardly mattered. Turk ordered all available guns on the starboard side to open fire. This time, however, the weapon was running deeper and despite the 20mm guns alone expending 2500 rounds of ammunition, all failed to score a hit. Undeflected from its course, the torpedo detonated with a massive explosion in *Robert J. Walker*'s empty No. 4 hold. A huge fountain of oil and water was thrown up, both sides of the ship were blown out, the deck was buckled, and a lifeboat was blown off its davits. According to MacRae, the explosion left holes so large that 'two Army trucks could have driven in one side of the ship and out the other.'[12] The damage extended down some 2m below the waterline, leaving the master with no option but to give the order to abandon ship. Turk's Armed Guard Unit had put up a commendable defence, and had gained the ship's crew vital time to outfit and ready themselves for possible abandonment, but the last explosion had severed the after 5-inch gun from its mounting and there was now little point in defending the doomed vessel. Turk passed his own order to abandon ship a few minutes after MacRae.

The final explosion also produced three casualties. A section of hatch cover struck ordinary seaman Jack Vickers across the back of the legs and knocked him semi-conscious. A 1.5 ton hatch strongback thrown 10m into the air hit Ernest Ballard, a crew messman serving as an ammunition runner to the gun stations, shattering his spine and leaving large open wounds in his neck and back. Also helping bring up ammunition was a Chinese utility man named Chew Toon. After the explosion Mahoy saw a man who was probably Toon astern of the ship screaming and waving his hands. One of the gun's crew threw a lifebuoy to him, but the man was not seen again.

Besides the Armed Guard, *Robert J. Walker* had on board 42 merchant crew and one passenger. The departure from the ship was orderly and most reached the safety of either the lifeboats or rafts within four minutes of the order to leave. However, abandoning ship was not without its dangers—and corresponding acts of bravery. Seaman 1st Class Marvin Taylor USNR, after helping to lower a life raft, found that it had drifted too far astern for him to reach it. Taylor—a non-swimmer—was wearing a life jacket and jumped into the sea in an attempt to reach the life raft. The water was thick with oil and instead of reaching safety, Taylor found himself drifting steadily towards the large hole in the steering engine room and in imminent danger of being sucked back inside the ship:

> At this time I faced the raft and saw Bernard Hulihee, Acting A.B., Merchant Seaman, strip off his clothes, dive into the water, swam over to me and grabbed hold of my wrist. Hulihee then pulled hard and we gradually edged away from the hole in the ship. Hulihee then assisted me all the way back to the raft, through the rough water, and helped in hoisting me aboard. My clothing was completely soaked with oil and water, and I was in a very exhausted condition. Hulihee, who was then hoisted aboard, appeared to be extremely tired, as though the ordeal had cost him a great deal of energy.[13]

Of the injured, only Ballard, who was unconscious and bleeding heavily, was assessed as too ill to be moved. It fell to MacRae to make the final decision to leave Ballard where he lay, and the young man from Denver, Colorado, died alone. Mahoy and the third engineer were the last of the crew to leave the ship. They jumped over the side and swam to a raft, picking up another six men from the water. The survivors got away in three lifeboats and four rafts, and MacRae set about organising the scattered groups. He ordered them to row some two miles away from the sinking ship and await rescue. At about 0900 they lost sight of their vessel as it drifted southwards into the haze.[14]

After confirming that *Robert J. Walker* was at last sinking, Timm turned *U 862* away and pondered his alternatives once more. Aircraft were now on the scene and the hunt was undoubtedly building in intensity. *U 862* had again used up much of her battery charge and Timm appreciated that opportunities to surface or use the *Schnorchel* would be limited at the very least. The U-boat was in an extremely vulnerable situation. Even with purification the fresh air *U 862* took down when she dived was barely sufficient for 40 hours. The more the U-boat was harried and hunted the faster the air and batteries would be exhausted. Timm did his best to limit his crew's exertions. He postponed the Christmas party, sent all who could be spared to their bunks, left on only the essential lighting and equipment, and at dead slow submerged, took the U-boat farther out to sea.

Though not as quickly as either MacRae hoped or Timm expected, the Australians were by this time moving into action. However, with assets of limited capability, no combined or integrated command arrangements between the RAN and RAAF, and limited practical experience, it could be argued that the outcome had already been decided. The last submarine attack off the Australian east coast had occurred in June 1943 and once it was clear that the Japanese were no longer capable of threatening Australian waters, coastal convoys had ceased in February 1944. The number of escort vessels available to Admiral Royle, which had reached 58 in September 1943—with plans for more than 100 by March 1944—thereafter began to fall as forces were reallocated for duties with forward-deployed Allied fleets. As the Allies advanced, so too Royle's area of responsibility expanded, but this also meant he could seldom focus his attention on local matters. The Naval Board, moreover, was attempting to cope with myriad other concerns. These ranged from the immediate problems of preparing Australian bases for use by the soon-to-arrive British Pacific Fleet (BPF) to the longer-term creation of a balanced postwar Navy.

With the bulk of Australia's ships and professional officers serving against the Japanese—where the threat now came more often from the air than from below the water—such vessels as remained in Australian waters were usually those too small or old to be of use elsewhere. They were often manned by reservists rather than permanent personnel. Not that the reserves were incapable, but even the most enthusiastic commander found it difficult to forge an efficient team when their tools were no longer appropriate and the appearance of even a friendly submarine was a rare event. A certain amount of complacency had set in and, as Air Commodore Charlesworth, Air Officer Commanding RAAF Eastern Area, was to complain in mid-1944, 'This has resulted in a general slackening off in procedure; ships are seldom where they should be, and a minority of merchant ships identify themselves to aircraft.'[15]

Indeed, by December 1944 the creation of even an *ad hoc* 'hunter-killer' group, as NOIC Fremantle had attempted, seemed beyond the resources of Pope's equivalent in Sydney, Acting Rear Admiral G.D. Moore RAN.[16] Moore, aged 51, had spent the years 1942–1944 behind a desk as Second Naval Member, but was an experienced seaman, having previously commanded both of the RAN's heavy cruisers, HMA Ships *Australia* and *Canberra*. What he appears to have lacked is experience in anti-submarine warfare, and though he may well have wished to do more, Moore's preparations prior to *U 862*'s arrival consisted solely of a request to Royle to reallocate three motor launches currently on coastal patrol duties.[17] NOIC Sydney planned instead to devote these vessels to the anti-submarine protection of HMAS *Hobart* while the light cruiser was in Jervis Bay working up.[18]

The RAAF similarly suffered from a lack of modern assets and practical experience. A junior partner in the Allied war effort and well down the list in aircraft allocation, Australia had its requirements met only when they would not detract from the European effort. Though RAAF squadrons participated in the destruction of at least thirteen U-boats in the Atlantic, aircraft in Australian waters made fewer than twenty attacks on possible submarines in 1942–1943 and failed to sink or damage even one.[19] The RAN and RAAF also had their differences on how best to apply maritime air power. Despite their heavy involvement in the protection of shipping, the RAAF officially preferred 'offensive sweeps' and searches of threatened areas, rather than the supposedly 'defensive policy' of close escort.[20] Unfortunately, no amount of aggressive spirit could make up for a lack of real-time contact. An extract from the RAAF Tactical Bulletin of June 1943 remained just as relevant eighteen months later:

> Few RAAF crews have ever had any great experience with enemy submarines. Indeed very few have ever seen even one of our own at sea. Targets are fleeting and you may spend hundreds of hours 'stooging' around without one sighting, and then suddenly you may see a submarine which appears and disappears in less time than it takes to write about it, and in that short time you have to destroy it.[21]

To Charlesworth's credit, however, he had at least taken the threat posed by *U 862* seriously. After the attack on *Ilissos* the RAAF had calculated that the offending U-boat could be in Eastern Area waters by mid-December, and offensive anti-submarine patrols soon covered the New South Wales coast from Sugarloaf Point to Beecroft Head and 40 miles to seaward. From 11 December patrols were extended to Batemans Bay, one commencing at dawn and one to terminate at dusk. From 14 December intelligence estimated that the submarine could have reached the Brisbane area, and patrols in Queensland were accordingly stretched to cover Double Island Point to Cape Byron and 60 miles to seaward.

The first flaw in the RAAF plan appeared when the attack on *Robert J. Walker* occurred just outside the southernmost extremity of the then covered area. In fact, the first intimation of the attack came from NOIC Sydney's staff, who at 0328 advised the Air Operations Room Eastern Area that an 'SSS' signal had been

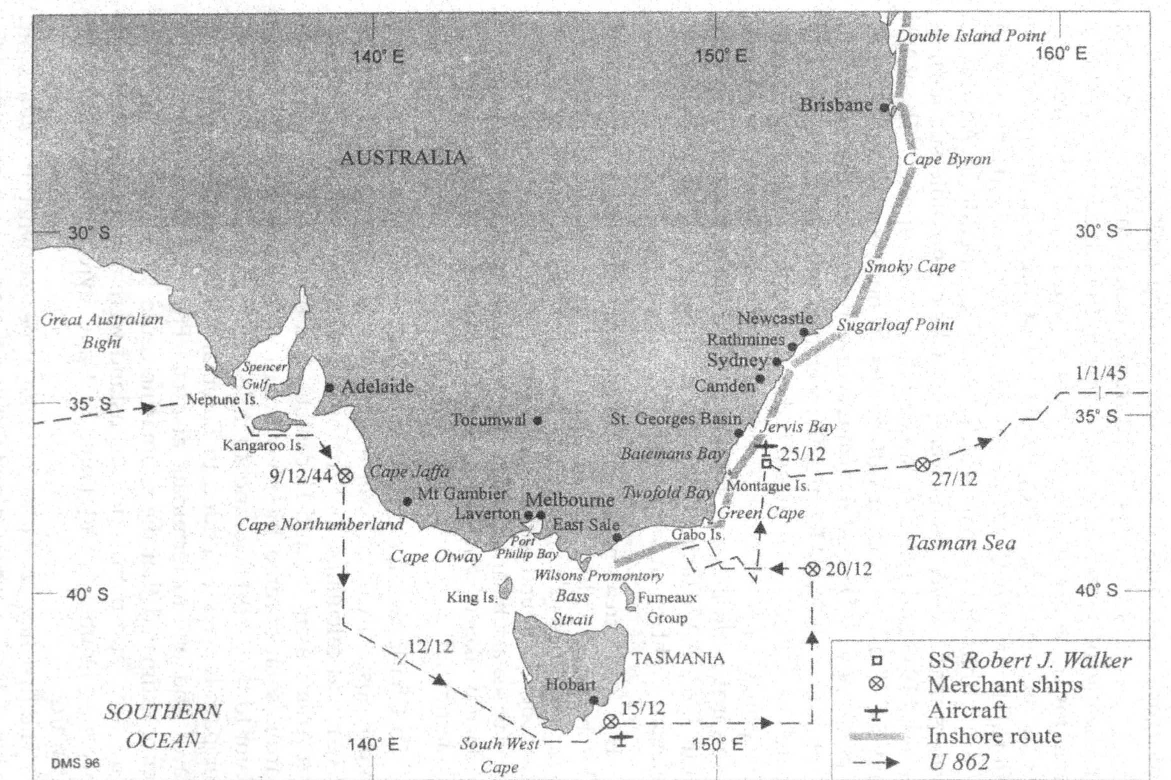

Operations off southeastern Australia, December 1944

received.[22] The RAAF expected to have some aircraft on the scene by 0530, but a succession of problems then intervened. Delays in booking telephone calls owing to the Christmas holiday period were compounded by the serious prevailing dust storms. Not until 0355 did No. 15 Squadron at Camden receive instructions to begin an expanding square search with the three Beauforts held on standby. Unfortunately the entry of dust into their flight instruments rendered the first two Beauforts unserviceable. The surviving Beaufort did not get airborne until more than an hour after it received orders to take off, and finally arrived over the Liberty ship some ten minutes after the last and fatal torpedo had struck home.[23] With visibility now down to one mile, the pilot appears to have placed the safety of the survivors ahead of the submarine hunt and after finding a lifeboat ended his first report with the simple statement, 'Standing by.'[24]

Meanwhile, at 0408 No. 11 Squadron at Rathmines received its orders to get the standby Catalina airborne. This aircraft reached the *Robert J. Walker* shortly after the Beaufort. The first aircraft handed over the position of the survivors, but an accompanying attempt by the Catalina to drop a medical kit and rations failed because of the bad weather. To complete the immediate effort, the Air Operations Room ordered a Kingfisher aircraft from No. 107 Squadron at St Georges Basin to cover and report the condition of the stricken ship.[25] The Kingfisher's base was only an hour's flying time from *Robert J. Walker*'s position and it is not clear why it did not arrive until after the other two aircraft. However, by the end of the day the search had involved another four Beauforts, three Catalinas and five Kingfishers. None of them made contact with the U-boat, and in the bad visibility the watch on the lifeboats was rarely continuous. Nevertheless, patrols returned regularly to the survivors' approximate position until they were recovered.

Finding no sign of the U-boat in the immediate area, Charlesworth extended Eastern Area's anti-submarine patrols south to Green Cape, but the searches remained limited to within 40 miles of the coast. Along with these 'normal searches', however, were increased demands for air cover for warships and important military shipping. Thus another 189 'special searches' had been flown by the time the hunt was finally abandoned on 9 January.[26] At least initially, *U 862* could not help but be aware of all this effort:

Dead quiet in the boat, from the Wardroom you can hear the men

> in the forward compartment snoring. At dusk surfaced for charging. After a short time we are discovered by an aircraft. Yes, they are looking for us now, this was only to be expected. Alarm—down to the cellar. This, however, gets on the nerves. Shortly before the meal, '*Flieger, Flieger*!' *Verdammt*, if an attack is underway at night then there must be an aircraft already very near. In the boat everything is galvanised, as each expects the bomb to drop in the next few seconds. Each metallic noise in the boat fills us with fear. It turns out, that the aircraft alarm was an error! The *Obersteuermann*, who stood in the control room, thought that the bridge had called out '*Flieger*,' and has therefore immediately activated the alarm. A typical case, where through a thoughtless or similarly sounding word a false alarm is triggered. It has, however, given us a severe fright! This is truly no child's game. Subsequently, no one could taste the meal, so very hard has the false alarm hit us in the stomach.[27]

Stress and exhaustion also beset the RAAF crews, and their task was not achieved without cost. During thunderstorms on 27 December a Beaufort and its four-man crew failed to return to base, and searches to locate wreckage or survivors proved fruitless. In return, the RAAF would take credit for a number of possible submarine sightings and two depth-charge attacks. However, after assessment, intelligence regarded only one of these attacks as a highly probable contact with the U-boat. On 29 December at 0444, Warrant Officer H.T. Moores, the captain of Kingfisher A48–9, sighted a narrow oil slick about half-a-mile long 30 miles off Batemans Bay. He altered course to investigate and thirteen minutes later, just as the aircraft had passed over the slick at 1200 feet, what looked like the narrow, V-shaped wake of a submarine's periscope appeared about 1000–1500m away. Moores released two depth charges over the wake and reported:

> Following the explosion a brownish stain appeared on the water and shortly afterwards oil was seen to slowly rise from the side of this until about an hour later. It covered an area about ¼ mile in diameter. A sea marker was then dropped to the centre of the patch as a guide for the relieving aircraft.[28]

If the RAAF felt that it had come closest to catching *U 862*, the RAN had at least not been idle. At the time of *U 862*'s attack *Hobart* was still at sea south of Sydney on 'shake-down' exercises. Cruisers were not equipped for anti-submarine warfare and Royle saw her as a liability rather than an asset. When *Robert J. Walker* reported the enemy attacking for the second time, CSWPSF ordered the cruiser to return to Sydney forthwith, and her commanding officer 'made all steam for the safety of Sydney Harbour'.[29] As soon as *Hobart* was on its way, Moore instructed her anti-submarine protection, the Fairmiles *ML 822* and *ML 829* and the even smaller harbour defence motor launch *HDML 1341*, to proceed to *Robert J. Walker*'s last known position and operate against the enemy submarine.[30] Joining them from Twofold Bay was another Fairmile, *ML 810*.

The small craft were only an interim measure, but were the best available until Moore could get vessels to the area from Sydney. First of these to reach the scene was the American patrol craft USS *PC-597*, which sailed at 0830 with a RAN salvage officer on board. She reached *Robert J. Walker* at 1830 by which time the stricken vessel was 20 metres down by the stern with her bow three metres in the air and her bridge awash. With no hope of saving her, *PC-597* began the search for survivors. Also sent from Sydney in what became known around the port as the 'Christmas scare' were the Q class destroyer HMAS *Quickmatch*, the requisitioned patrol craft HMAS *Yandra*, carrying salvage pumps, and the corvette HMAS *Kiama*. The first two were ordered to operate against the submarine and *Kiama* to take the Liberty ship in tow.[31]

Quickmatch, under Commander Otto Becher RAN, was completing her annual refit at the time of the attack and her ship's company were on extended weekend leave. The destroyer received her sailing orders at 0500 on 25 December. By 1300 she had raised steam, and within two hours sufficient ratings had returned on board or been lent from ships in harbour for her to proceed. *Quickmatch* reached the still slowly sinking *Robert J. Walker* at 2300. There was still no sign of the survivors, and Becher commenced a search for them.[32] Radar contact with the Liberty ship was lost abruptly at 0300 on 26 December, when she was assumed to have sunk. Two hours later a Catalina on anti-submarine patrol resighted the lifeboats and rafts and guided *Quickmatch, Kiama* and *PC-597* to their position.[33] With the aircraft maintaining a patrol of the surrounding area, *Quickmatch* picked up Captain MacRae and the 66 surviving members of his crew at about 0545.

Aware of the paucity of forces available to Moore, Royle had also been busy. With a succession of major ship movements underway as the BPF began its deployment to the Pacific, Royle was fortunate to have the four Q class destroyers of the 4th Destroyer Flotilla alongside in Melbourne. The destroyers had arrived during the very early hours of 24 December after screening the passage of the battleship HMS *Howe*—flagship of the

HMAS Yandra, *a small coaster of 990 GRT and maximum speed of 12 knots, was one of 37 vessels acquired by the RAN for the coastal patrol force between 1939 and 1943. In her naval role she was armed with one 4-inch gun, one .303 Vickers machine-gun, one .303 Maxim and one 2 pdr. For anti-submarine work she carried two depth-charge throwers and two depth-charge rails. Built in 1920, she was commissioned into the RAN in September 1940 and finally paid off in March 1946.* (RAN)

BPF—from Colombo to Fremantle and then escorting the CVEs HM Ships *Atheling, Battler, Striker* and *Fencer.*[34] At 0441 on 25 December Captain R.G. Onslow RN, in HMS *Quilliam,* was informed of *Robert J. Walker*'s position and ordered by CSWPSF to 'Take *Quilliam, Quiberon, Quality, Quadrant* under your orders and proceed with all despatch to area to search and hunt possible submarine.'[35]

Also still in Melbourne were the three corvettes of the 21st Minesweeping Flotilla that NOIC Port Melbourne had intended to use as a strike and search force. *Ballarat*, under Commander F.B. Morris RAN (Senior Officer 21st Minesweeping Flotilla), *Goulburn* and *Kalgoorlie* were immediately ordered by Royle to raise steam and proceed to Jervis Bay at best speed.[36] On the way north the corvettes were instructed to sweep for mines along the inshore shipping route from south of Gabo Island to Green Cape.[37] The four corvettes remaining in Melbourne were ordered to expedite maintenance, but were not expected to be available until 28 December. As a final measure Royle ordered all merchant shipping to zig-zag between Brisbane and Adelaide, extinguish navigation lights and sail on separate north and south inshore routes.[38]

Quilliam, Quality and *Quadrant* sailed from Melbourne at 0830 on 25 December with instructions to carry out an anti-submarine sweep passing 75 miles east of Gabo Island.[39] Captain Onslow then planned to head north and reach, *Robert J. Walker* at daylight on 26 December. He ordered *Quiberon,* which departed a few hours later, to do a sweep of her own and join the other three destroyers as soon as possible.[40] On arrival at the scene Onslow took command of all forces, sending *PC-597* back to Sydney, attaching *Quickmatch* to his formation and then using the five Q class to carry out a coordinated Asdic sweep. *Kiama,* with a much slower searching speed, was ordered to join *Yandra* and patrol between Montague Island and Green Cape. Onslow also attempted to coordinate his efforts with the RAAF patrols but found communications on the hunting frequency frustratingly poor.[41]

The search for the U-boat continued until late on 26 December, when Moore ordered it abandoned, directing the destroyers, motor launches and *Kiama* to return to Sydney while carrying out final sweeps along the way.[42] Working at a much slower pace, Morris' corvettes continued minesweeping until 28 December. When this search also proved negative Moore ordered them back to Sydney. The corvettes made their way slowly back up the coast, anchoring in Jervis Bay overnight and leaving *Yandra* alone to continue a patrol along the inshore routes between Sydney and Twofold Bay.

The attack by Moores' Kingfisher on 29 December forced a re-evaluation of the situation. Though the oil patch the pilot saw was in a position very close to where *Robert J. Walker* had sunk, Rear Admiral Moore presumably placed greater credence in the report of a periscope. He ordered *Quiberon,* the duty destroyer in Sydney, to proceed with all despatch and investigate the sighting. To assist the destroyer, NOIC Sydney also allocated *Yandra, ML 810,* and *Whyalla, Burnie,* and *Maryborough,* which were by now on passage through the area from Melbourne.[43] *Quiberon*'s captain, Commander W.H. Harrington RAN, would later report somewhat ruefully to Moore, 'In fact I made no contact with *ML 810,* HMAS *Whyalla* reported that her Asdic was out of action and *Maryborough*'s was unreliable.'[44] NOIC Sydney, however, had already passed command of the search to Commander Morris in *Ballarat,* which, with *Kalgoorlie* and *Goulburn,* had been ordered out from Jervis Bay. Harrington joined with Morris' flotilla on the afternoon of 29 December and the combined forces swept east in formation until midnight. The weather was yet again 'most unpleasant', producing poor Asdic conditions and limiting their speed to only 7kts. Even at this speed the corvettes pitched considerably and their Asdic domes were frequently out of the water. The force then swept north—briefly detaching *Quiberon* to investigate a disappearing ASV contact—until Moore cancelled the operation on the morning of 30 December.

Though it had been the longest and most extensive hunt for a submarine ever conducted off the Australian coast, the searchers again found no trace of Timm's U-boat. Excuses can be found in the weather and lack of suitable capability, and in fairness the RAN and RAAF's first priority appears to have been protection of the inshore shipping routes. Nevertheless, the impression remains that despite more than five years of war Australia's largest naval base and busiest waters were woefully unprepared for an enemy incursion. Without the fortunate presence of the BPF's 4th Destroyer Flotilla and 21st Minesweeping Flotilla—both ostensibly British assets despite the presence of Australian-manned ships—Royle and Moore were left with virtually no anti-submarine forces worthy of the name.[45]

Timm had indeed decided to move on, but this was unknown to anyone outside *U 862* and there were certainly no clues to indicate where the U-boat might next strike. Further compounding what already seemed a dangerous situation, on 27 December General MacArthur, as CinC SWPA, issued the following directive: 'Because of critical shortage of shipping which will permit no delay in turn about, it is desired, whenever necessary to avoid delay, that unloaded cargo ships be returned from Leyte [in the Philippines] to rear areas without escort.'[46] It is difficult to escape the conclusion that it was extremely fortunate for Allied shipping in the SWPA that Timm was alone and acting with extreme caution.

As for the air effort, like its Southern Area counterpart, RAAF Eastern Area had discovered that the simultaneous requirement for both regular patrols and air escort of shipping left very few aircraft available for offensive action. A further reserve, to carry out a serious 'hunt to exhaustion' should something be found, was simply beyond its capability. Though the RAAF did rather optimistically describe its efforts as 'searches to exhaustion', the effects had actually lasted much less than 24 hours.[47] By 26 December radar alerts had ceased, and Timm and his crew found time for at least a partial celebration.

> Our Christmas lamp is put on the table, it gives a very romantic, softened light. Pies and Christmas pastries stand on the mess-table. Quiet submerged cruising. The men in the forward compartment have turned on the electrically illuminated Christmas tree and decorated the entire compartment very nicely with war flags. There were also coffee and cakes for them. After two hours they took the tree to the *Unteroffizier*'s Mess and sat together in the control room. We took our lamp to the *Oberfeldwebel*'s Mess. Because of such an exciting night we haven't celebrated Christmas officially and we are determined to make it up for New Years Eve. Surfaced—thick fog—and carried on.[48]

By 27 December, two days before the Kingfisher's attack on a 'highly probable' contact, *U 862* was already almost 150 miles out into the Tasman Sea and well outside the range of RAAF searches. While the Australians fondly believed they were keeping the Germans terrified and out of harm's way, Timm was already manoeuvring his U-boat for another attack.

13 Neuseeland

Thousands of nautical miles away from home and from the southeast base, U 862 *dragged her way through the sea alone. Alone against the rest of the world.*

—*Maschinenobergefreiten* Albert Schirrmann

Dissolved on 19 November 1944, the essentially defensive British Eastern Fleet was formally replaced three days later by a separate East Indies Fleet and British Pacific Fleet (BPF). The first of these new fleets was established to support Admiral the Lord Louis Mountbatten's South East Asia Command and maintain a presence in the Indian Ocean. The second was a much larger concern, strongly reinforced and geared to demonstrate British military and political commitment to the main Allied theatre of war against the Japanese. After detailed consultation with the Australians, the British Admiralty designated Sydney as the BPF's principal base. The main body of the BPF, centred on the fleet aircraft carriers HM Ships *Indomitable, Illustrious, Indefatigable* and *Victorious,* and including the battleship HMS *King George V,* arrived in Sydney on 10–11 February 1945. Designated Force 63, these ships came from Ceylon via Fremantle, after carrying out a series of strike operations against Japanese oil refineries in Sumatra.

Throughout December and January other support and operational elements of the BPF had also been on the move. With the northern route through the Timor and Arafura Seas inadequately surveyed, they all came by way of southern Australia. The exploits and disappearance of *U 862* would undoubtedly have caused continuing consternation not only for Royle and the

ACNB, but also for the CinC BPF, Admiral Sir Bruce Fraser, and his staff. The British had certainly not been expecting to confront a U-boat in a supposedly safe rear area. In July 1944 the British Naval Liaison Party in Australia, headed by Rear Admiral C.S Daniel RN, had made its own report to the Admiralty on the state of the anti-submarine effort in the SWPA. The report had concluded that in comparison with the Atlantic, 'anti U-boat warfare is not pursued with the same degree of priority either by the US Navy or RAN' and that 'anti-U-boat training is not treated as of major importance in the RAAF'. Daniel had nevertheless regarded this attitude as understandable in view of the poor performance of Japanese submarines and the practice of the German U-boats in Penang to operate only in the Indian Ocean.[1]

The major units of the BPF were fully escorted and the Australians were doing everything they could to ensure their safe deployment, but Fraser had his own priorities and was obviously determined to leave nothing to chance. On 2 January he found it necessary to bypass the Australian Naval Board and write directly to Daniel, who was now the commander of the RN administrative headquarters in Melbourne, seeking information on the anti-U-boat defences of Sydney.[2] Though unsourced intelligence suggested that the U-boat might attempt to return to Jakarta through Torres Strait, the truth was that Timm could have been anywhere.[3] As late as mid-January the best Australian intelligence available to Fraser could note only that the U-boat might 'still be operating in Australian waters, as it is not due back at its base in Sourabaya [sic] until the latter end of February'.[4]

Royle continued to arrange for important shipping to be escorted by the Q class and corvettes whenever possible. However, with heavy commitments continuing elsewhere in the Pacific, there remained a general lack of suitable vessels. The Australians were already maintaining eight escort groups, each of three or four ships, in the New Guinea area, and CSWPSF had just made several Australian frigates available for use around the Philippines. Royle now felt he could not afford to make a permanent allocation of vessels for local defence.[5] Thus, though the Naval Board soon placed the corvettes *Bathurst* and *Bowen* under NOIC Sydney's operational control, the intention was to retain them in Sydney only until the submarine situation clarified.

Rear Admiral Moore had meanwhile attempted to set up a standing patrol along the inshore route between Newcastle and Jervis Bay using one of the corvettes of the 21st Minesweeping Flotilla. Unfortunately even these vessels were not considered to be in full operational state and Admiral Fraser preferred to keep them all together 'because of the necessity for intensive training as a flotilla'.[6] Though the corvettes were not actually transferred to the operational and administrative control of CinC BPF until 26 January, after 10 January Fraser would only allow them to be used for anti-submarine operations in an emergency.

Several incidents provided just enough tension to keep the forces alert. One of the first was a Beaufort report of a disappearing radar contact 30 miles off Newcastle on 2 January. This brought HMAS *Goulburn* out to investigate, but a more worrying development appeared in an urgent signal from RAAF Intelligence to RAAF Southern Area on 6 January stating that a submarine had possibly entered an area immediately east of Bass Strait and was proceeding westward. Assured that the source was 'highly reliable', NOIC Port Melbourne promptly proclaimed a temporary area of probability 60 miles wide and 150 miles east of Hobart.

There was no merchant shipping in the area, but Commander Heriot's initial concern was the safety of the troopship SS *Empress of Scotland*, carrying 3500 reinforcements for the New Zealand Division in Europe. She had left Wellington for Hobart on 6 January closely escorted by *Quiberon* and *Quickmatch*. RAAF Southern Area did its best to help Heriot, and allocated two Ansons and two Beauforts to search ten miles either side of the troopship's track during daylight hours. *Empress of Scotland*'s passage remained uninterrupted, but adding further credibility to the initial intelligence was a report on 11 January from the Liberty ship SS *Alcee Fortier* that she had sighted torpedo tracks 200 miles west of Hobart.[7]

With the U-boat possibly on the move, and continuing pressure from Fraser not to involve BPF assets, Moore reduced his inshore requirement to a corvette patrol 'on not more than 3 days a week'.[8] However, demonstrating that even experienced teams could make mistakes, the RAN's anti-submarine training ship HMAS *Kybra* made a good contact on 13 January, 8 miles off Sydney. *Quadrant, Lismore* and a Catalina were despatched and searched until the following afternoon without success.

It was another week before more specific intelligence concerning *U 862* arrived. Sounding a little relieved, the ACNB in a letter to Fraser on 19 January noted: 'Reliable information indicates that this craft is now on her way back to Javanese waters and it is therefore improbable that any enemy submarines are now operating in South East Australian waters.'[9] It was reliable intelligence

HMAS Quickmatch *at speed. Built for the RN she was transferred to the RAN upon completion in 1942 together with her sister HMAS* Quiberon. *A further three Q class destroyers were transferred to the RAN in late 1945.* Quickmatch *was converted to a fast anti-submarine frigate in the 1950s and sold for scrap in 1972.* (RAN)

because it had come directly from the decryption of a signal from *BdU* to Timm, but it was nevertheless a little premature for the ACNB to conclude that the U-boat was already safely out of the way.

Though *U 862* had in fact left Royle's area of responsibility, Timm was going to have to pass back through Australian waters to get home. For the previous two weeks he had been operating off New Zealand, and it was while crossing the Tasman Sea on 27 December that he had made his next attack:

> Around 2015 ahead to port a ship silhouette is sighted! Assume combat station. We increase to high speed. The steamship is heading for Bass Strait and regularly alters course by around 40 degrees every half hour. Since the moonlight is too bright for a surfaced attack, we dive for a submerged attack. We approach to a range of 500m from the steamship; the commander wants to fire straight away, the steamship alters away again. *Verdammt*, a juicy, fat, morsel of 8000–10 000 GRT. We have fallen behind, surface and set after him again. The wind has increased . . . Very difficult and slow progress. At dawn we are not far enough ahead because we are east of the steamship and have the light horizon behind us. We must therefore dive as it gets lighter. We calculate his zig-zag course ahead, our calculations are correct, the steamship alters towards us again, we are in a good firing position. At a

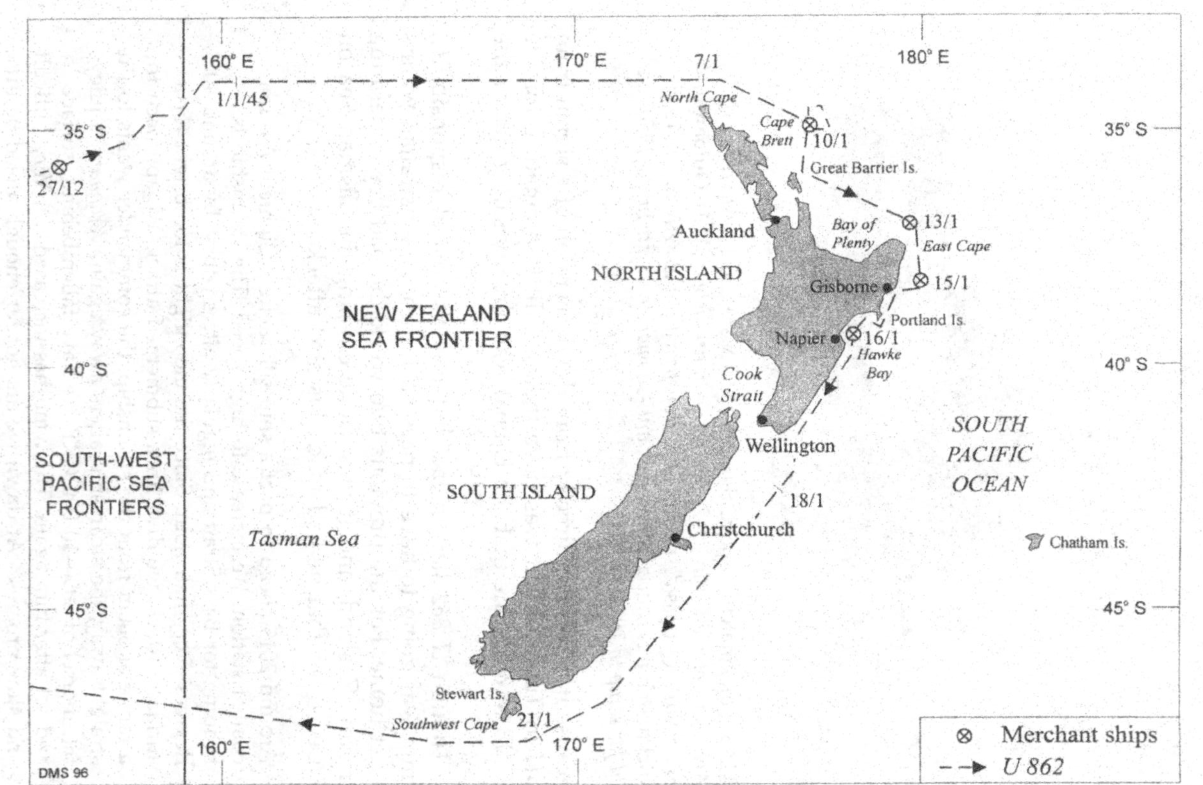

New Zealand, January 1945

range of 1200m an electro torpedo is launched, however, soon after it had left the torpedo tube and 300m from our own boat it detonates unexpectedly. In the boat a hard shock is felt. For a few moments we are dumbstruck. Premature detonation. The steamship, which naturally has also seen the explosion, thereupon shows its heels and flees at high speed. We run on submerged. After two hours aircraft bombs are dropped at a great distance from us. The aircraft supposes we are very near to the steamship and drops bombs all around.[10]

No merchant ship reported unexplained explosions that day, and if *U 862* did detect the sound of bombs they were not deliberately directed at her. The rattling effect was there nonetheless, and the presence of a full moon ensured that the U-boat spent minimal time on the surface and maintained a sharp lookout. Rough weather continued to make progress difficult and not until 30 December, when a thick fog appeared, did Timm feel confident that the Australians had given up their pursuit.

The following day the U-boat celebrated the coming of 1945:

The boat is proceeding with difficulty in the rough sea. Lunch is a catastrophe; in the galley the pots hop around and just at the moment the *Kommandant* wishes us a 'Happy New Year' on the loudspeaker, the last pot of vanilla sauce overturns. Here's to the New Year! We dive and have a small celebration in the forward compartment, where for the first time we formally light the Christmas tree.[11]

For the next week *U 862* struggled on through poor visibility and heavy seas.[12] Finally the weather began to clear and on 6 January those on the bridge basked in their first early morning sunlight for several weeks. They remained on the surface until thick cloud cover reappeared and the danger of surprise attack from the air drove them down again. On 7 January the U-boat rounded the tip of New Zealand's North Island and headed southeast to follow the shipping route. Reiffenstuhl made sure that the torpedo mechanics checked the remaining torpedoes thoroughly, for 'it may be that we will need them in the next few days'.[13] For a change the sea was mirror-smooth and while the weather remained calm Timm patrolled some 40 miles from North Cape, using the lighthouse to fix their position. The crew listened intently for any sign of the expected traffic. Detecting nothing, they moved closer to the coast and on 10 January were presented with their next opportunity to strike.

We are close to the shore in the approaches to Auckland. At night

> the Cape Brett Light is a good and continuing navigational aid. Again a very dark night, wind from the east which becomes stronger at midnight. Nothing to hear, nothing to see. One hour later the hydrophones detect an engine noise. Surfaced and looked out—it is a medium size steamship which is running parallel to the coast. Heavy squalls, it is very hard to see it. We have positioned ourselves out of sight of the steamship and then lost him again. Either we have either miscalculated, or the steamship is only part of the coastal traffic and has gone into a small harbour north of Cape Brett. Still, we dive ahead of the calculated interception point, however, nothing found. There is a strong westerly set and because of this we approach to within 8 nm of the mainland.[14]

Timm positioned the U-boat off Cape Brett Light again and briefly waited for the next passing steamship. But still nothing came, so he moved farther south. By the evening of 11 January they were travelling close to an unfamiliar coast dotted with several small islands. It was a particularly dark night and the sky remained overcast, preventing a fix of their position. Heavy rain squalls made matters worse, at times reducing visibility to less than a metre. As dawn approached, Reiffenstuhl was horrified to see land directly ahead of the U-boat and only a mile away. It had been a close brush with disaster, and the continuing lack of targets only added to Timm's problems. Perhaps intending a play on words, Reiffenstuhl wrote that night in his journal that it was 'the morale of the crew that has sunk'.[15]

Timm discussed the situation with his officers. They had two apparent options. The first would be to go back north, continue on past New Guinea, and attempt to intercept Allied traffic from Australia to the Philippines theatre before taking the U-boat on to Japan. The second option was to continue south, rounding New Zealand's South Island before making a further raid on the Sydney area and then returning to Java. This last proposal was closer to the plans discussed before their departure and Timm decided to stick with it, since fuel and above all provisions were already getting short.

During the day *U 862* skirted submerged along the edge of Great Barrier Island and crossed the Bay of Plenty that night. By the early morning of 13 January the Germans had reached a position close off East Cape. Here at last they found another target. It was a medium-sized vessel heading southeast along the coast, and Timm tried hard to manoeuvre into an attack position before dawn. He failed. His orders prohibited him from making an attack close to an enemy coast if there was any risk of being seen from land.

After nine weeks at sea excessive caution had allowed yet another steamship to escape. Soon, however, Timm would demonstrate a more reckless side to his character. On 15 January, with no sign of defensive patrols and with New Zealand merchant traffic seemingly unwilling to come out from the coast, he decided to take his U-boat as close as he could to the town of Gisborne. Reiffenstuhl recorded that their excursion was simply to see whether any ships were at anchor or alongside, but it is easy to believe that Timm also intended a display of bravado to impress his weary crew. Gisborne's port is shallow, and larger ships must be unloaded from tenders in the bay outside. Whether Timm had visited the harbour during his time in the merchant navy is unknown, but a submerged approach in daylight would still require careful manoeuvring:

> The navigation is indeed a matter of groping about, since we only have a little water under the keel. During the day you can see, through the periscope, people walking down the street. A man makes a fire on the beach. At dusk we are outside the harbour entrance, nothing is to be seen, the night is again very dark. Surfaced and charged the batteries outside the harbour. Went into the harbour. The docks are brightly illuminated, behind them a large factory. You can see the cars with their headlights driving along the streets. The street lighting itself is also very bright, we are blinded by it. The houses are all brightly illuminated, it looks to us like Christmas. Our hopes however were not fulfilled, there were no worthwhile steamships at anchor or in the dock, for us to sink. Yes, the people here are all so wonderfully unsuspecting. Reversed course; carefully we creep out of the harbour and unseen we are swallowed up by the open sea again.[16]

The value of Timm's excursion was questionable to say the least, and with only a few metres of water to spare *U 862* could not have escaped easily if discovered. They had seen only one ship underway, the SS *Pukeko* of 742 GRT, which had passed them at midday just outside the harbour entrance. Judging it not worth a torpedo, Timm had also decided against using his deck gun because, as in the attack on *Ilissos,* this would only have given their position away. 'Let it run,' he decided. 'It is like the others in there, not a thousand tons.'[17] Despite the disappointment, Timm decided to repeat the exercise the following day. After rounding Portland Island he ordered the U-boat to run in to Hawke Bay to examine a coaling pier. A heavy sea was running, and with the water less than 30m deep they found submerged steering difficult. Discovering no ship coaling, Timm that night moved on to the town of Napier on the southwest shore of the bay. He kept the U-boat on the surface as they approached:

> There is no darkening anywhere. You can see the street cafes illuminated with bright red lights, couples move to the old tunes played by the dance music. The town lies on a hill and glitters with a thousand lights. We do not go completely into the roadstead because the beacons, for inexplicable reasons, are not burning and there is a very bright and unpleasant phosphorescence. We lie there stopped and want to first examine the store.[18]

With no other shipping movements obvious, Timm decided it was safe to remain on the surface. He even allowed those men normally confined below to briefly come up on deck in small groups. They looked around in astonishment at the forgotten signs of a town at peace. Only half a mile from the shore and with the diesels quiet, the breeze brought them the unaccustomed staccato of jazz rhythms still forbidden in Germany. It was a unique experience—one they would never forget.

> After a short time a small steamship comes out of the harbour, he even has his peacetime steaming lights set. They appear to feel very sure of themselves in New Zealand. Ah, well! What is simpler to pursue than a steamship burning its steaming lights. We follow him out from the harbour . . . Dived to attack at dawn—the *Kommandant* misses the shot. At this short range the steamship has probably seen the brief exposure of our periscope or the torpedo track and sped off. Immediately he began to telegraph the signal station on Portland Island. Now we have been noticed here and must get away.[19]

Once again the Germans were mistaken. The New Zealanders remained unaware of their presence, and since they had no previous evidence of patrols, either by aircraft or warships, Timm seems to have missed the perfect opportunity to stir up trouble in a distant area. A few well-placed rounds with the deck gun would almost certainly have caused a public outcry, conceivably lowering enemy morale and no doubt forcing the redeployment or reinforcement of New Zealand's limited assets. Overall it would have had little military significance, but such missions were a staple of British submarines in both Mediterranean and Far Eastern backwaters, particularly when seaborne targets failed to appear. Even the Japanese had engaged in submarine gunnery attacks on isolated Pacific outposts as a diversionary measure.[20] If Timm was being honest with himself, there was little else he could realistically hope to achieve. It is only conjecture, but perhaps he had already shifted his viewpoint to his prospects after a German defeat. The 'terror' shelling of civilian property might be unfavourably considered by the triumphant Allies. As it was, the extended operation had been a waste of effort and, save to a small group of cryptanalysts, *U 862*'s journey around New Zealand would remain unknown until after the war.

Thinking that aircraft must by now be looking for them, the Germans moved farther out to sea and sailed southwards parallel to the coast. Timm planned to continue to Wellington, but the day after their sojourn in Napier, a message from *BdU* brought *U 862*'s New Zealand operation to an abrupt conclusion. The signal came directly to the point. 'Von der Esch, Ganzer, Schrewe, Timm return to Jakarta *immediately*.'[21] Along with the commanders of *U 862* and *U 537*, the names were those of the commanders of *U 863* and *U 871*, supposedly still on intermediate operations on their way out from Europe. However, unknown to *BdU*, Timm was the only one of the four still alive. There was nothing else in the message to explain the recall and, as Timm later explained, 'If it had said, "return", then that would have still left me a little bit more time, but that "immediately" forced me to do the same'.[22] By 21 January *U 862* had rounded New Zealand's South Island and begun her battle back to the west.

The general assumption in the U-boat was that ominous developments in Europe had caused Dönitz to request their return. However, the decision appears instead to have originated in the Far East, where in addition to the expected fall of the Philippines, the Japanese position in the East Indies–Malaya area was now also seen to be deteriorating. Already a problem for the Germans, the Penang base had suffered a major blow to its viability as early as 27 October, when British Liberators had laid 60 mines in the approach channels.[23] Minesweeping measures by the Japanese were as inadequate as their anti-submarine response, and with this practical demonstration that the base was now within reach of Allied air power, *Vizeadmiral* Wenneker issued instructions that U-boats could in future use Penang only in cases of emergency.[24] On 24 November Berlin followed up with a statement that Jakarta was henceforth to be considered the primary German U-boat base in East Asia.[25] On 20 December *Korvettenkapitän* Dommes took up a new appointment as *Chef der U-Bootsstützpunkte in Südraum*

(Chief of U-boat bases in Southern Area) at the Seletar naval base in Singapore.[26]

Soon afterwards, Dommes was informed by the Japanese that they expected a combined fleet and air attack on Singapore, and he appreciated that both it and Penang might soon become untenable.[27] Preparations to move facilities from Penang were already well underway, but the island remained the site of the only German-operated wireless station that the Japanese had allowed outside Tokyo.[28] Both *BdU* and Dommes worried that a rapid Allied advance might well cut off communications with the U-boats at sea. It was for this reason that they ordered the submarines to return to Java as soon as possible.

To avoid any chance encounters with the Australians, Timm charted a course well south of the continent. This would be clear of both aircraft and ships, but it left the U-boat exposed to some of the worst weather imaginable. The onslaught began as soon as *U 862* entered the Tasman Sea. The Germans' experiences on their journey east were as nothing in comparison. At first the U-boat rolled uncontrollably in response to the gale-strength wind and waves coming directly from the south. Soon, however, they were heading directly into a huge swell coming from the west. Those on the bridge looked on helplessly as 'the boat rises high out of the sea then slams with all its force into the troughs of the waves. At times you think that the hydroplanes must have broken away.'[29] Timm ordered the boat trimmed well down by the stern. Years later he was to recall almost fondly the conditions in the Southern Ocean: 'we bore up bone dry against these sky-high mountains. A great seamanship experience.'[30] On 26 January 1945, however, strapped to the bridge with the rest of his watch and feeling like a 'dripping wet poodle', Reiffenstuhl was less enthusiastic:

> The wind has increased further, very heavy sea, which we must continue to battle through. Often you think, that the boat will not be able to struggle to climb to the peak of a gigantic wave, then it is carried no more and slides down again. I have never believed before, that there are house-sized waves, but today I have personally seen them (over 10 m!). In the forward compartment it feels as if you are in a lift, which is running continuously up and down to the third floor. Already this has been happening for almost one week![31]

Cold salt water cascaded into the control room from the conning tower hatch every time it was opened, and the bilge pumps ran continuously. The violent and constant motion made everyday tasks like eating and sleeping almost impossible. A succession of hearty curses and hollow laughs would often issue from the messes as a man laboriously scraped the remnants of his meal from the deck, his comrades finding amusement in his misfortune. As Reiffenstuhl quipped, 'Yes, these are the delights and despairs of a seafarer.'[32]

Despite Timm's anxiety to return, the weather and the need to economise on fuel forced him to reduce speed. Their progress west slowed to a crawl. The perverse thrill of the U-boat's acute movements did little to relieve the monotony. For a few days *Dichteritis* or poetry composing became endemic as all on board tried to talk only in verse. Though *BdU* had expected *U 862* to arrive back in Jakarta by about 3 February, Timm was already well behind schedule.[33] Not until 2 February, as the U-boat finally altered course to the north, did the conditions improve and allow Timm to increase speed. On 4 February, however, another message from the Japanese radio intelligence service, warning of an 'English fleet cruising outside the Sunda Strait', brought *U 862*'s speed back to a cautious advance.[34]

To the tense and weary crew, what must have seemed the final blow was still to come. The cans of meat and mushrooms embarked in Jakarta were found to be tainted. On 5 February the first men reported sick with high temperatures and diarrhoea. The outbreak of dysentery spread rapidly through the boat. In the U-boat's oppressively smelly, damp, noisy and claustrophobic atmosphere, the ordeal of those who fell ill was almost indescribable. As Reiffenstuhl wrote after being forced to his bunk:

> Sweating heavily. Sickness in a U-boat is something dreadful. You lie in your own juice, can't wash properly, not to mention can't bathe, can't change any bedding and can't maintain a correct diet. The conditions in the heads are of course hideous. In the evening Kuddel, the IIWO, took to his bunk with a temperature over 38°, four officers have now fallen out. The *Kommandant* must go on watch. If a hostile ship comes now, we are not well prepared.[35]

If Reiffenstuhl was tempting fate he was not to be disappointed, for this last assertion would all too soon be put to the test.

14 SS Peter Silvester

> *As a result of the element of surprise by which it is characterised, the submarine—apart from direct naval successes which it is sought to obtain by its use—exercises a great influence on the military and strategical position, because the enemy must everywhere reckon with its appearance, and is influenced in a correspondingly high degree in his strategical decisions and military operations (detours, defensive measures, safety patrols, zig-zag course).*
>
> —*U-boat Commander's Handbook*, 1943 edition

It was the morning of 6 February 1945. In eastern Europe, Russian mechanised armies were establishing bridgeheads across the Oder, the last major river obstacle before Berlin. In western Europe, after the containment of the German Ardennes offensive, Allied troops were about to begin their own campaign to seize the Rhineland. In the Pacific, American operations to regain the main Philippine island of Luzon continued and amphibious forces were being assembled to invade Iwo Jima. The Indian Ocean, in contrast, was relatively quiet. It had now been three months since the last submarine attack by either of the two Axis partners.[1] On board *U 862*, more men had succumbed to dysentery, but all would soon need to raise themselves from their sickbeds.

> During the *Kommandant*'s watch tops of masts are sighted bearing 190°!! At a range of 700 nm from the coast a Liberty ship of 7000 GRT! A welcome feast still, before we return. It is the same '*Kaisersarg*' that we sank before off Sydney. I fire three torpedoes at him, all three of which hit (one at the foremast, one at the leading edge of the bridge and one almost in the same hole, the

> steamship is stopped after two hits). The steamship is thickly enveloped in smoke. Probable that he will not last much longer. After the smoke had cleared, you can still see him lying there! The fore part of course lies deeper in the water. We wait, however, to see whether perhaps he will still sink, which he doesn't. If we hadn't had the experience of that '*Kaisersarg*' off Sydney we would wonder now, but so . . . Now he lies there stopped and blows steam. He therefore needs a finishing shot.
>
> Since it is quite light and the fellow has two 10.5cm guns and four machine guns fitted on the deck, we attack him submerged. Hit in front of the bridge. A heavy explosion, the whole forward section breaks off and sinks. The other half of the steamship, however, still floats. Devil take him, what is he loaded with, that he will not sink? These are the ships, 'that fall apart at launching' as the German commentator Fritsche believes. We again go up to the wreck and hope to shoot some ventilation holes in the ship's side with the gun. But our main gun can't do it, the heavy sea has probably misaligned it. We approach to a range of 100m from the wreck, it has been completely abandoned. In the interim it has become dark again, everything looks eerie in the moonlight. You can see completely inside the front of the ship. Below, in the lower decks, the side passageways are painted with luminous paint. You can see all the internal arrangements exactly. The flag still waves proudly at the ensign staff. I would have willingly boarded the shipwreck to get the secret material out, but the *Kommandant* does not want to because the sea is too rough. Two magazines from the 2cm guns are swept over the decks and down. It is assumed, that in the worsening heavy sea the wreck will sink—An exciting night. Continue passage at high speed. Dead tired in the bunk, however, I am still not at all well.[2]

To the Liberty ship SS *Peter Silvester* fell the dubious privilege of being the last Allied ship to be sunk by enemy action in the Indian Ocean. She had left San Francisco in early January bound eventually for Colombo and had passed through Melbourne only the week before the attack. One of several Liberty ships converted to animal transports, *Peter Silvester* was carrying 317 army mules intended to become pack animals in Burma, and 2700 tons of cargo—mostly hay. She was manned by a crew of 42 together with 26 Naval Armed Guard, and carried another 106 American servicemen as passengers. Many of the men were from the US Army Air Corps, and by a quirk of fate their surnames all began with the letter 'H'; the result of an administrative decision that had seen their places in an earlier transport taken by emergency Red Cross personnel. Others belonged to the cavalry and were on board to look after the mules. Among the latter group were Privates Tom Tschirhart and Ray Laenen, two 18-year-olds who

SS Peter Silvester, *belonging to Pacific Far East Lines of San Francisco, photographed sometime in 1943 before her conversion to an animal transport. The mules were carried in stalls built on the forward and after decks. In Liberty ships the deck space was as important as the under-deck areas for the carriage of cargo and normally, except for the midships house and gun platforms, there were no important obstructions for the whole of the vessel's length.* (Project Liberty Ship 26 749)

had been close friends since their schooldays in Detroit. Against the odds they had remained together through induction into the Army, training and first assignment.

The night of the attack was dark, with the moon obscured. *Peter Silvester* had received no warnings of submarine activity and was taking no extra precautions.[3] Below decks, crew and passengers had settled down to their regular evening routine. Tschirhart, who normally joined a group playing poker on top of one of the lower hatch covers, had decided to retire early. At about 2140, *U 862*'s first salvo struck on the starboard side of No. 3 hold. The explosion put all lights and communication systems out of order, ruptured the main deck and 'blew all those hatch covers like a bunch of corks, right up through the ship'.[4] Everyone in Tschirhart's regular card group was killed. Many others were thrown from their bunks and all were plunged into darkness. The force was so great that Russ Hoover, a B-29 bombardier on his way to India, was blown through the two bunks above him into the deckhead. He then fell 4m to the deck and had his foot severely burned by escaping steam.[5] Both the damaged hold and the engine room flooded, and the bow settled rapidly. Men floundered about searching for ladders, yelling for their mates and assailed by the fear that they might be imprisoned and go down with the vessel. Tschirhart and Laenen struggled separately to the upper deck and were directed to their battle stations.

The second attack came just over half an hour after the first. Two more torpedoes struck *Peter Silvester*'s starboard side between Nos. 2 and 3 holds. Captain Bernard C. Dennis, the vessel's master, gave the order to abandon ship. Two of the starboard rafts had been blown overboard by the explosions, but the crew managed to launch four lifeboats and six other rafts. At about 2230, with men still abandoning ship, a final torpedo struck at No. 1 hold. Shortly after this the ship split in two forward of the midship house. The forward end sank immediately. Discipline during the evacuation had been good, with the able-bodied willingly helping those who could not walk by themselves. Crew member Burdette Burch went back into the hulk several times and alone rescued at least six of his fellows. In all, 32 men were lost in the sinking, many killed by the initial explosions, others probably drowned when the bow went down.

The survivors struggled in a sea full of fuel oil, cargo crates, and mules who were just as anxious about saving themselves. Tschirhart and Laenen had gone over the side at different times and positions, but fate directed them to the same lifeboat. Both later recalled the terrible noise of the mules 'screaming', and the continuing struggle to knock the big animals off as they tried to get aboard. Another survivor described the mules as being 'like a school of fish. When we put the boat hook out to pick up the men, if something didn't grab hold of it we knew it was a mule and would hit it on the head. They got in between the rafts and we had to knock them out.'[6]

In the midst of the wreckage, *U 862* surfaced and appeared to cruise around looking for something. The Americans did not know whether it was a Japanese or German submarine but expected the worst: '. . . we weren't sure whether they would machine-gun us or just what they might do. We were all a bit terrified, because certainly we were sitting ducks in the water. They just chug-chug-chugged around, and we could see the conning tower and the light and some men standing in it.'[7] Several survivors doused their emergency lights and even some of those already recovered got back into the water and stayed quiet.

According to Sergeant Barton Hoover the men in his raft didn't breathe 'for the rest of the night because [the enemy] . . . were so close we could spit on them'.[8]

Most of the men had swallowed oil and were violently sick; some were severely injured, many were clad only in their underwear and were shivering in the freezing night air. 'We was just one big pile at the bottom of the raft,' recalled Charles Hoar at a reunion in 1983.[9] The rafts, 'made of railroad ties and covered with canvas', were less than 6m square and in the rough seas prevailing were in constant danger of breaking apart. Water was buffeting the occupants up to their hips. Those who had either managed to save cigarettes or found cartons in the flotsam chain-smoked so they could stuff the packs in the cracks to keep the rafts from sinking.[10] The rafts were so overcrowded men could neither lie down nor stretch, and most managed to doze only fitfully while sitting bolt upright, virtually cheek to cheek. Conditions in the 8m long lifeboats were almost as bad. Two had capsized when launched and most required steady bailing.

The coming of day provided little relief. The sun beat down mercilessly and before long the thoughts of all survivors turned to 'every glass of water you left undrunk'.[11] The effects of constant immersion and exposure caused feet and legs to swell, but there was almost nothing they could do to relieve the discomfort. The men were alive but their situation was not good. Since the first attack had put *Peter Silvester*'s wireless and auxiliary equipment out of action, no distress signal had been sent. With no reason to suspect that anything was wrong, it might be weeks before the authorities began a search. The senior survivors in each group took stock of provisions. In theory the lifeboats carried sufficient food and water for 30 days, but some provisions had been lost and to give everyone a fair chance it would be necessary to distribute the survivors more evenly among the boats. An officer decided that Tschirhart and Laenen's lifeboat was overloaded and directed half the men into another boat close by. Though reluctant to leave his friend, Tom Tschirhart was one of those chosen to move.

Rationing began on the second day. The basic allowance was around 2oz of water and two malted milk tablets per man twice a day, though the lifeboats, being slightly better provisioned, were able to divide small cans of pemmican to add to the diet. The exception was the lifeboat commanded by Captain Dennis. Alone among the scattered groups, its occupants had managed to reboard the after section of *Peter Silvester* on the morning of 8

February. Dennis ordered the lifeboat restocked with plenty of provisions, then instructed his men to row for the Australian coast.

Attempts were made to keep the other small clusters of survivors together, but it was hard work. It took an entire day for those on one raft to paddle the 300m to another. As their strength ebbed, the vessels began to gradually drift apart again. By noon on the second day the survivors were in six separate groups and most had lost sight of one another. As Laenen watched Tschirhart's boat disappear over the horizon he wondered if he would ever see his friend again. All that most of them could do now was wait and hope.

The Australians had meanwhile attempted to maintain a track on *U 862*'s progress. Unfortunately, with imperfect intelligence, they found that even the mere threat of an enemy submarine required a large and ongoing commitment. With all commands ordered to remain alert, the number of submarine-related incidents in local waters and reported to CSWPSF rose to more than 20 in January, while the RAAF Eastern Area Appreciation that month made particular note of the 'heavy' operations resulting from suspected sightings.[12] Nor was the effect limited solely to eastern and southern Australia. On 15 January NOIC Darwin promulgated a message stating that no fewer than seven submarines had been sighted west of Darwin. As a result, four vessels surveying an important new channel through Scott Reef were instead detailed to carry out an anti-submarine sweep and search.[13] Similarly, on the morning of 22 January aircraft made two separate sightings of a probable enemy submarine in Bass Strait.[14] Notwithstanding previous assessments that the U-boat was by now farther west, Southern Area responded by dispatching a striking force of one Catalina, six Beauforts and four Ansons all equipped with ASV. A constant aerial patrol of coastal waters was already being maintained to cover BPF movements, and owing to the continuing shortage of suitable serviceable aircraft only two units of the strike force actually came from Southern Area. The search continued for over 24 hours but, with *U 862* still half way between New Zealand and Tasmania, naturally found no further trace of a submarine.

A more likely indication occurred on 28 January, when the Western Area intelligence section received notice of a 'possible enemy submarine' southwest of Fremantle and heading northwest.[15] The Beauforts of Western Area's No. 14 Squadron still maintained their daily anti-submarine patrol of the Fremantle sector but, like Southern Area, were now also struggling with the additional escort commitments brought on by the passage of the BPF. To assist, some of the Liberator bombers belonging to the newly formed No. 25 Squadron at Cunderdin were used. Between 29 and 31 January the Liberators searched out to 160 miles southwest and west of Cape Leeuwin.

Again no contact was made with the U-boat, but the Liberators at least had some idea of what to expect when on 10 February the SS *Cape Edmont*, on its way from Colombo to Melbourne, reported that she had recovered a lifeboat from the *Peter Silvester*. The steamship had sighted the boat and its fifteen occupants at first light on 9 February, the survivors having drifted 45 miles from the position of the sinking. *Cape Edmont* then spent the rest of the day searching for more survivors, maintaining radio silence in case the U-boat was still nearby. The discovery of the lifeboat was therefore only broadcast to the RAN when the streamship resumed its passage.

With the alarm at last raised, a search for the remaining survivors was rapidly initiated under the direction of NOIC Fremantle. Claims were later made that this was the largest and most thorough rescue search mounted during the war. At one stage it involved, virtually every Allied warship or merchant ship in the eastern Indian Ocean. It began when Commodore Pope sailed the corvette HMAS *Dubbo* and the patrol frigate USS *Corpus Christi* from Fremantle on 10 February. Two days later their respective sister ships, HMAS *Warrnambool* and USS *Hutchinson*, followed. The search was under Pope's control, but the diversion of other warships variously required the authority of the CinCs of both the BPF and the East Indies Fleet, the US Seventh Fleet and the ACNB. Aircraft were at first provided by the RAAF and RAF but soon included those on the BPF ferry carriers HM Ships *Slinger* and *Speaker*. Diverted from their passage from Trincomalee to Sydney, the two CVEs arrived in the search area on 14 February. Multiplicity of control was inevitable, yet there was remarkably little red tape, and the search was touted as proof of the spirit of cooperation that had finally been engendered between the Allies.

The honour of finding the next group of survivors fell to the RAAF. This in itself was no easy feat. The weather over the search area was deteriorating and visibility at sea was down to two miles with a cloud ceiling of only 150m. The search area was already large and to reach it the aircraft faced a long overwater flight with only the stars as a guide. Initially allotted to the task were two Liberators from No. 25 Squadron and two Catalinas from No. 205

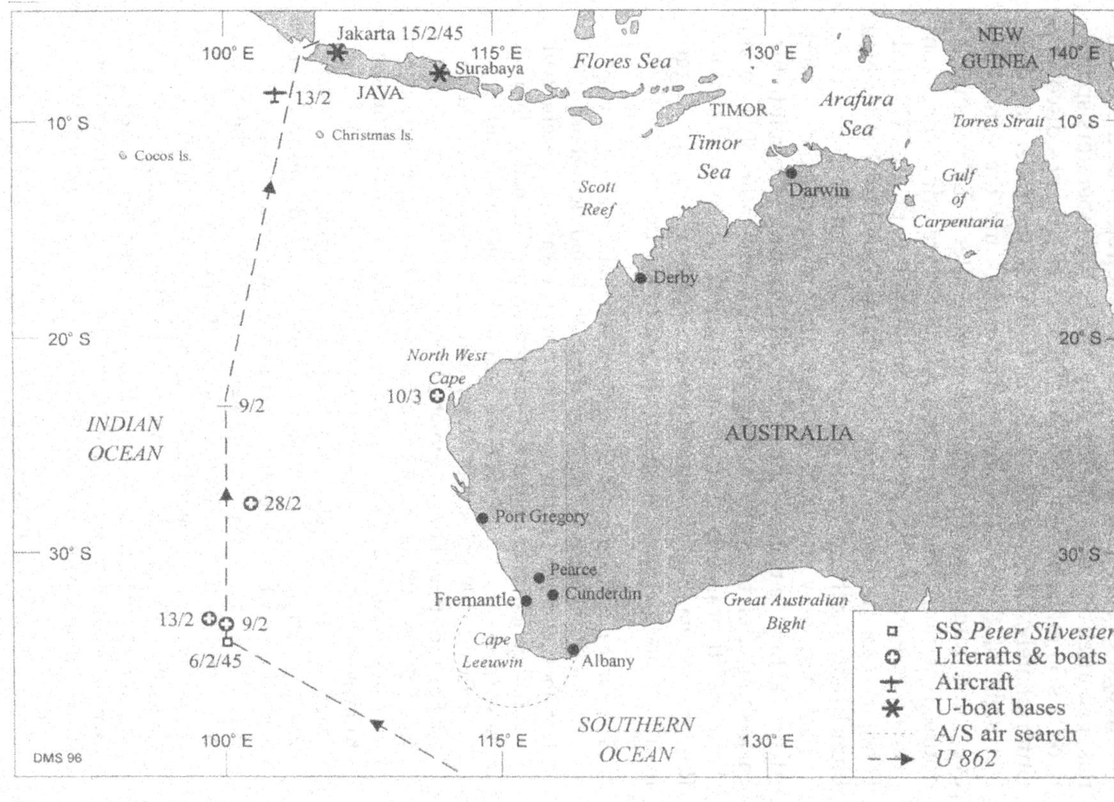

Western Australia, February–March 1945

Squadron RAF, the Liberators carrying a flexible auxiliary fuel tank in the bomb bay to increase their range.

Though engine troubles soon caused the return of the Catalinas, just after dawn on 11 February one of the Liberators spotted two rafts 30 miles farther northwest than *Cape Edmont*'s discovery. Unfortunately, the weather was so bad that the Liberator crew lost sight of them after only ten minutes, and the conditions eventually forced the aircraft back to base after a flight lasting 17 hours. Not until the following midnight were wind conditions deemed acceptable enough to risk another attempt. At 0330 on 13 February Liberator A72–156, captained by Squadron Leader Neil Blunck, and another aircraft took off from Pearce. For Blunck and his ten-man crew it would be their first mission from Western Australia. Engine troubles in the second Liberator forced it to turn back soon after take-off, leaving Blunck's navigator, 30-year-old Warrant Officer George (Rud) Rimes, to find the search area alone. Rimes, who was later to describe the flight as one of the 'biggest thrills' of his life, put the details down in a letter to his wife:

> The sun came up about 5 o'clock and we found we were flying over a sea of cloud. We soon got beneath it, and flew about 2000 feet above the sea for the next four hours. I was very careful with my navigation as everything depended on me. We had to find these specks on the ocean, in an area of 40 miles by 20 miles, after flying 1000 miles over water, and men's lives depended on us. So, after three hours I replotted all of my work from the start. Good thing I did, because I found a slight error. By ten o'clock the boys were awake (they'd had a good sleep). I took a sun shot to make certain of my position. At 11 o'clock we started our search and immediately noticed a piece of wreckage. This cheered us up for a bit. We turned back to examine it, and it proved to be a piece of mast. A couple of minutes later we noticed a ship on the horizon, so we went off to have a look at it. It was the Yank Navy ship on the job. We signalled to it and left them to get back to our search. I happened to be standing beside the pilot, and immediately noticed a red flare on the water, just a half mile to our left. Do you think I was excited? We circled them—they were two rafts—and the men waved frantically. Imagine nineteen men in two double beds, and you get some idea how cramped they would be.
>
> While we circled, I got its position ready, Merv coded it and sent it out to ship and base, but got no reply, and we dropped some supplies to them by parachute. However, though it dropped only 30 yards from them, whether from exhaustion or the current, they could not reach it. Just then someone noticed a light flashing in the distance,

so off we went to examine it, and we found a life-boat with eleven men on it. These seemed to be in a pretty good condition, and, of course, they waved madly, as they hadn't seen any aircraft for so many days. We circled them and dropped supplies which they were able to pick up by rowing. We had been very careful to note the exact bearing and distance of the boat and rafts, so we had very little difficulty in locating the rafts again. In fact we flew from one to other about three times and found they were about ten miles apart. Goodness knows if they knew of the other's existence. Probably not, because the visibility was only about five miles and any swell would hide a small raft.

After an hour, seeing that the rescue ship had not arrived, we decided to go and find it . . . I set course for the ship and was surprised to see it after two minutes. Apparently they had intercepted our message and were already steaming full speed for the position I had given. Peter flashed them this message by Aldis lamp. 'Rafts 180T—4 miles from you and boat 270—10 miles from rafts.' They acknowledged it and followed us. We went on ahead, because a ship has great difficulty in spotting a raft, being so low in the water. Having run across it again by good luck, we fired coloured cartridges to attract the ship's attention, which immediately turned for it. Boy, you should have seen the sailors stand up in the raft and jump for joy!

Before leaving, I asked the ship her position and my position only varied 10 miles from hers. You can imagine how bucked I was that my navigation was so accurate. I felt very tired and excited, so I had a sleep and let Clive navigate. We picked up a message on the way home saying the ship had reached the survivors, so that was that. We landed after being in the air sixteen hours. Operations crowd were simply purring and the Air Officer commanding had rang up and congratulated the squadron on the good job. Mac reckons we will all have to get new hats! Naturally we had a feed and quite a few drinks to celebrate the success. The crushing blow was this morning when we were awakened to clean up the kite about eleven o'clock. Yours truly had to clean out the lavatory which I used on the trip. I think I'll use the cake tin method next time.[16]

Corpus Christi was the rescuing vessel and the lifeboat had been the one commanded by Captain Dennis. Later the same day the American ship reported that she had picked up another 62 survivors from four rafts lashed together. Nothwithstanding Rimes' observations, many of the men could no longer walk and several were so ill that they could only take soup broth. Russ Hoover was one of the worst afflicted. He remained in hospital for several months and lost 68 pounds before he began to recover.

Though more than 100 of *Peter Silvester*'s complement had now been rescued, two lifeboats remained missing and NOIC Fremantle directed the search to continue. *Slinger* and *Speaker* had shortly to resume their voyages to Sydney, but Pope diverted HMAS *Castlemaine* and several suitable merchantmen so that their new courses passed through the current search area. Naval Headquarters in Fremantle had set up a detailed plot that displayed the position of the sinking, areas already searched, and probable course and speed of the two missing lifeboats based on the prevailing wind and sea. Search areas were then picked for the following days and instructions radioed to participants. Soon the overall search area extended over an expanse equivalent to one-third the size of Western Australia. Unfortunately, the extra heavy fuel loads required by aircraft made take-offs in the prevailing winds particularly hazardous. Tragically, on 14 February a Liberator crashed and burned about 800m from the end of the runway.[17] Five of the crew were killed. Thereafter the RAAF cancelled additional participation by the Liberators.

By 22 February, with no further trace of survivors, NOIC Fremantle formally abandoned the surface search. However, Western Area maintained a coastal air patrol with Beauforts, and ships and aircraft operating off the west coast remained on watch. Coastal authorities as far north as Derby were also alerted in case the missing boats were making for Australia. On 28 February, 22 days after the sinking, HMS *Activity*, another CVE *en route* from the East Indies Station to Sydney, reported that one of her planes had sighted a lifeboat. The 20 survivors on board had drifted 500 miles north-northeast from the initial site of the attack. They had suffered through two tremendous storms and eaten the last of their meagre provisions four days before being recovered. On board was Ray Laenen, happy to be rescued but immediately concerned that it was Tom Tschirhart's boat that remained missing. Laenen and the others were sent to a military hospital in Perth to recuperate. Aware of their own poor condition, they knew that every additional day reduced the chances of anyone else being found alive.

The position of Laenen's boat indicated that the earlier searches might have been centred too far east. CinC East Indies Fleet therefore ordered the carrier HMS *Formidable* and cruiser HMS *Uganda* to pass through the area of *Activity*'s sighting on their passage to Australia. They found nothing and ten days after his own rescue Laenen had practically given up hope. However, the next morning he returned after a few minutes away from his ward to find a new man in the bed next to his: 'It appeared to

Private Ray Laenen (arrowed) and fellow survivors of SS Peter Silvester *as found by the escort carrier HMS* Activity *after 22 days adrift. Though a few cans of water still remained, they had run out of food 18 days after the sinking. Laenen had lost 45 lbs by the time he was recovered.*

be Japanese—thin, emaciated, dark close-cropped hair.'[18] It took a few moments for Laenen to appreciate that the dark-skinned figure was his best friend. Tschirhart and the other fourteen occupants of his boat had been found by the submarine USS *Rock* on 10 March, 32 days after the sinking and only 20 miles from North West Cape.[19] One severely injured man had died on the first night after *U 862*'s attack, but the others had rigged a make-shift sail and sailed and drifted nearly 1100 miles. They had run out of food after only twelve days and milk tablets a week later. Thereafter there had been nothing but water. Yet on their last night adrift they had seen a lighthouse and next morning imagined they could see 'a big, beautiful sandy beach'.[20] Despite their pitiful condition they had brought out the oars, and it was while engaged in this last desperate row that the submarine had appeared alongside.

Contemporary accounts highlighted the organisation and effectiveness of the search. 'An epic narrative of persistence and co-operation between Allies' was one newspaper's opinion.[21] Nevertheless, the initial alert had been entirely a matter of chance, and other than those recovered by *Corpus Christi*, all other survivors had been picked up by ships not taking part in the organised search. The 143 men saved from *Peter Silvester* certainly had reason to be thankful for the preponderance of friendly forces in the Indian Ocean. The news of the sinking and successful search did not appear in the media until April, and no mention was made of the large role chance had played in the discovery of the survivors. There remains the suspicion that the favourable publicity may have helped divert public attention from what had in effect been an enemy success in an ocean supposedly now under Allied control.

While the search went on for the crew of *Peter Silvester, U 862* continued on her way back to Java. Notwithstanding her battering in the Great Australian Bight and the hunt she had left floundering in her wake, it would be the last few days of the voyage that would be the most dangerous. Though initially confused over which U-boat had sunk *Peter Silvester,* Allied intelligence made every effort to obtain a new fix on *U 862.* They knew that Timm would soon have to break radio silence to warn Jakarta of his return. The Allies, moreover, only required a rendezvous date, for Dommes had already helpfully broadcast his latest instructions to U-boats approaching Jakarta:

> (a) Proceed at night south of Krakatau and Dwars on Den Weg Island arriving at 05.50S 106.17E at dawn, when recognition signal is to be exchanged with escort. U-boat is then to proceed submerged on an easterly course to 106.30, where pilot is to be embarked.
> (b) Air cover will be supplied by Arado 196 or Japanese *Reishiki* aircraft, and U-boats may expect air reconnaissance in Sunda Strait from the day before their arrival.
> (c) Allied aircraft fly over Cocos on passage between Australia and India.[22]

Assuming the timely interception and decipherment of Timm's message, Rear Admiral Christie would have little difficulty arranging his own less friendly reception.

Though the crew of *U 862* were not aware their movements were quite so open to discovery, they certainly believed that the deployment of Allied units to their north was increasing. The previous week they had received the depressing news of the BPF's heavy carrier strikes on the oil installations at Palembang in Sumatra. They were also no doubt aware of the Southern Area's increasing isolation.

On 6 February, *Vizeadmiral* Wenneker provided Berlin with a rundown on the fighting in the Philippines, noting the Japanese acknowledgment that although southern Luzon could no longer be held, they still intended to hold northern Luzon for as long as possible. Wenneker then concluded: 'since it is practically impossible to keep this area effectively supplied, no military importance is to be attached to this remaining Japanese stronghold. To all intents and purposes the Southern Area must be considered as cut off.'[22] With German concerns increasing over the fate of the four *Monsun* U-boats they believed still at sea, *BdU* sent a request to all to break radio silence: '*U 862, U 863, U 871* and *U 537*. Owing to situation in Southern Area, transmit estimated time of arrival as early as possible. All boats make for Sunda Strait. Carrier aircraft must be expected everywhere.'[24]

The BPF carriers had actually arrived in Fremantle on 4 February, but either Timm did not receive *BdU*'s message or, with the suspected presence of an Allied Fleet in the area, he decided to remain quiet for a while longer. Not until 9 February did he finally release a message providing a short breakdown of his achievements and reporting *U 862*'s arrival at the rendezvous point on 15 February.[25] In response, Dommes passed the best intelligence he could:

1 According to Radio Intelligence there are again enemy forces between Australia and Cocos Islands.
2 In Sunda Strait there is constant danger of enemy submarines.[26]

Two days later he repeated the caution:

1 Exercise the greatest care at the Sunda Strait approach. Be prepared for carrier-borne aircraft and enemy submarines everywhere. Proceed submerged by day as far as possible.
2 There are now Arados at Jakarta and they have taken over protection.[27]

Timm needed no encouragement to remain cautious. He continued submerged during the day, but surfaced and ordered high speed at night to maintain progress. The Germans made no sight or sound contacts and, while a series of practical jokes helped to reduce the tension for some, others kept busy preparing post-patrol reports and listing maintenance requirements and stores requests. As Reiffenstuhl succinctly put it: 'The paper war blooms.'[28]

On the evening of 13 February Tunis brought them back to reality with a helpful warning that an aircraft was up and searching. A crash-dive followed, but the onset of a series of heavy rain squalls convinced Timm that he could continue his passage on the surface for the remainder of the night. Early the next morning *U 862* was at the entrance to Sunda Strait:

> At high speed we zig-zag up to Krakatau. There we went to the cellar then surfaced shortly afterwards again. We continue to zig-zag so we will not become a meal for a hostile submarine. Around 17.00 *Oblt.* Nietschke with his Arado arrives and provides us with air escort. A good feeling, to finally see something German again. Very good lookout for hostile periscopes. Broke through on the surface to Dwarsindenweg [sic]. Very, very hot in the boat during the underwater passage now necessary.[29]

Following in the wake of a Japanese escort, *U 862* crept safely into Tanjong Priok on the morning of 15 February. Timm's run of good luck had still not deserted him. Though HM Submarines *Storm* and *Sirdar*, were nearby they made no contact.[30] Nevertheless, on the day following *U 862*'s entry, FRUMEL provided yet another demonstration of its detailed appreciation of her movements and how close a call it had been:

> At 1023 on 14th February *U 862* was submerged in Sunda Strait and would surface in the vicinity of Krakatau Island. This U-boat was informed at 1127 that there was a wreck in position 05.50S: 106.16E and to proceed on the surface in that area. At dawn on 15th February *U 862* was 13 miles east of Babi Island enroute Jakarta.[31]

The scene that greeted *U 862* at Tanjong Priok gave the crew little comfort. On 27 December a Japanese ammunition ship had blown up while loading, and the clean-up had hardly begun. The rumours pointed to the activities of the 'British Secret Service', but the more likely cause was simply careless handling of explosives.[32] The result, however, was wholesale destruction of both harbour and dockyard installations. The German provisions store and torpedo-adjusting station were damaged, storehouses for raw and technical materials were covered with debris, and there were many casualties. Being lower down, the three U-boats in harbour at the time had escaped relatively unscathed, although *U 219* received slight damage and the watch detail suffered bruises and punctured eardrums.

U 862 remained in Jakarta for only a few days. The base staff had arranged a hectic program of parties and receptions, but Timm and his men knew they would soon need to move on. The immediate threat of a British invasion or attack was over and Dommes was now happy for them to refit the boat in Singapore.

On 18 February they sailed from Jakarta and cleared the danger area near the approaches at high speed. Dommes had told the German supply ship *Bogota* to reckon on *U 862* passing during the night and to take up its escort. Another German vessel, *Horsburgh,* would take over at 0800 on 19 February to escort the U-boat through the Bangka Strait. The Allied cryptanalysts in Melbourne and elsewhere recovered the message, but for unknown reasons the intelligence was not available for promulgation until 26 February.[33]

However, it may be that the much-maligned Japanese anti-submarine defences also lent a hand in *U 862*'s good fortune. On 30 January the Dutch submarine *Zwaardvisch,* responsible for sinking *U 168* and still commanded by Lieutenant Commander Goossens, left Fremantle for her fourth patrol in Far Eastern waters and her third in the SWPA. She made a safe transit of the Lombok Strait on 6 February and after unsuccessfully tangling with two Japanese destroyers in the Java Sea arrived on 13 February in her patrol area just east of Singapore. *Zwaardvisch* remained there until 16 February, when she was taken by surprise by an aircraft emerging from cloud cover and bombed as she dived. The explosions shook the boat severely, causing considerable internal damage that included leaks in the search periscope. Not until 19 February was Goossens ready to resume his duties and then only briefly. That evening the port engine went out of action. With the starboard engine also shaky, Goossens was reluctantly forced to call off his patrol.[34]

On 20 February *U 862* safely entered Singapore. The next day Reiffenstuhl entered the last comments in his journal, his final sentence reflecting the deep sense of relief felt by all on board: 'Secured in Shonan. End of the war cruise in East Asia. We live.'[35]

15 Lübeck

My U-boat men!

Six years of U-boat war lie behind us. You have fought like lions. A crushing material superiority has forced us into a narrow area. A continuation of the fight from the remaining bases is no longer possible.

U-boat men! Undefeated and spotless you lay down your arms after a heroic battle without equal. We remember in deep respect our fallen comrades, who have sealed with death their loyalty to Führer *and Fatherland.*

Comrades! Preserve your U-boat spirit, with which you have fought courageously, stubbornly and imperturbably through the years for the good of the Fatherland.

Long live Germany!

Your *Großadmiral,* 4 May 1945.

As soon as she arrived back in Singapore, work began on getting *U 862* ready for the return voyage to Germany. The overhaul would not be quick or easy. The batteries were in a poor state, and impurities in the Japanese diesel oil the U-boat had used had caused severe damage to her engines.[1] The stresses of the just-completed voyage imposed a similar need for recuperation on her crew. *U 862*'s maintenance period in Singapore had soon stretched out to the end of April. While working and waiting, the Germans listened to the news from the Fatherland and tried to imagine what it meant. Many had heard nothing from their families for months. The Christmas mail for the Far East had been lost in *Kapitänleutnant* Ganzer's *U 871*, and only a trickle of mail had arrived in other U-boats. Timm did his best to keep his crew's spirits up.[2]

Simultaneously, plans were being thrashed out between *BdU*, Wenneker and Dommes on the best way to employ *U 862* on her return to Europe. Despite assurances to the Japanese that offensive actions would continue, and Timm's end-of-cruise recommendation that the area off Sydney 'would repay a generously planned operation with several boats', Dönitz had by early 1945 relegated cooperation with the Japanese to a secondary consideration.[3] For the U-boats outside the Atlantic, the need to transport cargo now replaced even the tying down of enemy forces.

In June 1944 a review of essential raw materials required by the German war economy had concluded that except in the case of fuel, existing stocks and home production of most commodities were sufficient to last until June 1945. However, other 'miscellaneous goods', including bismuth, selenium, cassiterite, quinine and opium, were required immediately. If industry was not to be brought to a standstill, the boats arriving from Asia would have to import these goods at the rate of 12 tons a month. Furthermore, if *BdU* designated all returning operational boats for cargo carrying—which meant only two torpedoes each and no guns—the June deadline might be extended until enough of the new Type XXI U-boats were available to take on the import program.[4]

Unfortunately, losses and delays among the *Monsun* boats made even these modest targets impossible to achieve. By the beginning of 1945 there were only eight U-boats in the Far East with any chance of making the voyage back to Europe.[5] Dönitz ordered Wenneker and Dommes to do everything they could to ensure that at least three of these were ready to leave by 15 January. The lack of any possibility of refuelling in the Atlantic remained the greatest hurdle, but the Germans managed to improvise. The shorter-ranged and slower Type IXC U-boats, *U 510* and *U 532*, sailed from Jakarta on 11 and 13 January respectively. On 14 January they were followed by *U 861*, a Type IXD2 that left from Surabaya with orders to overtake and fuel *U 510*, then carry on to Europe herself. The Type IXD1, *U 195*, sailed from Jakarta on 26 January on a similar mission, but after refuelling *U 532*, *BdU* scheduled her to return to Surabaya for essential maintenance.

Timm was aware of *BdU*'s requirements but, again seemingly on his own initiative, requested an additional torpedo outfit to allow him to carry out intermediate operations off the coast of southeast Africa. Dommes was supportive, and in early March *BdU* approved a total allocation of eight torpedoes. Berlin, though, continued to emphasise the prime objective of the voyage: 'Oper-

A Type IXD2, U 861, *and an unidentified Type VII U-boat outside the bomb-proof submarine pens at Trondheim at the end of the war. The great difference in size between the two major U-boat types is very clear.* U 861 *sailed from Surabaya on 14 January 1945 and on 18 April became the last* Monsun *U-boat to reach a European port before the German capitulation.* (IWM BU6382)

ation is to be carried out only to an extent which will allow return home (to Germany) without fail, even with the U-boat's low battery capacity of 66 per cent. In addition take on as much rubber as possible. If it is discovered before departure that the battery has gone down even further, reduce the number of torpedoes.'[6]

However, Japanese logistics in Singapore were steadily becoming worse. Bombing raids by American B-29 Superfortresses from Calcutta (a 4000-mile round trip) destroyed much of the naval infrastructure, and burning warehouses full of rubber produced both a noxious thick smoke and a terrible fallout of black tar and dirt.[7] A succession of delays stalled work on *U 862*, and to the Germans, the Japanese attitude grew 'more and more icy'.[8] The U-boat's first main engine test was not completed until 25 April and Timm's sailing date was set back until May. In the interim the IJN had introduced its own last-minute suggestions for U-boat operations.

Notwithstanding Dönitz's new priorities, he and Wenneker still attempted to maintain the illusion of German support for the Japanese. In late January Vice Admiral Abe reported an interview with the CinC in which Dönitz stated that the *Kriegsmarine* was willing to send as many submarines as possible to take part in Japanese operations off the Philippines.[9] Tokyo asked Abe to convey 'an expression of our profound gratitude for the German Navy's intention to allow its submarines to take part in Pacific operations' and set about finalising details of operational areas, command and joint procedures with the German attaché.[10] Yet even before his meeting with Abe, Dönitz had stressed to Wenneker that the return of boats to Europe was to take priority.[11] In the event only *U 183*, now under *Kapitänleutnant* Fritz Schneewind, was made available to assist in the Pacific.

U 183 was the longest serving of the *Monsun* boats and after two patrols in the Indian Ocean had in October 1944 gone to Kobe to fit new batteries. Schneewind sailed from Japan on 22 February 1945 to embark fuel and torpedoes in Jakarta, then proceeded to an area north of Dutch New Guinea to operate against the American supply lines. *U 183* left Jakarta on the evening of 21 April having, according to FRUMEL, 'promulgated her noon positions for 22nd to 27th inclusive and her recognition signals'.[12] Despite zig-zagging radically during her passage, Schneewind's boat was hit by at least one of six torpedoes fired by USS *Besugo* at 1426 on 23 April. The explosion ruptured the U-boat's hull and she sank in one or two seconds, two miles west of her plotted position in the Java Sea. The American submarine recovered just one survivor. Among the dead was *Leutnant zur See* Walter Spieth, who had transferred across from *U 862* only the previous month.[13]

A second Japanese initiative concerned *U 862* directly. On 24 March Wenneker signalled Berlin expressing his support for a Japanese proposal that had recently been passed to him from Dommes: 'Japanese Fleet Staff Officer informed us: (it is planned) to have agent(s) landed on Madras coast by German U-boat. For this purpose it is intended to use Timm (862) on his return cruise. Carrying out of this task is important for German position in Southern Area. Immediate decision is necessary.'[14]

Unwilling to make any further concessions, *BdU* regretfully refused the Japanese proposal, citing the danger involved in approaching a coast patrolled by enemy air. Instead Berlin instructed Timm to head for his operation off the South African coast by the shortest route.[15] Dommes, though, had grown closer than most Germans to his contacts in the IJN and, after renewed conversations at the Japanese Fleet Headquarters in Seletar, determined to stand his ground:

1) Jap Navy lays great value on the accomplishment of the mission. Since all Jap U-boats have been withdrawn for the Philippine action, they have no more U-boats of their own in the area.
2) Refusal has not yet been communicated, since especially in the present situation it would seriously impair cooperation with the Jap Fleet command, which is now running smoothly.
3) Since there has been no U-boat in the area concerned for months, it is to be expected that the mission can be carried out by Timm as a *Schnorchel* U-boat without being observed.
4) Commanding officer requests permission to carry out the mission.[16]

A few days later Dommes repeated his pleas. He now argued that the Japanese Navy had already given 'far reaching assurances' to the Army, and concluded that 'Refusal would complicate position of German Navy in Southern Area and put me in an impossible situation as CO there, especially as in December 1944 similar missions were carried out in the same area without a mishap by Jap U-boats which were inferior to ours and according to this the carrying out of the mission offers good chances of success for Timm.'[17]

BdU finally granted its reluctant approval in mid-April. After completion of *U 862*'s refit on 12 May she would leave Singapore for Jakarta, fuel and proceed directly to the Madras coast.[18] But the issue was swiftly becoming of only academic interest. The war in Europe was coming to an end and events were moving far faster than the planners could predict. The final battle for Berlin was underway, and on 24 April Hitler ordered Dönitz and the rest of his staff to leave the city and set up in Plön in Schleswig-Holstein. The final disposition of the U-boat fleet, both in Europe and Asia, now occupied *BdU*'s attention.

The Japanese held no illusions concerning German prospects, and were quick to offer their own helpful suggestions.[19] On 19 April they put it to Wenneker in Tokyo that since it was more difficult for German U-boats to operate from home bases, as many as possible should be transferred to East Asia, where the IJN 'would devote itself fully' to their service. 'In view of the uncertain fate of Southern Area', Wenneker felt that he could not recommend this proposal.[20] Dönitz, in a meeting with Abe on 20 April, was just as quick to reject the offer, noting that because of the lack of oil Japan could expect only two or three Type IXs in the near future.[21] He was nevertheless happy for the Japanese to have the benefit of those U-boats still in the Far East. On 27 April *BdU* relayed the *Großadmiral*'s decision that though *Kapitän zur See* Freiwald and *U 181* should return to Germany as soon as possible, 'The remaining 4 U-boats (*U 183*, *U 195*, *U 219*, *U 862*) will remain for the time being as combat and transport U-boats for Japan in the Southern Area. Operation (to be directed by) CO Southern Area or Naval Attaché Tokyo.'[22]

Why Dönitz should request the return of Freiwald in particular is unclear, but the *Kapitän* had served on the *BdU* staff before joining *U 181*. In any case, Dönitz's concern with such trivialities serves as an illuminating contrast with the momentous events happening around him. Berlin was falling, and Russian and American forces joined hands south of the city on 25 April. Despite the fanaticism and self-deception he had displayed throughout the war, even Dönitz was by now convinced that further resistance would be futile. As recently as 11 April he had issued a decree to the Navy maintaining that 'The *Kriegsmarine* will fight to the end,' yet by 28 April he was confiding to his son-in-law, *Fregattenkapitän* Günther Hessler, that he had decided to surrender the Navy on his own responsibility.[23] On 30 April the *BdU* staff moved to Flensburg in the face of the Allied advance, leaving Dönitz in Plön determined to seek 'death in battle'. However, the *Großadmiral* was to be cheated of the chance to expiate his intended act of surrender. On the afternoon of 30 April Adolf Hitler committed suicide in the ruins of his Berlin headquarters. To his surprise Dönitz found himself nominated by the *Führer* as his successor as head of state and CinC of the *Wehrmacht*.

Freed from his oath of loyalty to Hitler, the new *Führer* struggled to maintain some semblance of order as German resistance crumbled. The situation offered no hope, and on 4 May a delegation from Dönitz signed a declaration of unconditional surrender of all German forces in northwestern Europe. That same day *BdU* ordered the 43 U-boats at sea to cease hostilities and return to base. This was not enough for the Allies, and further instructions were sent for the U-boats to surface, report their positions and proceed to designated Allied ports flying a black surrender flag.

With little information now emanating from the Fatherland, Allied radio was closely monitored in Singapore for news of the expected capitulation of Germany. The Southern Area received advice of Hitler's death on 2 May and even at this late stage the German personnel keenly felt his loss. The following afternoon Dommes arranged a memorial service:

> The Führer's picture was displayed, framed with green leaf and black silk garlands. Soldiers stood at attention when the Japanese commander, Lieutenant General Tomoyuki Yamashita . . . and many other high-ranking Japanese officers arrived. They bowed deeply before the Führer's picture . . . Wreaths were placed in front of the picture and . . . Captain Dommes, made a solemn speech. In final tribute, our soldiers fired salutes over the blue waters of the beach at Pasir Panjang.[24]

Wenneker replied to the order to end the U-boat campaign on 5 May in a message addressed personally to Dönitz: 'Combat action of East Asia U-boats has ceased. Return of U-boats impossible, since they are not ready for travelling.'[25] Dönitz either found this reply unacceptable or in the confusion of the final days perhaps failed even to receive the communication. Ignoring the terms of the Allied ceasefire and still strangely desperate to get Freiwald home, *BdU* on 7 May sent virtually its last message to Tokyo:

> 1) Give U-boats to Japanese except one. Send your proposal in regard to charging for them or sinking them (giving them as a present). Remove crews.
> 2) Freiwald is to return to Germany. If his own U-boat is not ready, he is to board another U-boat. Send this one to Germany.[26]

It was already too late, and Wenneker had no opportunity to respond. The final unconditional surrender of German forces in all areas came into effect at midnight on 8 May, and communications between Germany and Japan abruptly ceased. These last days were not only confusing for the Germans. The Japanese were also somewhat bewildered, and could not be entirely confident in the reactions of German forces in East Asia. Of all parties it was almost certainly the Allies who possessed the best overall picture of events. In early May the final disposition of the Far East U-boats merited a detailed summary by Washington:

> On 29th April shortly after a Honolulu broadcast announced a German surrender proposal, Tokyo instructed naval commands at Batavia and Surabaya to be fully prepared to take emergency measures toward German Navy in Southern East Asia. Less than two hours later, the CinC of the Tenth Area Fleet informed Tokyo that the top German Navy Commander in the southern area (Commander Dommes) had just 'pledged that, despite the deplorable fall of Germany, German submarines and naval personnel in the southern occupied areas would continue to cooperate to the bitter end in carrying out joint operations.'
>
> Despite this seeming willingness of the German Commander to

forfeit recourse to the rights of belligerents under international law in the event of capture by the Allies, German Naval Attache Wenneker at Tokyo appears to have intended otherwise, for on 6th May he addressed (at least to Kobe) the following despatch: 'Carry out order "Luebeck" at 1100 on 6th May and report.'

Six hours later he addressed 'All Hands' as follows:

'Comrades: Fate has decided against us. After fighting a war of unexampled heroism Germany has been overcome by superior enemy power and has laid down the arms which she bore honorably to the last.

'The decision "Luebeck" means for crews of East Asia submarines an impending dubious fortune. I, myself, deplore this most deeply. But the decision was necessary in the interest of maintaining the Navy's self-respect before her erstwhile ally and at the same time in the interest of Germany particularly. It will eventually find complete justification when the history of the war is written.

'I am fully convinced that the Japanese Navy will fully recognize the great sacrifice and will show their appreciation by their future attitude toward us. For all of us there is now nothing left but to act like upright men and German soldiers and bear with composure and dignity the fate that has been laid upon us, and by steadfast comradeship and discipline to present to our homeland, our hosts and the world an example to show that Germans know how to master even a hopeless situation. Only in this way can we today still (serve?) our homeland and stand up before the judgment of our dead and of history. Germany in spite of everything can and will survive.

'I thank you for your loyalty and say goodbye in the hope of seeing you again in the homeland (signed Wenneker).'[27]

Though easily overlooked by the victorious Allied powers, the six U-boats remaining at Japanese ports in May 1945 theoretically came under the terms of the general German surrender. Allied intelligence therefore assessed that the *Lübeck* order was simply a thinly disguised means of permitting Japan to 'seize' the submarines, the objective being the transfer of control in a manner that would afford no proof of violation of the surrender agreement, while still demonstrating the continued loyalty of Germany to her Axis partner.[28]

Dommes had made his decision to fight 'to the bitter end' after an officers' meeting at his headquarters that included representatives from the two U-boats currently in Singapore, *U 181* and *U 862*. There was apparently some disagreement among those present, but which side Timm upheld is not known.[29] Given his overall concern for the welfare of his crew, it certainly seems unlikely that he would have been keen to risk them further, particularly since subsequent action would help no cause but that of the Japanese.

The direction from Wenneker resolved any conflict there may have been, and on the morning of 6 May Timm passed the order to *U 862*'s crew to assemble on board. Just before noon the senior Japanese naval officer in Singapore, Vice Admiral Shigeru Fukudome, and his staff called on Dommes, Timm and Freiwald, and informed them of the imminent internment of all German service personnel.[30] During the afternoon some trucks drew up on the wharf and a fully armed detachment of Japanese soldiers formed up opposite the U-boat. For a brief moment it appeared to the Germans that the Japanese intended to take *U 862* by force. The situation, however, was strictly under control and within a few minutes the *Kriegsmarine* ensign had been lowered, the rising sun hoisted and the U-boat renamed *I-502*. There was no ceremony attached and without a word the German crew disembarked and filed onto other trucks ready to be taken back to their quarters.

It has been said that a submarine does not provide a home for her crew. Unlike almost every other naval vessel, when it is in harbour no one lives on board. Still, it could not have been without some feelings of loss that *U 862*'s men were driven away from the wharf. Their *Überseekühe* may have been a strictly functional weapon of war, but she had also been a piece of their life, and each man knew her ways intimately. She was uncomfortable perhaps, but over two years she had brought them safely more than halfway around the world. Though some may have felt a sense of relief at having the burden of responsibility lifted, others felt regret as they finally lost control of the boat. *Obermaschinenmaat* Rudolf Herrmann, however, expressed the most immediate anxiety, 'Now we are without a boat. When will we see Germany again??'[31]

Though the war was over in Europe, in Asia it might continue for many more months. For the Germans, marooned in a foreign land and with little status in Japanese eyes, the future was uncertain. Doubts over the Japanese attitude had been growing for some time, and Wenneker had already relayed his opinion to Berlin earlier in the year, 'Mistrust of whites is deeply rooted. We Germans are tolerated only as long as we are fighting on the same side and are of material use.'[32]

Despite Wenneker's misgivings, the Japanese made no move to turn on their former partners. The official directive from Tokyo ordered a continuing show of magnanimity to 'German officials, citizens and their interests in East Asia'.[33] The Japanese were cold

I-501 *(ex-*U 181*) and* I-502 *(ex-*U 862*) alongside the damaged IJN cruiser* Myoko *at Singapore in August 1945. In December 1944* Myoko *had her stern blown off after a torpedo hit from the submarine USS* Bergall. *In July 1946 the cruiser was scuttled by the Royal Navy in the Malacca Strait.* (D. Vincent)

but correct; they had their priorities and were content to let the Germans look after themselves. Shelter was still available and even the supply of provisions posed few problems. Fortunately the base staff had amassed considerable credit with the local traders, though it did not prevent one rumour circulating through the German ranks that Dommes had received 1 million yen for *U 862*.[34]

In Europe the *Kriegsmarine* had ceased to exist, and Dommes arranged for certificates of service to be drawn up for all naval personnel to 7 May. Nevertheless, the existing rank and administrative structure provided an essential means of maintaining discipline and remained in force. As senior officer, Freiwald now became the leader and advocate of all German forces in Singapore. Timm briefly became camp commander at Pasir Panjang, and what soon became a familiar pattern of incarceration was established. 'In the Camp we have very little to do. Usually sport in the afternoon. We have received no news from Germany and what we hear is not particularly pleasing. In Shonan we are not permitted to do anything. The only thing here is "jungle". There is now, however, something else that makes us absolutely inconsolable. There is no more to drink!'[35]

On 20 May the Japanese transported all German citizens not needed in Singapore to the Batu Pahat internment camp, 80 miles from the island, on the southwest coast of the Malay peninsula. It eventually held more than 250 Germans. However, 24 of the ex–U-boat crew found themselves ordered to remain in Singapore to instruct the Japanese on *U 181* and *U 862*. The assignment was unpopular, and not only because the men again found themselves in the firing line. The Japanese had allocated 110 crew to each U-boat and the Germans soon found they had little in common. For the U-boat men, 'worlds lay between us and the Japanese. Punishment beating of subordinates by Japanese superiors was the order of the day. Surface exercises were accomplished, aircraft defence rehearsed, firing practice with the anti-aircraft guns and torpedoes.'[36]

The Allies continued to mount air raids on Singapore. Around the end of June a formation of American Lightning aircraft appeared, approaching the wharf where the U-boat lay at an altitude of only 50m. The alarm sounded, and without a second thought the German advisers loaded and manned the U-boat's *Flak* armament. One of the aircraft was successfully engaged and cartwheeled into the water. With all Germans supposed to have laid down their arms, it was no wonder that 'This matter was never spoken about again.'[37] It would be another six weeks and the war in Asia would be over before Rudolf Herrmann, who was assisting with the engineering aspects, could gratefully record, 'Thanks be to God, we are no longer needed on board.'[38]

Guerrilla troops were by now very active on the peninsula, and the Germans often heard fighting in the surrounding jungle. Though the internees at Batu Pahat were usually left in peace, any attempt at travel became hazardous. One day the last members of the German staff were en route there from Penang when the armed train on which they were travelling was ambushed and the Japanese guards killed. Most of the Germans managed to escape and on foot eventually reached a town 40 miles from Batu Pahat. After an extended wait, Freiwald sent a heavily armed expedition under Timm to bring them back. The first attempt failed, but a second soon after returned all the survivors safely to camp.

Elsewhere in Asia the Allies continued their advance. By July the local population were openly discussing with the Germans the speedy arrival of the British. Nevertheless, the general Japanese decision to surrender after the dropping of the atomic bombs in August took everyone by surprise. Local ceremonies soon followed. On 4 September Lieutenant General Itagaki and Vice Admiral Fukudome signed the surrender of all Japanese forces in the Singapore and Johore area on board the cruiser HMS *Sussex*. On 12 September the same two officers surrendered all Japanese forces in Southeast Asia in the presence of the Allied theatre commander, Admiral Lord Mountbatten. The Germans had been moved back to their old camp in Singapore at the end of August and were on hand to witness the British fleet's arrival. Though the sight made the hearts of more than a few of the U-boat men beat faster, it was sobering to see the huge number and range of warships available to the victors.

It took time for the liberating forces to become organised. The exact status of the Germans, whether 'prisoners of war' or 'surrendered enemy personnel', was still to be determined. The British took down personal details and some officers were temporarily imprisoned, but not until mid-October were the Germans allocated a permanent detachment of paratroops as guards. Relations were quite cordial to begin with, and far more spontaneous than they had ever been with the Japanese. Albert Schirrmann fondly recalled a soccer match between the former foes: 'At the victory celebration which followed we were well entertained. After sufficient beer and whisky were provided we sang an English tune. The Tommy's sang their Siegfried Line.'[39]

On 17 October the British relayed to Freiwald their decision that the Germans were to be marched across the island to the infamous Changi Prison. Though offered motor transport, the officers refused and joined with their men the following day on the seven-hour trek in 32° heat. If the German descriptions are accurate, the British intended the march as a suitable demonstration of final defeat. The Germans, however, maintained good order and for 30km kept their spirits up by whistling and singing. The local population turned out in their thousands to watch. Rather than showering the Germans with abuse and rotten fruit as the British expected, they instead cheered and threw flowers.

Reaching Changi, the Germans were also relieved to discover that they were to occupy the barracks used by the former prison guards and not the cells. Even so, there were no fittings, no running water, and the Japanese had left the floors covered in filth. The senior British officer was unsympathetic, but at least arranged for the Germans' camp equipment to be forwarded the next day. A friendly Chinese trader—still kept suitably reimbursed by Freiwald—maintained the supply of provisions and within a few days a workable organisation was in place. The Germans restored the water and electricity supplies, built a kitchen and dining areas, and planted gardens between the rows of barracks. According to Schirrmann, 'The English could not do without our technical personnel. The whole prison was soon under German management. Electricians, kitchen personnel, stock managers, all positions were occupied by Germans and all work was completed by Germans. It was as good as having no guards.'[40]

The British were also soon employing the Germans as work gangs in the naval base and beyond. The Germans relished the relative freedom and were happy to oblige. Terence Long, a Lieutenant RNVR at the time, recalls being given a small landing craft to recover quantities of teak logs that the Japanese had gathered on the upper reaches of the Malayan east coast river systems. For crew he was allocated a senior U-boat officer and four or five German seamen. Whether they came from *U 862*'s complement is uncertain, but the officer certainly regaled Long with exaggerated tales of their exploits in 'Wellington [sic] harbour' on Christmas Day 1944. Long found them 'a very tough tight-knit crew, totally loyal to their commander, a man whose laid-back approach to discipline was interesting to watch'. They showed no sense of German responsibility for the war and had the 'unanimous opinion that the Allies would rue the day they took sides with the Russians'. Long was also 'interested and a little appalled to find them so very racist in their attitude towards the general Asian population', letting it be known that 'the British were far too familiar with non-Aryans!' Strangely, Long found that 'None of the crew were eager to return to Germany and, indeed, wished to migrate to Australia.'[41]

The idea of being repatriated to Australia may have had something to do with *U 862*'s voyage, or possibly the Australian soldiers who had taken over the guard duties at Changi. The Germans had arrived in the bare concrete of their new accommodation exhausted, unfed and without any belongings. The Australians, showing no apparent bitterness, offered them tea and their week's ration of beer. But notwithstanding their desires for a better life, migration anywhere was never a serious option for the Germans. They remained the defeated party, and a few months later the Australians took over the now 'beautiful' German camp, leaving the Germans to move unceremoniously into tents.[42] A further brief interaction with some Australians came about when HMAS *Toowoomba* called in at Singapore in mid-1946. Bill Bulley, a junior sailor who had served previously in *Quickmatch*, later recalled being shown over Changi Prison.

Several of the Germans there could speak English and it turned out they were from the U-boat he had been hunting eighteen months before. According to Bulley, 'There was a great deal of very interesting reminiscing and I told them off for messing up a perfectly good 1944 Christmas.'[43]

With priority naturally going to the repatriation of Allied troops and former prisoners of war, the Germans in the Far East had to wait almost a year before receiving word of plans for their return. In the meantime their captors permitted them to write once a month (25 words only) to relatives through the Red Cross. In some cases letters back from Germany did not appear until June 1946. However, in that month the British advised that a vacant troop transport had arrived in Singapore. On 26 June the Germans were finally ordered to embark on the coincidentally named SS *Empress of Australia*. Allowed to take only one piece of luggage, those Germans 'who had used their coveted Singapore dollars to buy whisky, a good meal and pretty girls, could laugh. The other "Big Spenders", who had purchased souvenirs, silk and memorabilia had to sell their property at give-away prices to the local Chinese.'[44]

On 28 June, *Empress of Australia* sailed from Singapore, reaching Liverpool, England, on 20 July. The U-boat men had been led to expect that they would go straight on to Germany, but it was not to be. On arrival they were told that they had just missed the ship to Bremerhaven. Within a day the men from Singapore were with 3000 other inmates at a prisoner-of-war camp in Sudbury, Derbyshire. Behind barbed wire for the first time, confused and upset, the new arrivals awaited a decision:

> They don't know what to do with us here. We are not counted as prisoners, however we do sit behind barbed wire. The feeling of hunger remains the whole day. At the moment we are not allowed to write home either. They have said, it would be to no purpose since we would soon be leaving again. They can not force us to work and we do nothing voluntarily. We spend the whole day running around in circles and just wait for meals. In the afternoon we sleep until dinner. We are constantly freezing. We are just not used to the temperature in Europe any more. Let us hope that a decision on us will come from London this week.[45]

It came at last on 4 August 1946. The British ordered the separation of the officers and other ranks. Uniforms were put away and a cloth diamond denoting prisoner-of-war status was affixed to the Germans' work jackets. Austrian nationals were on their way home by the end of October, but for the remaining Germans it seemed that their return was becoming ever more distant. Soon they were scattered over England in various small camps and employed by local farmers to work the fields. The work was nothing special, but there was a certain amount of freedom, and the food was better than in the larger camps. Privileges were gradually restored. By November the Germans could move about freely within five miles of camp without guards, but the weeks still dragged by. Hospitalised for two months, Rudolf Herrmann spent Christmas 1946 away even from his comrades. In Europe, but still so far from home, the pangs of longing were deeply felt: 'We sat at the table, drank coffee and ate some pastries, sang two Christmas carols together, then each pursued his own thoughts. For many it is a long time since they celebrated at home with their loved ones. For me the last time was 1939.'[46]

Repatriation for the majority of Germans did not begin until 1947, and it was neither a fast nor, at least to the prisoners, a logical process. For those who, like Herrmann, were held up till the end of the year by the bureaucracy, the wait seemed interminable.[47] For Heinrich Timm it would be even longer. Thought to be unrelenting militarists by the British authorities, many U-boat commanders found themselves among the last prisoners of war to be released.

Not until April 1948, without his command and four long years after he had left, did Timm at last return home to Bremen. The circle of events that had begun in May 1944 was finally complete.

Epilogue

Let me say at the outset, that I hold no animosity or grudge toward you. After all, at the time our countries were at war and our duty and allegiance was to our respective country. In fact, I have always maintained a grateful and appreciative feeling towards your commander for not killing any of the survivors on that fateful night. As I sit here and reminisce, I can still see your submarine as it surfaced so closely to our lifeboat wondering if this would be the last day of my young life.

—Ray Laenen to Albert Schirrmann, 5 August 1995

Despite the restrictions imposed on the British Eastern Fleet and the limited assistance provided to the Japanese, the *Kriegsmarine*'s scheme to deploy U-boats to the Far East was essentially a hollow gesture. The boats achieved some limited sinkings, but they were kept in check and ultimately the theatre was irrelevant to the outcome of the war. Several historians of the German war against merchant shipping have consequently argued that the *Monsun* boats belonged in the Atlantic and fairly summarised U-boat operations in the Indian Ocean as 'misconceived, misdirected and tragically wasteful'.[1]

Yet one should not criticise Dönitz too harshly. Convinced of the righteousness of his cause, and without the benefit of hindsight, he was surely obligated to employ his U-boats in the most cost-effective manner possible. By the end of the first 'happy time' in the summer of 1941, the U-boats had already lost their chance for a knockout blow against Britain. After America's entry to the war in December 1941 and certainly by May 1943, even Dönitz was convinced he had lost the race to sink more shipping tonnage than the Allies could build. Thereafter, diverting Allied efforts away from areas more harmful to German interests was the only way to continue the U-boat campaign that made sense.

During the late-war 'sour pickle times', a U-boat's good fortune in escaping detection counted for much more than the skill of her commander. Thus the availability of another ten to twenty operational U-boats in the Atlantic would still have made no appreciable difference to the end result. Furthermore, if one accepts the essential indivisibility of the oceans, tying forces down in the Indian Ocean was just as relevant as occupying them in the Atlantic. It was certainly far safer, since in European waters the Allies had naval and air forces sufficient not only to protect convoys, but also to operate offensively. Indeed, it often seems forgotten that most of the *Monsun* boats were sunk in the Atlantic before they even reached the Indian Ocean. From this perspective, then, the East Asian deployment was a reasonable alternative for Dönitz, unquestionably worthy of a serious attempt.

U 862 was without doubt one of the most successful of the *Monsun* boats. However, even if it is accepted that her exploits in the Indian Ocean were inconsequential, the same should not be said of Timm's voyage to Australia. Rather than a series of disconnected incidents, the three-month period of *U 862*'s second war cruise was instead one prolonged three-sided battle between the U-boat, the elements, and the Australians and their allies. That Timm found few targets and sank only two ships during this operation is immaterial. The mere threat of his presence had occupied the attentions of more naval and air assets, for a longer period, than probably any single submarine has ever achieved before or since. Notwithstanding his mistakes and the role played by luck, Timm had skilfully led his crew through sickness, boredom, extremes of weather and moments of terror. In the final analysis it was his leadership that kept *U 862*'s crew motivated and brought them back unharmed. Surely Dönitz could have wished for no better. Hence it is unfortunate that *U 862*'s exploits have been too often trivialised in Australia in terms of 'secret landings' or a 'ruined Christmas'. They deserve much greater recognition both for their intrinsic worth and for the lessons they may yet hold.

The protection of sea communications was and remains a key element of the Australian Navy's role, and the threat to commerce posed by enemy submarines has occupied the attention of Australian defence planners since at least 1915. During World War II more than one-third of the RAN's resources in men and tonnage were devoted to escort work. However, Timm ably demonstrated that, even at the end of the war and with the considerable assistance of the RAAF—albeit largely uncoordinated—the RAN was incapable of defending its own waters against an unsupported U-boat operating at the very limits of her capabilities. In fact only one enemy submarine was sunk by local forces in Australian coastal waters between 1939 and 1945.[2] Though success in anti-submarine warfare cannot be measured simply by the sinking of submarines, commentators have often seen this result as disappointing. Nevertheless, in the circumstances it was not unusual and simply serves to illustrate that submarines have always been difficult to track and that localisation remains the key issue for the hunting forces.

Rather than apportioning blame to the participants, equipment and procedures, it is far more valuable to take note of the underlying lessons.[3] But, brought up on the imported analysis of the battle of the Atlantic—a far different scale of conflict—two generations of the Australian Navy and Air Force have ignored or forgotten what should have become a classic example of how a submarine threat forces expenditure far outweighing the danger posed, and in areas far removed from the ostensible 'front line'. Intelligence will always be imperfect, and in a post-Cold War world, where stealthy diesel submarines are proliferating, the lessons of *U 862*'s voyage remains as relevant today as they did in 1945.

Clearly, in the context of the entire U-boat war, with 733 U-boats sunk, 14 557 000 GRT of merchant shipping destroyed and more than 100 000 lives lost on both sides, the voyage of *U 862* is a mere footnote.[4] Yet on a personal level it was of course much more than that. For the individuals involved it was now a matter of rebuilding their interrupted and often shattered lives.

Karl Dönitz's acting German government had been dissolved by the Allied High Command on 23 May 1945 and the *Großadmiral* taken into custody. Charged at the Nuremberg war crimes trials on three separate counts, he was found not guilty of conspiracy to wage aggressive war, but guilty of both actively waging an aggressive war and violating the laws or customs of war. It was on the last count that Dönitz's fate depended, for the prosecution argued that he had ordered his U-boats to deliberately slaughter the survivors of torpedoed ships. Despite the finding, the *Großadmiral* escaped with his life, the Tribunal stating expressly 'that the sentence was *not* assessed on the ground of any breaches of the international law of submarine warfare'.[5] Sentenced to ten years imprisonment—the lightest punishment of all those found guilty—Dönitz was finally released from Spandau prison in 1956. The Third Reich's last head of state died on Christmas Eve 1980, having publicly acknowledged that the '*Führer*-principle' of political leadership was wrong, but unrepentant for his wartime role and still very much revered by the vast majority of his 'old comrades'.[6]

Like the other Germans from Singapore, *Fregattenkapitän* Wilhelm Dommes spent several years as a prisoner of war in England. Despite the enthusiasm he showed to continue the fight in May 1945, the passing years seem to have softened his outlook. *Kapitänleutnant* Fritz Schneewind had been a particularly good friend, and his powerlessness to prevent the deaths of those in *U 183* so close to the end of the war afflicted Dommes deeply. However, he did not blame his ally for the losses, always believing that 'the Japanese did all they could to help us'. Uncommonly among his compatriots, he had formed strong ties with his naval contacts in East Asia. Dommes was to maintain these relationships, 'founded on mutual respect and comradeship', even after he eventually retired to Hanover. Admiral Uozumi was a particular confidant, and they continued to correspond until the Admiral's death in 1963.[7]

One Japanese naval officer with whom Dommes had no opportunity to renew acquaintance was Captain Tatsunosuke Ariizumi. After leaving Penang he became commander of the First Submarine Division, a special-purpose formation of four very large submarines carrying a total of ten float planes.[8] Their first mission was planned to be a bomb and torpedo strike against the Panama Canal's vital Gatún Locks, but by June 1945 the attack was abandoned in favour of a strike against the American task forces assembling at Ulithi Atoll. However, while at sea on 15 August Ariizumi received the Emperor's dramatic radio message ending the war. Unwilling to accept surrender, the recalcitrant captain shot himself as his squadron was being escorted by US naval vessels to Yokosuka, a 'happy event' in the eyes of at least one American submarine admiral.[9]

Unlike the Japanese, German U-boat commanders saw no need to commit suicide to preserve their honour. *Korvettenkapitän* Heinrich Timm was a survivor. He had been in a position of command since the very beginning of the war and had eventually served in all the world's oceans. Even as a dedicated 'disciple of Dönitz', he ultimately seems to have achieved that difficult balance between reasoned responsibility for his command and compulsive loyalty to his nation. Timm's sense of duty remained after the war and, like many surviving *Kriegsmarine* officers, he joined the West German *Bundesmarine* when it formed in 1955. He spent another eleven years in his beloved sea service, in postings that included command of both the gunnery training ship *Scharnhorst* and the naval base at Flensburg. In the late 1950s Timm was at the naval base in Wilhelmshaven, where he met the commander of a nearby NATO air station, later to become Air Marshall Sir Rochford Hughes and one of New Zealand's most honoured servicemen. Timm enlightened the incredulous New Zealander on the details of his 1945 voyage, but also demonstrated his predilection for spinning a *Seemannsgarn* (seaman's yarn), adding that he had sent his crew ashore in Hawke Bay to obtain fresh milk. According to Hughes, '*Kapitän* Timm was the sort of chap I believed implicitly. His knowledge of our coast and admiration for the country was also impressive.'[10] Timm finally retired in 1966 as a *Fregattenkapitän*, and died in Bremen in 1974.[11]

To the end, Timm's men had fought and acted as they had been trained to do and as was expected of them. They had particular reason to be thankful to their *Kommandant*, for unlike so many other commanders, Timm had kept them on the right side of the thin line between life and death. After their release by the British, most of *U 862*'s crew returned to their own home towns, resumed their civilian occupations and usually retired in the same localities. Over the years they have remained a cohesive group, their common bond aptly described by Dönitz himself: 'Every submariner felt himself to be as rich as a king and would trade places with no man.' Unsurprisingly, after more than 50 years the ranks are thinning. Of the 65 who sailed from Kiel in May 1944, more than twenty had passed away at the time of writing, including *Oberleutnant zur See* Karl Steinhauser, *Leutnant (Ing.)* Walter Spindler, *Obermaschinist* Seppel Edelhäuser and *Bootsmaat* Freidrich Peitel. Albert Schirrmann lives in retirement in Bochum and maintains a part-time role as *U 862* 'contact-man'. In 1995, as a result of the research for this book, he was contacted by former cavalry Private Ray Laenen.

After four months recuperation in Western Australia, Laenen and Tom Tschirhart were assigned to the Philippines and spent the remainder of the war in the same office in Manila. They were discharged from the Army a year apart but were reunited back in Detroit. If anything, their friendship grew firmer over the succeeding years. Each acted as best man at the other's wedding, they attended college together, each had five children and later both became salesmen in the automotive industry. They still get together frequently and with several other survivors attend the regular *Peter Silvester* reunions that began in 1979.

Though not a survivor, another worthy comrade who kept in touch was Warrant Officer George Rimes. About a month after the rescue the American authorities in Fremantle held a party for the men of the *Corpus Christi*, any *Peter Silvester* survivors who were well enough to go, and the Australian Liberator crews. It was Rimes' first opportunity to meet some of the men he had helped save, and he was soon the proud possessor of several 'short snorts', signed ten-shilling notes that promised the recipient a free drink next time they met. Rimes eventually became a school principal and, after renewing contact with the Americans in 1972, maintained close ties with the survivors. He exchanged correspondence and the occasional visit in Australia and overseas until his death in Canberra in 1995.

As for *U 862*, she had made her last voyage many years before. The Japanese never used the U-boat operationally, and at the end of the war she was found by the British in Singapore along with her sister *U 181*.[12] The Allies had no need for the vessels, so to fulfil the requirements of the Anglo-American Soviet Agreement on the destruction of U-boats, the few surviving *Monsun* boats were ordered to be scuttled.

On the morning of 14 February 1946 the tugs *Growler* and *Assiduous* took the gutted *U 862* and *U 181* in tow and silently slipped out of Singapore harbour. Some of the U-boats' former crew were working as part of a harbour detail and stopped for a moment to watch the procession depart. In the bright sunlight the boats still gleamed a dull grey, but after months of neglect their casings were streaked with rust and their air of menace was long gone. Now they were in the company of the frigates HM Ships *Loch Lomond* and *Loch Glendhu*, new anti-submarine vessels described as 'the ultimate in Admiralty design and North Atlantic war experience'.[13]

The U-boats were taken to a position in the middle of the Strait of Malacca. *U 862* was the first to be disposed of, sunk at 1930 on 15 February in 52 fathoms of water.[14] *Loch Lomond* took the opportunity to test her anti-submarine weaponry and followed the descent of the U-boat's hulk with a single pattern from her Squid mortar. No longer reliant on an operator's fallibility, the targeting data was passed directly from the Asdic to the bombs and the firing sequence fully automated. Only three projectiles in triangular pattern were needed to finally crush the U-boat's hull. The frigate's captain later signalled that much wreckage was seen.

U 181 followed *U 862* unceremoniously to the bottom at 0545 the next morning. With their unmourned passing, the last vestiges of the *Kriegsmarine*'s operational presence in East Asia had gone.

Appendix 1: U 862

Work-up

(From *Kriegstagebuch U 862*, 7 October 1943 to 11 May 1944, captured Admiralty document PG/30768/1, NHS.)

7.10.43	Commissioning of boat in Deschimag dockyard in Bremen.
9.10	Passage to Hamburg for *FuMG* adjustment.
12.10	Sail to Kiel for ship and machinery trials.
15.10	Preliminary trim and compensation trials in Kiel Harbour.
18.10	Torpedo shots.
20.10	Trimming trials.
21.10	Radio tests in Kiel Förde.
23.10	Machinery trials in Kiel Bay.
26.10	Passage to Sonderburg.
27.10	Listening trials. Return passage to Kiel.
29.10	Sail to Swinemünde (full power). Secured Eichstaden. *Flak* training.
2.11	Target shooting. Subsequently sail to Stettin and secured U-boat base.
3.11	Sail to Danzig, and secured U-boat base. Tests with U-Boat Acceptance Group, Danzig.
5.11	Shallow dives.
6.11	Sail measured mile, on surface and dived, combined with crash-dives.
7.11	Sail to Pillau, secured second harbour basin. Dry runs for pre-tactical exercise for the first-time crew members.
8.11	Passage to Gotenhafen. Torpedo testing command tests.
9.11	TEK (Torpedo testing command) tests. Secured in Hela.
10.11	Begin training with the *Agru-Front*.
5.12	Complete training with the *Agru-Front*.

7.12	Passage to Pillau.
8.12	Begin pre-tactical exercise.
17.12	End of pre-tactical exercise.
26.12	Begin torpedo firings in Pillau.
9.1.44	End torpedo firings.
12.1	Begin tactical exercise.
18.1	End tactical exercise. Secured in Gotenhafen.
20.1	Passage to Bremen.
23.1	Secured in Deschimag dockyard in Bremen. Begin maintenance period.
6.4	Complete maintenance period, passage to Kiel.
8.4	*Schnorchel* tests.
15.4	Sail to Swinemünde.
16.4–22.4	*Flak* training.
23.4	Sail to Hela
24.4–26.4	Training with the *Agru-Front*
26.4	Sail to Kiel
29.4	*FuMO* trials. Subsequently secure in Howald dockyard.
9.5	*FuMO* trials.
10.5	*FuMO* trials.
11.5	Begin storing for the front.

First war patrol

(*U 862*'s short report sent after arrival in Penang and recorded in *Kriegstagebuch BdU* 14 September 1944, ANL and DEFE 3/743 pp. 87–92, PRO.)

1 Situation report:
Heavy single ship traffic in Mozambique Straits via KQ 2158, focal point KE 2946 then in direction of Comoro Islands. Slight day, no night air patrol. Air bases according to pilots captured log: Diego Suarez, Seychelles, Pamanzi (Comoro Islands), Tulear (Madagascar), Tombeau Bay (Mauritius), Durban, St Lucia (see para. 3).

2 Aircraft locations:
'Wanze': 20/8 LT 5933, LT 5666. On 21/8 in LT 5632, all 146 cm, 'Wanze' locations visible and audible.

3 Aircraft shot down:
On 20/8 in evening twilight [sic] Catalina shot down in LT 5969. Otherwise no sightings.

4 Sinkings:
At 0212/25/7 in FT 8461 Freighter Mexican?, Fully loaded with vegetable (oil), 7000 GRT, course 290 degrees, 11 knots. At 2103/13/8 in KQ 2158 collier of 5500 GRT, course 010 degrees, 9 knots. At 2103/16/8 in KE 3277 'Empire' freighter, mixed cargo, 8000 GRT, course 050 degrees, 12 knots. At 1937/18/8 in KE 2342 ammunition

ship of 5500 GRT, course 030 degrees, 11 knots. At 2036/19/8 in LT8946 'Bernat' type freighter, 5900 GRT, course 030 degrees, 11 knots.

5 Ship sightings:
At 0916/12/7 in ER 9998 tanker in ballast, course 280 degrees, over 16 knots.

6 Torpedo experience:
23 'eels' of which 3 'T-5', one circle runner, one hit, one miss, 11 electric torpedoes, 4 fans of which 2 misses, 1 failure. 9 air-driven torpedoes, 4 fans, of which 1 miss, 2 failures.

7 Flak guns:
3.7cm serviceable fully automatic for 5 weeks (corrupt group) only serviceable for single shots. Entirely unserviceable towards the end of the patrol. Defects could not be rectified with own resources. 2cm good. One guide ring ('Steuerring') broken, no spare on board.

8 Own damage:
Through impact of aircraft and simultaneous bomb explosion bow cap of tube 1 stiff, tube 2 stiff and leaky. Further damage not yet discovered.

9 W/T:
Everywhere good receiving conditions. From LT and LU tried in vain 3 times to transmit W/T message (Africa 2, 3, with high aerial and jumping wires). From Chagos onwards transmission of W/T messages possible on 'Taifun'. Observed no reaction on the part of the enemy after transmitting. 'Wanze' very liable to go wrong. One 'Wanze' broke down completely as a result of unserviceability of main transformer after burning out several times. Except for transformer there were enough spares on board. 'Tunis': bracket on D/F loop too weak. Cellon screen leaking. Bound with rubber. Set was used a great deal and proved its worth. Hohentwiel: no lasting influence through tropical climate. Set serviceable to the end. Maximum range against loaded freighter 72 hectometres.

10 Weather conditions:
Favourable in the operational area.

11 Boat's crew acquitted itself well. State of health good. Have begun return passage with one 'T-5' and two air-driven torpedoes.

Second war patrol

(*U 862*'s short report dated 27 February 1945 as intercepted by FRUMEL and recorded in B5553/1, AA and RG 457 Entry 9017, NA.)

2nd Operation

1 Left Jakarta on 18th November, course south. Then as far as Adelaide, continuing south of Tasmania and proceeding northwards.

From the latitude of Sydney east along route towards Auckland (New Zealand). East coast of New Zealand to southward. Operation was broken off in accordance with orders and return passage hauling off to southward. Steered for Sunda Strait from the south. Arrived Jakarta on 15th February.

2 Situation:
From the southwestern corner of Australia to Adelaide, off Adelaide and as far as the southern tip of Tasmania no traffic except for the first sighting (see under para 6), main traffic apparently keeping off far to the southward. Between eastern entrance to Bass Strait and Sydney heavy single-ship traffic at approximately 30 miles distance from coast. Counter measures on being observed.

Round New Zealand only small coastal freighters. Large traffic expected off Auckland and on approach routes not discovered despite long stay. All roadsteads of small towns of east coast empty, but towns brightly lighted. Course of steamship sunk on return passage confirms conjecture regarding passage south of Australia.

Mistake in planning operation was that sea area was too large. Better chances are to be expected by concentrating on traffic north and south of Sydney. Another visit to this area fell through on account of recall. The sea area would repay a generously planned operation with several boats.

Request remaining 'eels' available this area for operation on east coast of Africa during return passage.

Request 11 Iron Crosses class 2, and 11 Iron Crosses class 1.

3 Aircraft locations (Ortungen):
Tunis; on 25th November in JH4179 (34.33S 113.20E). On 25th December in VD8445 (34.45S 149.12E), VD8486 (35.03S 149.44E). All 9 to 12cm. On 13th February in KB1913 (08.33S 104.15E) (Tunis).

4 Aircraft sightings.
At 1425/22 in VR5921 (43.39S 148.05E), made flashing signals to boat, R/S5 white 3 red. At 2000/24/12 in VD8222 (36.27S 150.48E), aircraft making smoke screen around steamship which had been hit.

5 Sinkings:
At 2033/24/12 in VD8222 Liberty freighter, 7000 GRT, course 015, 12 knots.

At 1725/6/2 in JF6245 Liberty freighter, 7000 GRT, course 330, 12 knots.

6 Sightings:
At 0120/9/12 in VC8465 (37.45S 139.12E) coast freighter, 135 degrees, 10 knots. Gun attack was beaten off.

At 0800/15/12 in VR5921 (43.39S 148.05E), tanker, 065 degrees, 12 knots, attack hindered by aircraft.

At 2150/19/12 in VD9775 (38.57S 152.48E), freighter, 300 degrees, over 16 knots.

At 1215/27/12 in VD6814 (35.45S 153.52E), freighter, 6000 GRT, 240 degrees, 12 knots, premature.

At 2314/9/1 in VG5459 (35.09S 176.08E) off Auckland coast freighter inward-bound.

At 1610/13/1 in VG9423 (37.21S 178.32E), coastal freighter close under the coast, no chance to attack.

At 0020/15/1 in VG9753 (38.33S 178.32E), coastal freighter close under the coast, no chance to attack.

At 1840/16/1 off Napier, coastal freighter, close under the coast missed.

7 Torpedoes expended:
13 in all, of which one T-5 detonated after 3 min 4 sec without hitting target; 6 ATOS (air-driven torpedoes)—4 hits, 1 miss, 1 gyro failure; 6 ETOS (electric torpedoes)—4 hits, 1 miss, 1 premature detonator.

8 Flak small arms:
At the outset 3.7 was in order for single-shot firing, then out of order, as cartridges constantly jammed in barrel.
2 cm. (Strong indications good).

9 Battery capacity:
66 per cent

10 W/T:
East coast of Tasmania reception only at night, east of New Zealand even this was limited.

Shaft of Hohentwiel bent when crash-diving for aircraft.

11 Weather conditions:
South of Australia variable west wind drift weather, to eastward wetter. New Zealand good. Return passage, westerly gales.

12 Crew proved very satisfactory. State of health partly influenced by period in tropics.

Appendix 2: German U-boats allocated to the Far East

U-boat[a] *Type*	*Commander*	*Sailed*[b]	*Arrived*	*Sinkings*[c] *(gross tonnage)*	*Fate*	*Remarks*
U 178 IXD2	*KK* W. Dommes *KL* W. Spahr	Bordeaux 28.3.43 Penang 27.11.43	Penang 29.8.43 Bordeaux 24.5.44	1.6.43 *Salabangka* (6586) 4.7.43 *Breiviken* (2669) 4.7.43 *Michael Livanos* (4774) 11.7.43 *Mary Livanos* (4771) 14.7.43 *Robert Bacon* (7191) 16.7.43 *City of Canton* (6692) 27.12.43 *José Navarro* (7244)	Scuttled 25.8.44 in Bordeaux to prevent capture.	Detached from U-boats operating around Cape. Dommes relinquished command of *U 178* and subsequently became commander of the Penang base and later German Navy Commander in Southern Area. Spahr had been IWO of *U 178*.
U 511 IXC	*KL* F. Schneewind	Lorient 10.5.43	Penang 21.7.43 Kure 7.8.43	27.6.43 *Sebastiano Cermeno* (7194) *9.7.43 Samuel Heintzelman* (7176)	Surrendered 8.45 at Maizuru and sunk by USN in Maizuru Gulf 30.4.46.	'Marco Polo'. Transferred to Japanese Navy 16.9.43 and renamed *RO-500*.
U 200 IXD2	*KK* Schonder	Kiel 12.6.43			Sunk 24.6.43 southwest of Iceland by Liberator of 120 Sqn RAF.	1st *Monsun Group*. No survivors.
U 188 IXC/40	*KL* S. Lüdden	Lorient 30.6.43 Penang 9.1.44	Penang 31.10.43 Lorient 19.6.44	21.9.43 *Cornelia P Spencer* (7176) 20.1.44 *Fort Buckingham* (7122) 25.1.44 *Fort la Maune* (7130) 26.1.44 *Samouri* (7219) 26.1.44 *Surada* (5427) 29.1.44 *Olga E. Embiricos* (4677) 3.2.44 *Chung Cheng* (7176) 7–12.2.44 seven sailing vessels 9.2.44 *Viva* (3798)	Scuttled 25.8.44 in Bordeaux to prevent capture.	1st *Monsun Group*.

U-boat[a] Type	Commander	Sailed[b]	Arrived	Sinkings[c] (gross tonnage)	Fate	Remarks
U 168 IXC/40	*KL* H. Pich	Lorient 3.7.43 Penang 7.2.44 Jakarta 3.10.44	Penang 11.11.43 Jakarta 24.3.44	1–2.10.43 six sailing vessels 2.10.43 *Haiching* (2183) 14.2.44 *Salviking* (1440) 15.2.44 *Epaminondas C. Embiricos* (4385)	Sunk 6.10.44 north of Java by Dutch submarine *Zwaardvisch*.	1st *Monsun Group*. 27 survivors.
U 183 IXC/40	*KK* H. Schäfer *KL* F. Schneewind	Lorient 3.7.43 Penang 10.2.44 Penang 3.5.44 Jakarta 21.4.45	Penang 2.11.43 Penang 21.3.44 Penang 7.7.44	29.2.44 *Palma* (5419) 9.3.44 *British Loyalty* (6993) 5.6.44 *Helen Moller* (5259)	Sunk 23.4.45 in the Java Sea by USS *Besugo*.	1st *Monsun Group*. Schäfer died in Penang. Schneewind had been commander of *U 511*. One survivor.
U 509 IXC	*KL* W. Witte	Lorient 3.7.43			Sunk 15.7.43 northwest of Madeira by Avengers of VC-29 USS *Santee*.	1st *Monsun Group*. No survivors.
U 514 IXC	*KL* H. Auffermann	Lorient 3.7.43			Sunk 8.7.43 northeast of Cape Finisterre by Liberator of 224 Sqn RAF.	1st *Monsun Group*. No survivors.
U 532 IXC/40	*FK* O. Junker	Lorient 3.7.43 Penang 4.1.44 Jakarta 13.1.45	Penang 2.11.43 Penang 19.4.44	19.9.43 *Fort Longueuil* (7128) 29.9.43 *Banffshire* (6479) 1.10.43 *Tahsinia* (7267) 11.10.43 *Jalabala* (3610) 26.1.44 *Walter Camp* (7130) 27.3.44 *Tulagi* (2281) 10.3.45 *Baron Jedburgh* (3656)* 28.3.45 *Oklahoma* (9298)*	Surrendered 13.5.45 at Loch Eriboll and scuttled in North Atlantic 1946.	1st *Monsun Group*.

U-boat[a] *Type*	*Commander*	*Sailed*[b]	*Arrived*	*Sinkings*[c] *(gross tonnage)*	*Fate*	*Remarks*
U 506 IXC	*KL* E. Würdemann	Lorient 6.7 43			Sunk 12.7.43 west of Vigo by Liberator of 1st A/S Sqn USAAF.	1st *Monsun Group* Six survivors
U 533 IXC/40	*KL* H. Hennig	Lorient 6.7.43			Sunk 16.10.43 in Gulf of Oman by two Bisley aircraft of 244 Sqn RAF.	1st *Monsun Group*. One survivor.
U 516 IXC	*KL* H Tillessen	Lorient 8.7.43	Lorient 23 8 43		Surrendered 14 5.45 in Lough Foyle and scuttled in North Atlantic 1946.	1st *Monsun Group*. Withdrawn from operation after refuelling *U 532* and *U 533*.
U 847 IXD2	*KL* H. Kuppisch	Bergen 29.7.43			Sunk 27.8.43 in Saragossa Sea by aircraft of VC-1 USS *Card*.	1st *Monsun Group*. Diverted for emergency refuelling duties. Kuppisch was to have been commander of the Penang Base No survivors.
UIT 23	*OL* Striegler	Bordeaux 5.43 Singapore 13.2.44	Sebang 7.43		Sunk 14.2.44 in Malacca Strait by HMS *Tally Ho*.	*Merkator* boat. Ex-*Reginaldo Giuliani*, taken over by Germany after Italian surrender and used for transport. 14 survivors.

U-boat[a] *Type*	*Commander*	*Sailed*[b]	*Arrived*	*Sinkings*[c] *(gross tonnage)*	*Fate*	*Remarks*
UIT 24	*KL* Pahls *OL* W. Striegler	Bordeaux 5.43 Penang 8 2 44	Sebang 11.7.43 Penang 5 4.44		Surrendered 8.45 at Kobe. Scuttled at Kii Suido 16.4.46	*Merkator* boat. Ex-*Commandante Alfredo Cappellini.* Seized by Japanese 7.5.45 and renamed *I-503.*
UIT 25	*OL* D Spliedt *OL* Meier	Bordeaux 6.43	Singapore 30.8.43		Surrendered 8.45 at Kobe. Scuttled at Kii Suido 15.4.46.	*Merkator* boat. Ex-*Luigi Torelli.* Seized by Japanese 7.5.45 and renamed *I-504.* In November 1944 Spliedt, was replaced after 'fisticuffs' with a German vice-consul in a bar in Kobe. Meier had been IWO of *U 183.*
U 848 IXD2	*KK* W Rollmann	Kiel 18 9.43		2.11.43 *Baron Semple* (4573)*	Sunk 5.11.43 southwest of Ascension Island by USN Liberators and USAAF Mitchells of VB-107 and Compron 1.	One survivor was picked up by USS *Marblehead* 3.12.43, but died three days later.
U 849 IXD2	*KL* H. Schultze	Kiel 2.10.43			Sunk 25 11.43 west of Congo estuary by USN Liberator of VB-107.	No survivors.

U-boat[a] *Type*	*Commander*	*Sailed*[b]	*Arrived*	*Sinkings*[c] *(gross tonnage)*	*Fate*	*Remarks*
U 510 IXC	*KL* A. Eick	Lorient 3.11.43 Jakarta 26.11.44 Jakarta 11.1.45	Penang 5.4.44 Jakarta 3.12.44 St Nazaire 25.4.45	22.2.44 *San Alvaro* (7385) 22.2.44 *E. G. Seubert* (9181) 7.3.44 *Tarifa* (7229) 19.3.44 *John A. Poor* (7176) 24.3.44 sailing vessel 27.3.44 HMT *Maaloy* (249) 23.2.45 *Point Pleasant Park* (7136)*	Surrendered 10.5.45 at St Nazaire. Renamed *Bouan* by French. Stricken in 1959 and broken up 1960.	
U 850 IXD2	*KL* K. Ewerth	Kiel 18.11.43			Sunk 20.12.43 west of Madeira by aircraft of VC-19 USS *Bogue*.	No survivors.
U 172 IXC	*KL* E. Hoffmann	St Nazaire 22.11.43			Sunk 12.12.43 northwest of Cape Verde by aircraft of VC-19 USS *Bogue* and USS *George E. Badger*, *George W. Ingram*, *Clemson* and *Dupont*.	46 survivors.
UIT 22	*KL* Wunderlich	Bordeaux 24.1.44			Sunk 11.3.44 off Cape of Good Hope by Catalinas of 279 and 262 Sqns SAAF.	*Merkator* boat. Ex-*Alpino Attilio Bagnolini* taken over by Germany 9.43. No survivors.
U 177 IXD2	*KK* H. Buchholz	Pallice 2.1.44			Sunk 6.2.44 southwest of Ascension Island by USN Liberator of VB-107.	14 survivors.

U-boat[a] *Type*	*Commander*	*Sailed*[b]	*Arrived*	*Sinkings*[c] *(gross tonnage)*	*Fate*	*Remarks*
U 1062 VIIF	*OL* F. Albrecht	Bergen 3.1.44 Penang 19.6.44 Penang 15.7.44	Penang 19.4.44 Penang 2.7.44		Sunk 30.9.44 southwest of Cape Verde Islands by USS *Fessenden* and *Mission Bay.*	Transport U-boat. 22 torpedoes for Penang.
U 852 IXD2	*KL* H. Eck	Kiel 18.1.44		13.3.44 *Peleus* (4695)* 1.4.44 *Dahomian* (5277)	Forced aground 2.5.44 off Somaliland after attacks by Wellingtons of 8 and 621 Sqns RAF.	59 survivors. After the war Eck and two others were executed for ordering lifeboats from *Peleus* to be fired upon.
U 1059 VIIF	*OL* G. Leupold	Kiel 4.2.44			Sunk 19.3.44 southwest of Cape Verde Islands by two Avenger aircraft of VC-6 USS *Block Island.*	Transport U-boat. 25 torpedoes for Penang. Boat was surprised while crew taking a morning swim. Eight survivors, but one died a short time after recovery.
U 843 IXC/40	*KL* O. Herwartz	Lorient 19.2.44 Jakarta 10.12.44	Jakarta 13.6.44 Bergen 3.4.45	8.4.44 *Nebraska* (8261)	Sunk 9.4.45 in the Kattegat by Mosquitoes of 143, 235 and 248 Sqns RAF.	13 survivors.
U 851 IXD2	*KL* H. Weingärtner	Kiel 26.2.44			Lost after 27.3.44 in central Atlantic to unknown causes.	No survivors.

U-boat[a] *Type*	*Commander*	*Sailed*[b]	*Arrived*	*Sinkings*[c] *(gross tonnage)*	*Fate*	*Remarks*
U 181 IXD2	*KzS* K. Freiwald	Bordeaux 16.3.44 Jakarta 19.10.44	Penang 8.8.44 Jakarta 6.1.45	1.5.44 *Janeta* (5312)* 19.6.44 *Garoet* (7118) 15.7.44 *Tanda* (7174) 19.7.44 *King Frederick* (5265) 1.11.44 *Fort Lee* (10198)	Surrendered 16.8.45 at Singapore. Scuttled in Malacca Strait 16.2.46.	Seized by Japan 7.5.45 and renamed *I-501*.
U 196 IXD2	*KK* F. Kentrat *OL* W Striegler	Bordeaux 16.3.44 Jakarta 30.11.44	Penang 10.8.44	9.7.44 *Shahzada* (5454)	Lost after 30.11.44 in vicinity Sunda Strait. Cause unknown.	Carried 14 torpedoes for Penang. After a long illness Kentrat was posted to Japan as commander of a battery renewal facility in Kobe and assistant to the Naval Attaché in Tokyo. Striegler had survived sinking of *UIT 23* and after time in *UIT 25* assumed command of *U 196* in September 1944. No survivors.
U 537 IXC/40	*KL* P. Schrewe	Lorient 25.3.44 Surabaya 9.11.44	Jakarta 2.8.44		Sunk 9.11.44 north of Lombok Strait by USS *Flounder*.	No survivors.
U 1224 IXC/40	Norita	Kiel 30.3.44			Sunk 13.5.44 northwest of Cape Verde Islands by USS *Francis M. Robinson*.	'Marco Polo 2'. Transferred to the Japanese Navy 28.2 44 in Europe and renamed *RO-501*. No survivors.

U-boat[a] Type	Commander	Sailed[b]	Arrived	Sinkings[c] (gross tonnage)	Fate	Remarks
U 859 IXD2	*KK* J. Jebsen	Kiel 4.4.44		26.4.44 *Colin* (6255)* 28.8.44 *John Barry* (7176) 1.9.44 *Troilus* (7422)	Sunk 23.9.44 approaching Penang by HMS *Trenchant*.	11 survivors picked up by *Trenchant* and eight by Japanese.
U 860 IXD2	*KL* P. Büchel	Kiel 11.4.44			Sunk 15.6.44 south of St Helena by seven Avengers of VC-9 USS *Solomons*.	20 survivors.
U 198 IXD2	*OL* B. Heusinger von Waldegg	Pallice 20.4.44		16.6.44 *Columbine* (3268) 15.7.44 *Director* (5107) 5 or 6.8.44 *Empire City* (7295) 7.8.44 *Empire Day* (7242)	Sunk12.8.44 northwest of Seychelles by HMIS *Godavari*, HMS *Findhorn* and *Parret*.	No survivors.
U 861 IXD2	*KK* J. Oesten	Kiel 20.4.44 Jakarta 14.1.45	Penang 22.9.44 Trondheim 18.4.45	20.7.44 *Vital de Oliveira* (1737)* 24.7.44 *William Gaston* (7177)* 20.8.44 *Berwickshire* (7464) 5.9.44 *Ioannis Fafalios* (5670)	Surrendered 6.5.45 at Trondheim. Scuttled North Atlantic 1946.	
U 490 XIV	*OL* W. Gerlach	Kiel 4.5.44			Sunk 11.6.44 northwest of the Azores by aircraft of VC-95 USS *Croatan*, USS *Frost*, *Inch* and *Huse*.	Transport U-boat. Carried fuel and lubricating oil to refuel other U-boats enroute. 60 survivors.
U 862 IXD2	*KK* H. Timm	Kiel 21.5.44 Jakarta 18.11.44	Penang 9.9.44 Jakarta 15.2.45	25.7.44 *Robin Goodfellow** (6885) 13.8.44 *Radbury* (3614) 16.8.44 *Empire Lancer* (7037) 18.8.44 *Nairung* (5414) 19.8.44 *Wayfarer* (5068) 24.12.44 *Robert J. Walker* (7180) 6.2.45 *Peter Silvester* (7176)	Surrendered 8.45 at Singapore. Scuttled in Malacca Strait 15.2.46.	Seized by Japan 7.5.45 and renamed *I-502*.

U-boat[a] Type	Commander	Sailed[b]	Arrived	Sinkings[c] (gross tonnage)	Fate	Remarks
U 863 IXD2	*KL* D. von der Esch	Kiel 3.7.44			Sunk 29.9.44 southeast of Ascension by two USN Liberators of VB-107.	No survivors.
U 180 IXD1	*OL* R. Riesen	Bordeaux 21.8.44			Sunk 22.8.44 west of Bordeaux after striking a mine.	Transport U-boat. No survivors.
U 195 IXD1	*OL* Steinfeld	Bordeaux 21.8.44 Jakarta 26.1.45	Jakarta 28.12.44 Jakarta 4.3.45		Surrendered 8.45 at Surabaya. Broken up 1947.	Transport U-boat. Seized by Japan 7.5.45 and renamed *I-506*.
U 219 XB	*KK* W. Burghagen	Bordeaux 23.8.44	Jakarta 11.12.44		Surrendered 8.45 at Surabaya. Broken up 1948.	Minelaying U-boat converted to cargo carrier. Seized by Japan 8.5.45 and renamed *I-505*. Burghagen at 54 was the oldest U-boat commander to serve during the war.
U 871 IXD2	*KL* E. Ganzer	Trondheim 31.8.44			Sunk 26.9.44 northwest of the Azores by Fortress of 220 Sqn RAF.	No survivors.

U-boat[a] Type	Commander	Sailed[b]	Arrived	Sinkings[c] (gross tonnage)	Fate	Remarks
U 864 IXD2	*KK* R. Wolfram	Kiel 5.12.44 Bergen 5.2.45			Sunk 9.2.45 west of Bergen by HMS *Venturer*.	Transport U-boat. Departure delayed two months because of *Schnorchel* trouble and after running aground. No survivors.
U 234 XB	*KL* J. Fehler	Christiansand 16.4.45			Surrendered 14.5.45 in mid-Atlantic to USS *Sutton*. Used by USN as experimental vessel and expended as target 11.46.	Transport U-boat. Fifteen Japanese and German passengers on board.
U 873 IXD2	*KL* F. Steinhoff				Surrendered 11.5.45 in mid-Atlantic to USS *Vance*. Broken up 1948.	Transport U-boat. Cargo for Japan loaded but voyage cancelled prior to sailing.
U 876 IXD2	*KL* R. Bahn				Scuttled 3.5.45 in Eckernförde.	Damaged by aircraft 9.4.45 in Kiel. Voyage cancelled. Only eight torpedoes carried in favour of cargo.

a U-boats are listed in order of departure from Europe.
b Dates refer to patrols and do not include all movements between ports.
c '*' denotes sinking in the Atlantic Ocean.

Notes

Preface

1 See L. Lind, *Toku Tai*, Kangaroo Press, Maryborough, 1992, pp. 111–118 and 'Nazis popped in for NZ milkshake', *Sydney Morning Herald*, 17 January 1994, p. 1.
2 According to British Prime Minister Winston Churchill, 'U-boats are those dastardly villains who sink our ships, while submarines are those gallant and noble craft which sink theirs.'
3 P. Padfield, *Dönitz The Last Führer*, Victor Gollancz, London, 1993, pp. 464–465.
4 N. Monsarrat, foreword to H. Schaeffer, *U 977*, William Kimber, London, 1952, p. 8.
5 Letter, W. Hirschmann to author, 4 December 1995.
6 J. Mallmann Showell, *U-boats Under the Swastika*, Ian Allan, London, 1973. p. 25.
7 P. Padfield, 'Grand Admiral Karl Dönitz German Navy' in *Men of War*, S. Howarth ed., Weidenfeld & Nicolson, London, 1992, p. 186.
8 In contrast, British merchant ships lost almost 23 000 men in U-boat attacks.

Chapter 1 *Unterseeboot 862*

1 K. Dönitz, *Memoirs: Ten Years and Twenty Days*, Weidenfeld & Nicolson, London, 1959, p. 4.
2 ibid. p. 7.
3 Record of conversation, Raeder with the *Führer*, June 1934, MP1587/1 168F, Australian Archives (AA).
4 The treaty allowed the Germans to build a submarine service up to 45 per cent as large as the Royal Navy's and up to parity should it be deemed desirable by the Germans and the British agreed.

5 Dönitz, p. 4.
6 E. Rössler, *The U-boat*, Arms and Armour Press, London, 1989, p. 103.
7 Letter, Dönitz to Supreme Naval Command, 8 September 1939, ibid. p. 146.
8 The first frontline patrols of the Type IXD1 boats demonstrated the disadvantages of the experimental propulsion system. It was subsequently removed and the boats converted to transport U-boats.
9 This range was based on a continuous economic speed of about 8kts. Under operational conditions the range was much less.
10 Twenty-eight variant D2 and one of the very similar D42.
11 *WAnz* G2 (*WellenAnzeiger* or spectrum display unit), also known as *FuMB 9 'Cypern II'*. Another aerial was mounted on top of the *Schnorchel*.
12 'Tunis' combined the dipole aerial *'Fliege'* for the 9cm wavelength and the horn radiator *'Mücke'* for 3cm radar.
13 '. . . a somewhat vulgar term for nose' (G. Hessler, *The U-Boat War in the Atlantic 1939–1945*, vol. III, HMSO, London, 1989, p. 58).
14 'Tube 7' was also used to refer to the tube used to eject the submarine bubble target, a chemical device designed to create a false Asdic echo. The tube was fitted in the after heads.
15 Though possibly apocryphal Mallmann Showell reports the case of *U 1206* (Commander Schlitt), sunk as a direct result of mishandling the toilet (*U-boats Under the Swastika*, p. 120).
16 The longest patrol ever carried out by a Type IXD2 was 225 days (*U 196*).

Chapter 2 *Kapitänleutnant* Heinrich Timm

1 Letter, A. Schirrmann to author, 15 December 1993.
2 Letter, O. Giese to author, 20 October 1995.
3 Heinrich Timm's biographical details are based on information provided by Frau Timm, the U-Boat Archive, Cuxhaven and the Royal Navy Historical Branch (NHB), London.
4 Though German naval records refer to Timm sailing the Australian route as a merchant navy officer, Timm's wife has written that he did not visit Australia in the pre-war period. See *Kriegstagebuch (KTB) BdU*, 14 September 1944 and letter, Frau Marga Timm to author, 27 December 1993. Frau Timm was unfortunately forced to rely on memory, since her home was bombed twice during the war and most of her husband's papers were destroyed.
5 E. Topp, *The Odyssey of a U-boat Commander*, Praeger, Westport, 1992, p. 95.
6 The account of this action is derived from BR 1736 (52) *Submarines* vol. 1, Naval Staff History, Historical Section Admiralty, 1953, p. 21, and *M 7*'s post-action report, 12 January 1940, held by NHB.

7 *KTB Skl*, 9 January 1940.
8 *M 7* survived the war and was taken by the USSR as a prize. She later served in the Black Sea Fleet but her final fate is unknown.
9 Padfield, 'Grand Admiral Karl Dönitz German Navy', p. 189.
10 Between August 1941 and May 1945, 87 Allied merchant ships and 19 warships were sunk in Arctic convoys, with the loss of 2644 lives.
11 *U 88, U 405, U 436, U 456, U 589* and *U 703*.
12 *KTB U 251*, 2 May 1942, PG/30 227/3, NHB.
13 *Jutland* had already been damaged by torpedo aircraft from I/KG 26 and some accounts portray her as a derelict at the time of Timm's attack.
14 *KTB U 251*, 3 May 1942.
15 *U 88, U 355, U 376, U 457* and *U 657*.
16 *KTB U 251*, 10 July 1942, PG/30 227/7, NHB.
17 *U 255, U 403, U 408, U 435, U 592* and *U 703*.
18 *U 251* was sunk on 19 April 1945 in the Kattegat by British and Norwegian aircraft. Thirty-nine of her crew, including her commander, were killed.

Chapter 3 *Die U-Boot-Fahrer*

1 Owing to the unfavourable weather conditions and stiff opposition, Dönitz did not feel that the deployment of U-boats to northern waters was worthwhile. He consistently pressed the Naval Staff to transfer the majority of boats to the Atlantic battle, (Hessler, vol. I, p. 73 and vol. II, p. 16).
2 Dönitz, p. 228.
3 Higher monthly peaks had been reached five times during 1942, (Hessler, vol. II, plan 60).
4 Raeder had resigned rather than implement Hitler's directive to scrap all German capital ships. Dönitz remained *BdU* but much of the day-to-day conduct of the U-boat war was directed by the *Chef der Operationsabteilung* (*BdU op*), *Konteradmiral* Godt.
5 A peak of 920 GRT had actually been reached in October 1940.
6 These biographical details are based on *curricula vitae* provided to the British authorities in Singapore in December 1945 and held by NHB.
7 In 1944 the average age of a U-boat commander was 26.8. There were fourteen U-boat commanders aged between 20 and 21, up from nine in 1943 and nil in previous years, (letter, W. Hirschmann to author, 13 December 1995).
8 As a member of the armed forces one could not be a party member, and Steinhauser had probably joined in civilian life, (letter, W. Hirschmann to author, 4 December 1995).

9 Message requesting German Cross in Gold, Tokyo to Berlin, 28 October 1944, RG 457, Entry 9017, National Archives (NA).

10 Sometime during this period Schäfer managed to complete his PhD on 'The nutrition of U-Boat men in war'.

11 Letter, Hirschmann to author, 4 December 1995.

12 Letter, Schirrmann to author, 4 April 1994.

13 A British study of January 1944 noted that roughly half of U-boat prisoners of war were aged 21 or younger, up from less than 7 per cent aged 20 or younger in December 1939 (T. Mulligan, 'German U-boat crews in World War II: Sociology of an elite', in *The Journal of Military History*, vol. 56, no. 2, April 1992, p. 266).

14 E. Topp, 'Manning and training the U-boat fleet' in *The Battle of the Atlantic 1939–1945*, S. Howarth and D. Law eds, Naval Institute Press, Annapolis, 1994, p. 216. A contrary view is provided by Werner Hirschmann, who in 1938–1939 was the Hitler Youth leader in his community of 10 000, and later *LI* of *U 190*: 'I don't think during that entire time did I ever touch on any National Socialist philosophy or other such indoctrination in discussions with my boys. But we had choirs, string quartets, folk dancing with the female organization, scouting, week-long bicycle trips, tenting, target shooting, sports etc and knew every joke about Göring circulating in Germany at those times.' (W. Hirschmann, 'Comments on Topp's "Manning and training the U-boat fleet", 1994, copy held by author).

15 Characteristics of Enemy Submarines, HQ CinC US Fleet 1943, MP1587/1 167D, AA.

16 For examples, see interrogation reports of survivors from: *U 168*, MP1587/1 167A, AA; *U 183*, MP1587/1 167D, AA; and *U 860*, NHB.

17 Admiralty Monthly Anti-Submarine Summary, January 1945, p. 16, NHB.

18 Since U-boat recruiting campaigns were pitched at craftsmen and engineers, particularly from the metal industries, the majority of crew members were probably quite well educated.

19 Mallmann Showell, *U-boats Under the Swastika*, p. 136; W. Lüth, 'Command of men in a U-Boat' in H. Busch, *U-Boats at War*, Putnam, London, 1955, p. 273; letter, Hirschmann to author, 4 December 1995.

20 Letter, Hirschmann to author, 4 December 1995.

21 W. Hirschmann, 'Comments on the movie "*Das Boot*" '. Copy held by author.

22 Timm was not alone in his musical subversion. In the U-boat base at Lorient the only radio station listened to was the English-based Radio Calais, which played jazz and swing (letter, Hirschmann to author, 4 December 1995).

23 In another *Monsun* boat, *U 181*, the Nazi salute was apparently given by plugging the right thumb into the pants pocket and raising the hand (O. Giese and J. Wise, *Shooting the War*, Naval Institute Press, Annapolis, 1994, p. 179).

24 Hirschmann, 'Comments on "*Das Boot*" '.

25 This is not to say that the *Agru-Front* did not have a sense of humour. An appropriate illumination of the spirit is perhaps contained in the official certification given to the *LI* of *U 190*:

> 'Diving Master Diploma. We Masters of the Guild of Trim Tamers and *LI*-Torturers herewith make known that the most worshipful *Leutnant* (*Ing.*) Hirschmann today before the undersigned took a submarine of medium size undamaged below the surface without danger for the galley and the nap of the training officer and moved same in moderate oscillations up and down so that now he has been found worthy and been admitted into the brotherhood of the glorious diving boat people. Given this 26.2 in the year 1943. The Chief Engineer Training Officers of the *Agru-Front*.'

26 *KTB U 862*, 11 May 1944, PG/30768/1, NHB.

Chapter 4 *Group Monsun*

1 Among these improvements were heavier anti-aircraft guns, anti-destroyer torpedoes, new search receivers and radar, and later the advanced-design electro-boats. See Hessler, vol. III, p. 4.

2 Minutes, Conference of the CinC Navy with the *Führer*, 31 May 1943, MP1587/1 168I, AA.

3 Hessler, vol. III, p. 14.

4 On 17 October 1943, *Michel* was sunk by three torpedoes from the submarine USS *Tarpon* 90 miles east of Yokohama.

5 Rössler, *The U-boat*, p. 64.

6 A.W. Saville, 'German Submarines in the Far East', in *United States Naval Institute Proceedings*, August 1961, p. 80.

7 NID 24/T51/45, German U-Boat Bases and Refuges in the Far East, 28 August 1945, ADM 223/51, Public Records Office (PRO).

8 W. Rahn, 'Japan and Germany 1941–1943: No common objective, no common plans, no basis of trust', in *Naval War College Review*, Summer 1993, p. 48.

9 Japanese Monograph No. 110, Submarine Operations in Second Phase Operations, Part I April–August 1942, Military History Section Headquarters Far East, Office of the Chief of Military History, Department of the Army, p. 46. The agreement was signed 18 January 1942.

10 BR 1736 (50) *War With Japan*, vol. IV, Historical Section Admiralty, 1965, p. 186.

11 W. Churchill, *The Second World War*, vol. 4, Houghton Mifflin, Boston, 1950, p. 936.

12 Rahn, p. 58.

13 NID 24/T51/45.

14 Hessler, vol. III, p. 15

15 Dönitz, p. 416.

16 Conference, Hitler with Ambassador Oshima, 21 January 1943, Magic

summary, no. 323, SRS 874 mfm 1593, National Library of Australia (ANL).

17 Admiral S. Fukutome, former Chief of Staff, Combined Fleet, described their gift as 'small . . . and therefore of little value to Japan'. (D. Gunton, *The Penang Submarines*, City Council of George Town, Penang, 1970, p. 51). However, Commander Shizuo Fukui, writing immediately after the war, noted, 'Very extensive research on characteristics, structures & every sorts of equipments were taken place in the Inland Sea with success, which resulted many developments in the design of Japanese submarines laid down in the later period of the war' (S. Fukui, *Japanese Naval Vessels at the End of World War II*, Greenhill Books, London, 1992, p. 30). In February 1944 another Type IXC, *U 1224*, was handed over to a Japanese crew in France.

18 *U 168, U 183, U 188, U 200, U 506, U 514, U 516, U 532, U 533, U 509* and *U 847*.

19 During her next attempt at passage, *U 847* was diverted to act as an emergency tanker and eventually sunk by carrier-borne aircraft at the end of August.

20 F. H. Hinsley, *British Intelligence in the Second World War*, vol. 3, Part 1, HMSO, London, 1984, p. 515.

21 Traffic analysis involved the study of enemy radio procedures, techniques and volume etc.

22 Hinsley, p. 213.

23 One CV and one CVE were assigned to Atlantic anti-submarine duties in the spring of 1943. Five CVEs were in action during the summer and autumn.

24 Hessler, vol. III, p. 48.

25 ibid. p. 59.

26 Eight days after the capture, divers recovered eight secret communications publications wrapped in an ordinary tablecloth. Though five had been printed with soluble ink, US Army chemists developed a new chemical solution which eventually recovered some 90 per cent of the text. Combined with Ultra material, the processed documents allowed Allied intelligence to set up a fairly complete folder on German and German–Japanese Far East communications and keep it up to date (J. Bray, *Ultra in the Atlantic*, vol. VI, Aegean Park Press, 1994, pp. 88–90).

27 For example, for a petty offence Eck had once ordered a *Maschinengefreiter* to be lashed to the 3.7cm gun for sixteen hours while the U-boat proceeded, surfaced, through a heavy sea ('Interrogation of *U 852* Survivors', November 1944, NHB).

28 Padfield, *Dönitz: The Last Führer*, pp. 353–357.

29 An entry in the *KTB BdU* for December 1942 notes, 'The killing of survivors is not desirable, not so much because of humanitarian reasons, but because of the damage to the morale of our own crews, who would expect a similar fate if roles were reversed.'

30 Though other reports of firing on survivors were received, it was usually judged that fire had actually been directed at the ship alone.
31 From decrypts, the Allies had established that the rendezvous would take place at one of two positions. To protect their source the Admiralty insisted that 'neither aircraft nor surface vessels would appear within 100 miles of the rendezvous positions unless previous contact had been made with the enemy and that surface vessels would not intervene unless D/F evidence about the enemy's whereabouts was obtained' (Hinsley, p. 230).
32 'Intelligence reports on the war in the Atlantic 1942–45', MF 28, ADFA, p. 135. Interestingly, German Naval Headquarters at Penang also assumed that the Allies were in possession of the radio codes ('Interrogation of survivors from *U 168*', MP1587/1 167A, AA).
33 'Experience with the *Eisbär* group had shown that Type IXC boats, even if refuelled in the South Atlantic, could not last out in the Cape area until all torpedoes were expended' (Hessler, vol. II, p. 83).
34 *U 1059* was caught completely by surprise, the U-boat lying stopped on the surface while some of the crew had an early-morning bathe.
35 Record Group 457, SRH-019, 'Blockade-running between Europe and the Far East by submarines', 1942–44, 1 December 1944, NA.
36 Hessler, vol. III, p. 65.

Chapter 5 *Erste Feindfahrt*

1 In an Admiralty intelligence report of 12 July 1944 which detailed the experience of U-boat commanders then on operations, Timm, at 17 months experience, was ranked number ten. At the time there were some 177 operational U-boats out of 429 in commission. ADM 223/172, PRO.
2 *KTB BdU*, 1 June 1944, p. 358.
3 ibid. p. 351.
4 Timm's cargo included supplies for the Penang base and *Fumberta*, *Fliege* and Tunis radar intercept sets.
5 CB 04051 (103), 'Interrogation of U-Boat survivors—cumulative edition', June 1944, Naval Intelligence Division, Admiralty, p. 35.
6 Hessler, vol. III, p. 59.
7 Between 16 May and 28 May six U-boats were sunk leaving Norway for the Atlantic. Nor was *U 862* the only boat to turn back on 26 May. *U 958* was in the vicinity and was also forced to return to Bergen after suffering damage and casualties after attack by two Mosquitos of No. 333 Squadron RAF.
8 *KTB BdU*, 26 May 1944.
9 Secret Intelligence summary, week ending 29 May 1944, ADM 223/172, PRO.
10 The former Norwegian royal yacht, *Stella-Polaris*, with unlimited hot

water, was 'the dream of U-boat men after a rough tour at sea' (Giese p. 136).

11 Allied plans for the A/S defence of the landings were based on a direct and immediate threat from 120 U-boats (M. Milner, *The U-Boat Hunters: The Royal Canadian Navy and the Offensive against Germany's Submarines*, Naval Institute Press, Annapolis, 1994, p. 138).

12 'The German U-Boat Command Handbook for U-Boat Captains', Admiralty Monthly Anti-Submarine Report, May 1944, NHB.

13 A. Schirrmann and F. Peitel, *Freie Jagd Im Indischen Ozean*, p.11.

14 *KTB BdU*, 21 July 1944.

15 In January 1944 *U 377* was sunk by her own acoustic torpedo.

16 *Robin Goodfellow* was reported overdue by Bahia on 6 August 1944, but not until the following day did the SS *Priam* report that she had picked up a distress message from the freighter saying that it was being torpedoed in 20°03'S 14°21'W at 0015Z 25 July (Admiralty War Diary (AWD), 7 August 1944, NHB).

17 G. Reiffenstuhl, *KTB U 862*, 3 August 1944.

18 *KTB BdU*, 8 August 1944.

19 Reiffenstuhl, 4 August 1944.

20 One shaft was kept running at half speed coupled to a diesel while the batteries were charged using the diesel dynamos. The remaining shaft was coupled to the motor with current from the batteries. With this arrangement the greatest range could be covered while proceeding at approximately 7kts.

21 FECB was an inter-service organisation under naval control. The cryptanalytical unit was also known to the US Navy as Fleet Radio Unit Eastern Fleet (FRUEF). Two days after FECB's report, the Americans reported the exact extent of *U 862*'s planned operations area in the Gulf of Aden. RG 457, SRMN 053 'OP-20-GI reports of German U-boats east of Cape Town', 8 August 1944, NA.

22 Message, CinC SA to CinC EF, 101031B, AWD, 10 August 1944.

23 Message, CinC EF to Force 66, 061318Z, AWD, 6 August 1944.

24 Message, CinC EF to CinC SA, 130525FG, AWD, 13 August 1944.

Chapter 6 *Paukenschlag*

1 Form, S. 1533, SS *Radbury*, 3 November 1944, ADM199/527, PRO.

2 Report, sinking of SS *Radbury*, undated, ADM199/2147, PRO.

3 The chief engineer was later submitted for the OBE in recognition of his outstanding conduct.

4 Form, S. 1533, SS *Empire Lancer*, undated, ADM199/527, PRO.

5 Reiffenstuhl, 16 August 1944.

6 ibid., 18 August 1944.

7 ibid.

8 Form, S. 1533, SS *Wayfarer*, 19 September 1944, ADM199/527, PRO.

9 Report, TD/139/2139, 16 January 1945, ADM199/2147, PRO
10 ibid.
11 Message, *BdU* to Timm, 19 August, RG 457, SRMN 053, 23 August, NA.
12 Reiffenstuhl, 19 August 1944.
13 Only one of the ships sunk and the ship damaged were in convoy. The escort consisted of only two trawlers and as Tait feared had proven unable to cope with the attacks by *U 861*.
14 'Summary of U-boat and anti U-boat operations in Indian Ocean', 25 August 1944, ADM219/201, PRO.
15 Report, 'Protection of shipping in the Indian Ocean', 7 April 1944, ADM219/116, PRO.
16 ADM 219/201, PRO.
17 The problem was always 'to decide whether or not to go into convoy by balancing the probable saving of shipping sunk against the loss of carrying capacity and the escorts used up by the convoy system'. ADM 1/15709, PRO.
18 The Admiralty argued that it was uneconomical to raise the scale of escort protection against what was never more than a 'small but steady drain' on shipping, (ADM 219/116, PRO). Somerville, moreover, declined a suggestion that he use frigates and sloops for escort because that would have delayed the formation of escort carrier groups and he wished to hunt the submarines with carriers rather than waiting for them to come to well-protected convoys.
19 Monthly Report of A/S Warfare, East Indies Station—October 1944, p. 6, NHB. The Hedgehog was a precision stand off weapon which could project a pattern of 24 small contact-fused bombs to a range of 250 yards.
20 Indian Ocean General Reconnaissance Operations, 'Summary of operations during August, September, October 1944', copy held by author.
21 The U-boat was assessed as 'in Mozambique Channel probably between 015° S and 010° S'; Message, CinC EF to multiple addressees, 200213Z, AWD 20 August 1944, NHB.
22 'Monthly Report of A/S Warfare', East Indies Station—October 1944, p. 21, NHB.
23 'German U-boat Command Handbook for U-boat Captains'.

Chapter 7 *Flieger, Flieger!*

1 Hessler, vol. II, p. 45.
2 Letter, RAF Air Historical Branch to author, 25 June 1993.
3 'Monthly Report of A/S Warfare—East Indies Station', October 1944, p. 21, NHB.
4 RG 457, SRMN 053, 30 August, NA.

Nevertheless, on 28 August shipping sailing between Aden and South Africa was again routed to pass through the Mozambique Channel (Eastern Fleet War Diary, August 1944, NHB).

6 This was almost certainly *U 859*.
7 Reiffenstuhl, 26 August 1944.
8 H. Busch, *U-Boats at War*, Putnam, London, 1955, p. 261.
9 Schirrmann, p. 14.
10 Message, ZTPGU/25246, DEFE3, PRO.
11 Message, Timm to *BdU*, 1105/4/9/44, ibid.
12 Message, *BdU* to all East Asia U-boats, 2012/14/7/44, ibid. The previous entry route had been compromised after the commander of the first *Monsun* boat to return to Europe, *U 188*, had been captured by the French Resistance while on his way to make his report (*KTB BdU*, 14 July 1944, p. 425).
13 A D/F fix was obtained on Timm's transmission of 4 September, though given the distance from the receiving stations it was not accurate enough for localisation and served only as an indication of movement ('Monthly Report of A/S Warfare East Indies Station', September 1944, p. 2, NHB).
14 Message, Penang to Timm, 0906/6/9/44, DEFE3, PRO.
15 Message, Penang to Timm, 1214/7/9/44, ibid.
16 The copy of Timm's message 1105/4/9/44 held in the PRO is annotated with the additional date/time group 1853/9/9/44.
17 The patrol dates for these submarines were as follows:
Statesman 15 August–5 September
Sirdar 19 August–18 September
Strongbow 19 August–10 September
Tantalus 25 August–27 September
18 Reiffenstuhl, 9 September 1944.
19 Schirrmann, p. 21.
20 R. Herrmann, *KTB U 862*, 9 September 1944.
21 Reiffenstuhl, 9 September 1944.
22 *Trenchant* was patrolling off the north coast of Sumatra on 22 September when suddenly ordered to intercept the U-boat. The British submarine made the passage on the surface at night and at full speed.

Chapter 8 Penang *und* Shonan

1 Saville, p. 88.
2 According to a report by Admiral Wenneker in Tokyo, 'The four Southern Area bases were built under greatest difficulties against opposition from the Japanese Army.' (Message, Tokyo to Berlin, 19 April 1945, RG 457 Entry no. 9017, NA).

3 'Interrogation of survivors from *U 168*', undated, MP1587/1 16[illegible] AA.
4 Giese, p. 201.
5 MP1587/1 167A, AA.
6 ibid.
7 On 26 March 1944, *I-8* sank the SS *Tjisalak*; 98 of the survivors were subsequently murdered by the submarine's crew. On 2 July the victims were the survivors of the SS *Jean Nicolet*. Some of the merchant seamen were killed outright, others had their hands tied behind their backs and were forced to run a gauntlet of Japanese sailors. The submarine then submerged with the remainder of the helpless men still on deck.
8 Giese, pp. 202–205.
9 MP1587/1 167A, AA.
10 Reiffenstuhl, 11 September. 1944.
11 ibid., 10 September 1944.
12 Despite the security precautions, the Allies were aware of the U-boat's passage. An American daily secret intelligence summary for 13 September records '*U 862* due to arrive Singapore from Penang 13/9' (RG 457, SRMN 053, 13 September, NA). Fortunately for *U 862*, HMS *Tantalus*, the only Allied submarine in the Malacca Strait area at the time, left patrol 12 September for Fremantle.
13 Schirrmann, p. 23.
14 Afterwards known as the 'Tiger Balm Gardens' after the medical ointment invented by the owners.
15 Reiffenstuhl, 15 September 1944.
16 From the beginning of the war the limit for the *Ritterkreuz* was 100000 GRT sunk for commanders operating in the Atlantic. After the summer of 1943 the limits were lowered considerably and finally no limit was set until the end of the war (letter, A. Niestlé to author, 20 April 1996).
17 Reiffenstuhl, 19 September 1944.
18 The exact quantity of mercury carried by *U 862* is not recorded, but sister boats carried up to 100 tons of freight (mercury or lead) in the keel.
19 Schirrmann, p. 20.
20 MP1587/1 167A, AA. Despite this apparent intention to restrict awareness, the records of Tokyo–Berlin communications contain at least one reference to 'The demotion of an enlisted man who caught venereal disease in a forbidden house' (15 December 1944, RG 457 Entry no. 9017, NA).
21 Rieffenstuhl, 10 September 1944.
22 Schirrmann, p.26.

apter 9 *Die Australien Operation*

1 *KTB BdU*, 14 September 1944.
2 'Captured German document dealing with S/M warfare in the Indian Ocean', 6 May 1944, MP1587/1 167A, AA.
3 ibid.
4 Message, *BdU* to Penang, 1846/14/9/44, DEFE 3/736, PRO.
5 Report, 'The U-boat phase of the Japanese war', 1 August 1945, ADM/219/232, PRO.
6 Combined Operations and Intelligence Centre, 'Weekly Summary of Naval Activities', 17 September 1944, MP1587/1 316L, AA.
7 Secret Telegram No. 842 071550, 7 September 1944, ADM 223/271, PRO.
8 Abe, as chief of the Naval Affairs Bureau, was the first among the top policy makers in the Navy Ministry to advocate that Japan conclude the Tripartite Alliance.
9 B5553/1, FRUMEL Periodic Summaries 1944–1945, 3 October 1944, AA.
10 Message, Berlin to Tokyo, 27 September 1944, RG 457 Entry 9017, NA.
11 RG 457 SRMN 051A, 'Memoranda to COMINCH F21 on German U-Boat Activities October 1943–May 1945', 15 October 1944, NA.
12 RG 457 SRMN 037, 'COMINCH File of U-Boat Intelligence Summaries January 1943–May 1945', 3 February 1945, NA.
13 Message, Japanese naval attaché, Germany, to Tokyo, 22 December 1944, B5553/1 AA.
14 J. Bray, *Ultra in the Atlantic*, vol. II, Aegean Park Press, Laguna Hills, 1994, p. 221.
15 Rössler, p. 239.
16 Message, *BdU* to Penang, 0729/27/9/44, DEFE 3/736, PRO.
17 Message, Tokyo to Berlin, 23 September 1944, RG 457 Entry 9017, NA. Dönitz may also have been unwilling to take the risk of torpedo loading from the upper deck containers while on patrol. This practice had been abandoned in the Atlantic in mid-1943.
18 B5553/1, 5 October 1944, AA.
19 MP1587/1 167A, AA.
20 Letter, Dommes to Royal Navy Submarine Museum, 29 November 1980, NHB.
21 C. Blair, *Silent Victory: The US Submarine War Against Japan*, J.B. Lippincott, Philadelphia, 1975, p. 743.
22 MP1587/1 167A, AA.
23 RG 457, Entry 9017, 13 October 1944, NA.
24 B.R. 1736 (52), vol. III, p. 78.
25 ibid.
26 *KTB BdU*, 13 Oct. 1944. On 21 October these orders were updated: 'On account of submarine danger, when proceeding into any East

Asia port close down, crew on upper deck with life jackets, offic[illegible] to wear no insignia as officers have been taken prisoner by enem[illegible] submarine' (Message, *BdU* to all East Asia U-boats, 1317/21/10/44, DEFE3, PRO).

27 Message, Berlin to Tokyo, 4 November 1944, RG457, Entry 9017, NA.

28 J. Brennecke, *Haie im Paradies,* Ernst Gerdes Verlag, Preetz/Holstein, undated, p. 259.

29 *Quito* was a small merchant vessel in varied and constant use by the Germans in East Asia.

30 Reiffenstuhl, 5 November 1944.

31 B5553/1, 6 November 1944.

32 Eastern Fleet submarines would patrol no farther than the upper reaches of the Malacca Strait down to One Fathom Bank. Only Fremantle-based submarines were allowed through the Sunda Strait and at the time of *U 862*'s passage HMS *Tantalus* was on patrol in the South China Sea between Singapore and Borneo. Fortunately for Timm, between 2 and 7 November the British submarine was diverted to air–sea rescue duties off the east coast of Malaya (BR I736 (52) vol. III, p. 81).

33 This volunteer defence force would become the core of the Republic's army during the postwar revolution.

34 Herrmann, 13 November 1944.

Chapter 10 *U 537 und U 196*

1 The notation 1612/15/9/44 appears on the bottom of the signal text which has a time of intercept of 1727/14/9/44. DEFE 3/736, PRO.

2 Message text appears in RG 457 'Declassified Traffic Intell Summaries of Japan Naval Forces', 17 Sep 1944, SRNS 1516, NA; extracts with slightly different wording appear in FRUMEL Periodic Summary, 18 September 1944, CRS B5553/1 AA, and RG 457, 'COMINCH U-Boat Intelligence Summaries', 23 September 1944, SRMN 037, NA.

3 G. Wheeler, *Kinkaid of the Seventh Fleet,* Naval Historical Center, Department of the Navy, Washington, 1995, p. 458.

4 Letter, Royle to Vice Admiral Carpender, 18 February 1943, MP1049/5 2026/10/1499, AA.

5 D. Horner, *High Command: Australia's Struggle for an Independent War Strategy, 1939–45,* Allen & Unwin, Sydney, 1992, p. 363.

6 Letter, Commander Allied Naval Forces SWPA to ACNB, 16 March 1943, MP1049/5 1844/2/12, AA.

7 Wheeler, p. 346.

8 F. Walker, *HMAS Armidale: The Ship That Had To Die,* Kingfisher Press, Budgewoi, 1990, p. 27.

9 Letter, NOIC Fremantle to ACNB, 25 September 1944, MP1185/8 2026/5/316, AA.

Message, NOIC Fremantle to CSWPSF, 180346ZSEP44, ibid.

F. Walker, *Corvettes—Little Ships for Big Men*, Kingfisher Press, Budgewoi, 1995, p. 25.

12 Eastern Fleet War Diary, September 1944, NHB.

13 Message, CSWPSF to multiple addressees, 190900ZSEP44, MP1185/8 2026/5/316, AA.

14 NOIC Fremantle War Diary, 1 October 1944 to 31 December 1944, AWM78 409/1, Australian War Memorial (AWM).

15 *Chanticleer* (ASR-7), of 1780 tons, was launched in 1942 as a submarine rescue vessel. the 710-ton *Isabel* (PY-10) had been built in 1917 as a yacht.

16 G. Odgers, *Air War Against Japan 1943–1945*, Australian War Memorial, Canberra, 1957, p. 349.

17 RAAF Maritime Trade Protection Narrative, AWM54 81/4/141, AWM.

18 Message, CSWPSF to all NOICs, 191358Z/SEP44, MP1185/8 2026/5/316, AA.

19 For example, on 29 September *Tamworth* reported confident Asdic contact 11 miles north of Rottnest and made several attacks. All sailings from Fremantle were suspended and the only known incoming ship diverted to Albany.

20 RAAF Maritime Trade Protection Narrative, p. 155.

21 B5553/1, 10 September 1944, AA.

22 The time that elapsed between CTF 71's taking action and FRUMEL's promulgating the information more widely illustrates the importance of the operational commander's direct access to Sigint.

23 USS *Flounder*, Report of Fourth War Patrol, mf 33 ADFA.

24 ibid. Second endorsement, 24 December 1944.

25 B5553/1, 14 November 1944, message, Penang to *U 537*, 10 November 1944, AA.

26 General Headquarters SWPA, Ultra Intelligence Bulletins, Special Intelligence Bulletin, 6 October 1944; copy held by author.

27 Message, CSWPSF to NOIC Fremantle & NOIC Darwin, 290514ZNOV44, MP1185/8 2026/5/316, AA.

28 Message, CSWPSF to NOIC Fremantle & NOIC Darwin, 300641ZNOV44, ibid.

29 After *U 196*'s initial failure to return, *BdU* assumed wireless difficulties and on 12 December ordered Striegler to refuel *U 843*, which had departed for Europe on 10 December.

30 *KTB BdU*, 22 December 1944.

31 Letter, A. Niestlé to author, 25 November 1995.

Chapter 11 *Zweite Feindfahrt*

1 RG 457, SRMN 053, 4 December, NA.

2 B5553/1, 27 & 28 November 1944, AA.
3 Between 23 October and 24 November the Dutch submarine *O.* [illegible] conducted a patrol that included the north coast of Java. She sailed south through the Lombok Strait on 19 November.
4 Reiffenstuhl, 19 November 1944.
5 ibid. 28 November 1944.
6 ibid. 29 November 1944.
7 RG 457, message, Tokyo to Berlin, 6 December 1944, Entry 9017, NA. On 4 December Reiffenstuhl described the imagined force as an 'English battleship group'.
8 An Allied assessment dated 8 December 1944 noted that though Germany–Japan exchanges had included information on D/F, traffic analysis and merchant navy codes there was no evidence of combined efforts to attack high-grade naval ciphers (J. Bray ed. *Ultra in the Atlantic*, vol. III, Aegean Park Press, 1994, pp. 65–82).
9 Addu Atoll was a secluded fleet anchorage at the southern end of the Maldive Islands. It was used as an alternative to Colombo 600 miles to the northeast.
10 Report by *OKM*, 13 January 1945, in *KTB BdU*, p. 853.
11 *KTB Skl*, 6 December 1944.
12 In fact *BdU* would continue to report *U 862* as operating off Albany for the duration of Timm's voyage. *KTB BdU*, 29 November 1944–January 15 1945.
13 Reiffenstuhl, 9 December 1944.
14 ibid.
15 Interview, Chief Engineer P. Kypriatas, MP 1049/5 2026/10/1771, AA.
16 Interview, Captain E. Svokos, ibid.
17 Interview, AB/SG Stanley Henry Martin, ibid.
18 Reiffenstuhl, 9 December 1944.
19 Southern Area Tactical Appreciation, December 1944, in RAAF Maritime Trade Protection Narrative, pp. 165–6.
20 ibid.
21 RAN Daily Narrative, 10 Dec 1944, NHS.
22 An 'A1' grading indicated a completely reliable source accepted as true.
23 The only confirmed indication of a German U-boat received by the RAN before this date was a D/F report, 'within 120 miles of 024°S. 086°E at 2217K/3rd December' (RAN Daily Narrative, 5 December 1944). This may have been *U 181*, which while attempting to return to Europe was forced back to Jakarta with a defective main bearing. Reiffenstuhl, writing on 28 November, was obviously already in an Australian mood, quipping, '*Kpt.* Freiwald's boat is a New South Wales boomerang'.
24 RAN Daily Narrative, 6 December 1944. The narrative also noted that Air Operations Room Southern Area did not intend to take action on the report. Sightings of suspected periscopes were not

uncommon and this report was actually well south of *U 862*'s position.

25 G.H. Gill, *The Royal Australian Navy, 1939–1945*, vol. II, Collins, Sydney, 1985, p. 551.

26 *RAN Daily Narrative*, 21 December 1944.

27 Reiffenstuhl, 15 December 1944.

28 ibid., 20 December 1944.

29 Herrmann, 19 December 1944. This incident was almost certainly the result of anomalous sound propogation.

30 Reiffenstuhl, 23 December 1944. Though Reiffenstuhl used local times in his journal, the U-boat's routine was run to German time, nine hours behind, thus 'lunch' actually occurred at night.

31 *U 862*'s war diary has not survived and the entry is Timm's postwar recollection as recorded in Brennecke's *Haie im Paradies*, p. 259. He is quoted as seeing 20–30 mast tops, but this is almost certainly an exaggeration. It is instead quite possible that Timm had detected the 21st Minesweeping Flotilla.

Chapter 12 *Sechte Kriegsweinacht*

1 Type XXI performance improvements included a normal operational depth of 150–200m, a crush depth of 330m, the ability to travel submerged at 16kts for one hour, and a minimum crash-dive time of 18 seconds. Unfortunately for Dönitz his decision to hasten their introduction meant many delays. Of the 118 Type XXIs that entered service between June 1944 and May 1945 only two sailed for an operational cruise.

2 Reiffenstuhl, 24 December 1944. This was arguably the most successful day of all for U-boats in the last part of the war. In terms of the 'tie-down resources' strategy there were near simultaneous sinkings in the English Channel, in North American waters and off Australia.

3 Liberty ships accounted for nearly three-quarters of America's total wartime construction of more than 40 million deadweight tons.

4 Interview with Murdoch Daniel MacRae, MP1587/1 153X, AA.

5 Message, *Robert J. Walker* to CSWPSF, 241652ZDEC44, ibid.

6 Message, *Robert J. Walker* to Navy Melbourne, 241805ZDEC44, ibid.

7 The possibility of a mine causing the damage persisted for some time. On 27 December, Vice Admiral Kinkaid, asked Royle for his evaluation of the attack 'in view of the improbability of submarine having reached position 36–20 South 150–45 East without prior attack on other ships' (Message, CTF 77 to CSWPSF, 271110/DEC44, ibid).

8 Interview with John Mahoy, ibid.

9 Reiffenstuhl, 24 December 1944.

10 'Command Handbook for U-boat Captains'; Admiralty Montl Anti-Submarine Report, May 1944, NHB.
11 Reiffenstuhl, 24 December 1944.
12 Interview with Murdoch Daniel MacRae, MP1587/1 153X, AA.
13 Statement by Marvin L. Taylor, 30 December 1944, ibid.
14 The survivors would later state that they believed the haze had prevented the enemy submarine from surfacing and shelling them in the lifeboats (Submission from *Daily Mirror*, 29 December 1944, SP109/3/1 309/26, AA).
15 Odgers, p. 349.
16 Moore's appointment was variously known as Flag Officer-in-Charge Sydney (FOIC Sydney) and Naval Officer-in-Charge Sydney (NOIC Sydney).
17 On 22 November 1944, with no threat apparent, another five MLs under NOIC Sydney's operational control had been paid off.
18 RAN Daily Narrative, 18 December 1944, NHS.
19 During this period the Japanese carried out some 40 patrols in Australian waters.
20 Eastern Area Operational Bulletin, July 1943, Box 5 6/5/9, 1969/100/2, AA.
21 RAAF Trade Protection Narrative, p. 219.
22 Report, Eastern Area Intelligence Section to RAAF HQ, undated, Box 5 6/2/25 1969/100/2, AA; RAN Daily Narrative 25 December 1944.
23 RAAF Trade Protection Narrative, pp. 161–2. MacRae complained, 'If an aircraft had arrived even as late as 5 a.m. it would in all probability have prevented the second [actually third] torpedo hit, and the ship could easily have been towed to safety' (Gill, p. 553). Air Vice-Marshal W.D. Bostock, air officer commanding RAAF Command, in a reply to the commander Allied Air Forces SWPA, General G.C. Kenny, claimed that the total time from receipt of information until first aircraft airborne was 91 minutes and said he did not consider this delay excessive (Odgers, p. 351).
24 RAN Daily Narrative, 25 December 1944.
25 Eastern Area (RAAF) Daily Intelligence Summary, no. 361, Box 5 6/2/25 1969/100/2, AA.
26 The 'special searches' comprised 106 Beaufort, 24 Catalina and 59 Kingfisher sorties ('Possible submarine sightings off Australian coast', AWM54 888/10/1, AWM).
27 Reiffenstuhl, 25 December 1944.
28 RAAF Trade Protection Narrative, pp. 222–223
29 L. Lind, *HMAS Hobart*, The Naval Historical Society of Australia, Sydney, 1971, p. 65.
30 Message, NOIC Sydney to ML's *822*, *823* and *810*, 241900ZDEC44, MP1587 153X, AA.
31 There was no naval tug in Sydney and because of the Christmas holidays difficulty was experienced obtaining a crew for a commercial tug. Partially manned by naval personnel, the *Aristell* finally

sailed 14 hours after *Robert J. Walker*'s distress message (RAN Daily Narrative, 26 December 1944).

2 HMAS *Quickmatch*, Monthly Report of Proceedings, January 1945, AWM78, AWM.

33 Incident sheet, AOIC Eastern Area, 25 December 1944, Box 5 6/2/25 1969/100/2, AA.

34 These carriers were not front-line units and were used for aircraft ferry and replenishment for the larger fleet carriers.

35 Message, CSWPSF to Capt. D4, 241841ZDEC44, MP1587 153X, AA.

36 RAN Daily Narrative, 25 December 1944.

37 Message, CSWPSF to SO 21st MS Flotilla, 250114ZDEC44, MP1587 153X, AA.

38 RAN Daily Narrative, 25 December 1944.

39 ibid., 26 December 1944.

40 Message, Capt. D4 to NOIC Sydney, 2506011ZDEC44, MP1587 153X, AA.

41 Message, Capt. D4 to NOIC Sydney, 252343ZDEC44, ibid.

42 Message, NOIC Sydney to Capt. D4, 261141ZDEC44, ibid.

43 Message, NOIC Sydney to *Quiberon*, 282031ZDEC44, ibid.

44 'Report on operation of 29 and 30 December 1944', Commanding Officer *Quiberon* to NOIC Sydney, 2 January 1944, copy held by author.

45 Australia provided base support but had no say in the employment of the BPF.

46 RAN Daily Narrative, 27 December 1944.

47 Maritime Trade Protection Narrative, p. 162.

48 Reiffenstuhl, 26 December 1944.

Chapter 13 *Neuseeland*

1 Report, British Naval Liaison Party to the Admiralty, 28 July 1944, MP1185/8 1932/3/44, AA.

2 Letter, ACNB to CinC BPF, 19 January 1945, MP1049/5 1855/15/2, AA.

3 'Enemy submarines on the Australian coast', 7 January 1945, AWM188/40, AWM.

4 Letter, ACNB to CinC BPF, 19 January 1945. An earlier American report was only slightly more specific, noting that *U 862* was 'probably in Melbourne–Sidney [sic] area (RG 457, SRMN 053, 8 January 1945, NA).

5 On 1 January, Commander Task Force 75 (Rear Admiral Berkey, USN) had complained that he had not even enough escorts to effect a regular convoy schedule between New Guinea and the forward area (RAN Daily Narrative, 1 January 1945, NHS).

6 ibid., 10 January 1945.

7 FRUMEL continued to credit *U 862* with an attack on *Alcee Fo*
until the end of the war ('*U 862*', DSD translations of cypher me
sages 1945–1946, B5555, AA).
8 RAN Daily Narrative, 10 January 1945.
9 Correction to letter, ACNB to CinC BPF, 19 January 1945, MP1049/5 1855/15/2 AA.
10 Reiffenstuhl, 27 December 1944.
11 ibid., 1 January 1945.
12 One of *U 862*'s crew members was married on 4 January. His bride was in the final stage of pregnancy making a hurried celebration necessary. He was only informed about his marriage on 23 January 1945, DEFE 3/740, PRO.
13 Reiffenstuhl, 7 January 1945.
14 ibid., 10 January 1945.
15 ibid., 11 January 1945.
16 ibid., 15 January 1945.
17 Brennecke, p. 261.
18 Reiffenstuhl, 16 January 1945.
19 ibid.
20 In the Australian context the most obvious examples are the gunnery attacks on Sydney and Newcastle after the midget submarine raid on Sydney Harbour in June 1942. Another less well-known incident occured on 28 January 1943, when *I-165* shelled Port Gregory in Western Australia, ostensibly to divert Allied attention from operations in Guadalcanal.
21 B5553/1, 22 February 1945, AA.
22 Brennecke, p. 261.
23 The Liberators were from No. 159 Squadron RAF and had flown from Kharagpur in India.
24 *KTB Skl*, 28 October 1944.
25 Special Intelligence Bulletin No. 586, 30 November 1944, copy held by author.
26 With Dommes' departure, *Korvettenkapitän* Erhardt briefly resumed duties as commander of the Penang base. In February, with no further U-boat operations expected from Penang, Erhardt returned to Singapore.
27 Message, Tokyo to Berlin, 15 January 1945, B5553/1, 26 January 1945, AA.
28 The Japanese maintained a formal objection to permitting German wireless stations in Japanese territory. In Penang they were prepared to agree to the erection of a transmitter, even operated by German personnel and working according to German procedure, only providing the Germans made the transmitter over to them so that the wireless station was nominally Japanese. In Singapore and Jakarta the Japanese made their own wireless stations available to the Germans at special routine times (Report, 'German–Japanese Radio Communications', 25 August 1945, ADM223/51, PRO).

Reiffenstuhl, 26 January 1945.
Brennecke, p. 262.
31 Reiffenstuhl, 27 January 1945.
32 ibid., 24 January 1945.
33 B5553/1, 26 January 1945, AA.
34 Herrmann, 4 February 1945.
35 Reiffenstuhl, 5 February 1945.

Chapter 14 SS *Peter Silvester*

1 SS *Marion Moller* was sunk by the Japanese submarine *RO-113* on 5 November 1944 east of India. SS *Fort Lee* was sunk by *U 181* on 2 November 1944 midway between Perth and Mauritius.
2 Reiffenstuhl, 6 February 1944. *Peter Silvester* actually mounted a standard Liberty ship armament. Fritsche was Goebbels' minister for Radio Propaganda.
3 The ammunition supply–issuing ship *Darvel*, attached to the BPF, sailed from Trincomalee for Fremantle in late January 1945. According to her third radio officer, a few days into her journey a message was received from the ACNB to the effect that as the southern Indian Ocean was free from submarines there was no further need to zig-zag. *En route Darvel* was tasked to look for *Peter Silvester* survivors. They found none but did sight 'debris and mules floating in a sea of oil'. Letter, D. Reynolds to author, 22 January 1995.
4 'Together . . . always together', *Detroit Free Press*, 3 February 1980.
5 'Nightmare of shipwreck recalled', *Big Spring Herald*, 27 June 1976.
6 'Report of LT Burch of the M/V "Peter Sylvester" [sic] MP 1587/1 1539', AA.
7 'Together . . . always together'.
8 'Survivors of World War II raft ordeal meet after 34 years', unknown newspaper, Charlotte North Carolina, 28 July 1979.
9 '*Silvester* survivors relive WWII ordeal at sea', *Sauk Valley Sun*, 17 August 1983.
10 Waterproof cartons of cigarettes were at first quite common among the debris.
11 '*Silvester* survivors relive WWII ordeal at sea'.
12 RAAF Trade Protection Narrative, p. 168.
13 The sightings came from three separate aircraft and were made from 1200 feet (RAN Daily Narrative, 16 January 1945). The surveys were needed to establish channels suitable for capital ships north of Australia and hence to shorten shipping routes between the Indian and Pacific Oceans.
14 One sighting was made by the pilot of a civil aircraft, the other by the crew of an RAAF Anson on a training flight (RAAF Trade Protection Narrative, p. 167).

15 Gill, p. 553. This intelligence would appear to have come from D/F fix, but there is no other evidence to indicate that Timm brok radio silence before 9 February.
16 Letter, 14 February 1945, copy held by author.
17 Liberator A72–124.
18 'Together . . . always together'.
19 *Rock* was returning from an unsuccessful patrol in the South China Sea.
20 'Together . . . always together'. The recovery position was actually still out of sight of land.
21 'Indian Ocean Sinking', unknown newspaper, 2 April 1945, copy held by author.
22 B5553/1, 17 January 1945, AA.
23 Message, Tokyo to Berlin, 060342 February 1945; ibid., 16 February 1945.
24 Message, 31 January 1945; ibid., 4 February 1945.
25 Message from *U 862*, 9 February 1945; ibid., 14 February 1945.
26 Message to *U 862*, 10 February 1945; ibid., 16 February 1945.
27 Message, Control to *U 862*, 13 February 1945; ibid.
28 Reiffenstuhl, 10 February 1945.
29 ibid., 14 February 1945.
30 *Storm* arrived off the Sunda Strait on 8 February; she saw nothing except a distant A/S patrol and two days later started to work up the Sumatran coast. She arrived in Trincomalee on 20 February. *Sirdar* left Fremantle on 8 February, passed through the Lombok Strait and spent fourteen days on the coastal route between Jakarta and Surabaya (BR 1736 (52), vol. III, p. 90).
31 B5553/1, 16 February, AA.
32 According to one of *U 219*'s officers a working detail of coolies had been negligently smoking. At the time of the explosion *U 219*'s crew had just finished the day's work and left for the city. On hearing the explosion they turned the lorries around to offer assistance. However, as the ship had belonged to the Army, Japanese naval officials were rather reluctant to allow rescue operations and the Germans had to be persistent in order to proceed (Letter, H. Krug to author, 9 December 1993).
33 B5553/1, 26 February, AA; SRMN 053 27 February; SRH 23: 22 February.
34 BR 1736 (52), vol. III, p. 89.
35 Reiffenstuhl, 21 February 1945.

Chapter 15 Lübeck

1 The Germans found the Japanese very careless in the refining and

handling of diesel oil, and the smoking of U-boat diesels while using this fuel could never be prevented completely.

2 In the case of *Bootsmaat* Kurt Delfs, who had received no news of his wife since leaving Kiel, Timm finally resorted to the official Tokyo–Berlin communications channel to obtain information (message, Tokyo to Berlin, 28 March 1945, NARG 457, SRH Entry No. 9017, NA). No reply was intercepted by the Allies.

3 *U 862* short report, B5553/1, 27 February, AA.

4 Hessler, vol. III, p. 65.

5 *U 181, U 183, U 195, U 219, U 510, U 532, U 861* and *U 862*. *UIT 24* and *UIT 25* had neither the range nor the mechanical reliability to make the journey.

6 Message, Berlin to Tokyo, 8 March 1945, RG 457, SRH Entry 9017, NA.

7 Raids by 20th Air Force B-29s began on 5 November 1944 and continued intermittently until 28 March 1945. The heaviest raid came on 24 February 1945, when an all-incendiary attack by 105 B-29s hit the Empire Dock, burning out some 40 per cent of the warehouse area (K. Carter, *The Army Air Forces in World War II*, Office of Air Force History, Headquarters USAF, 1973).

8 Schirrmann, p. 34.

9 B5553/1, 25 January 1945, AA.

10 Message, Tokyo to Abe, 27 January 1945, ibid.; agreement was reached as follows:
   a) German submarines shall as far as possible operate in an area south of 5.00N, subject to alteration according to circumstances.
   (b) Command shall be exercised by the German Navy.
   (c) Intelligence reports will be passed by the Japanese Navy to the German Attaché in Tokyo and to the Resident German Naval Officer at bases in the Southern area.

11 Message, Berlin to Tokyo, 30 December 1944, B5553/1, 5 January 1945, AA.

12 CRS B5555, DSD translations of cipher messages 1945–46, AA.

13 Spieth had been replaced as IIIWO in *U 862* by *Kapitänleutnant* Heinz Rasner, formerly of the base staff in Singapore. Rasner had originally come out in the *Hilfskreuzer Thor* and had no U-boat experience. In Singapore he had been something of a disciplinary problem for Dommes, with separate convictions in January and February 1944 for tardiness, negligence, overstaying leave and unmilitary bearing. (message, Tokyo to Berlin, 9 February 1945, RG 457, SRH Entry 9017, NA). The only other wartime loss from *U 862*'s crew appears to have been *Matrosenobergefreiter* Franz Arnoldi, transferred to *UIT 25* and killed during an air raid on Kobe on 17 March 1945.

14 Message, Tokyo to Berlin, 24 March 1945, RG 457 SRH 9017, NA. The agents were part of Japan's *Hikari* (bright ray) organisation, set up in May 1943. The group's mission was to assist the Indian Independence movement led by Chandra Bose. *I-26* landed twelve

men near Karachi on 21 December 1943 and *I-166* landed six n near Ceylon on 24 December 1943. Several other missions wei aborted or failed.

15 Message, Berlin to Tokyo, 31 March 1945, RG 457 SRH Entry 9017, NA.

16 Message, Tokyo to Berlin, 5 April 1945, ibid.

17 Message, Tokyo to Berlin, 9 April 1945, ibid.

18 Message, Berlin to Tokyo, 12 April 1945, ibid.

19 Even, the possibility of setting up a 'German Legion' in the Southern Area, directly under the control of the Japanese Army, was briefly mooted. Wenneker, though, was quick to voice his misgivings, arguing that the Germans could not be sufficiently armed and doubting the practicability of land war operations, 'In view of Japanese distrust of the white man and all his works and totally different way of thinking' (message, Tokyo to Berlin, 19 April 1945, ibid.).

20 RG 457, SRMN 037, 20 April, NA. Hitler, however, informed Abe that should Germany's situation 'take a turn for the better, it goes without saying that as a matter of principle we would respond to Japan's desires by sending the fleet to East Asia to cooperate in operations ('Japanese reaction to German defeat', in *Listening to the Enemy*, ed. R. Spector, Scholarly Resources Inc., Wilmington, 1988, p. 238).

21 ibid. A subsequent Japanese proposal to fuel the U-boats in the South Atlantic was simply ignored.

22 Message, Berlin to Tokyo, 27 April 1945, RG 457 SRH Entry 9017, NA.

23 Padfield, *Dönitz*, pp. 397–404.

24 Giese, p. 230.

25 Message, Tokyo to Dönitz, 5 May 1945, RG 457, SRH Entry 9017, NA.

26 Message, Germany to Tokyo (for CO Southern Area), 7 May 1945, ibid.

27 Spector, p. 239.

28 On 2 May Tokyo directed that German ships were to be utilised in the war with the Allies. 'When consent is refused we shall intern them.' Another directive on 5 May stated, 'Measures are to be taken for the seizure and internment of German vessels by the Japanese Navy. Strict secrecy is to be preserved in their seizure and use in the Far East out of consideration of relations with Soviet Russia' (ibid. p. 241).

29 Giese, p. 229.

30 Fukudome also earnestly promised the reconquest of Germany by Japanese forces (ibid. p. 234).

31 Herrmann, 6 May 1945.

32 Message, Tokyo to Berlin, 5 January 1945, RG 457, Entry 9017, NA.

33 Spector, p. 241.

34 Other than the message from *BdU* on 7 May quoted above, there is

no evidence that the Germans either asked for or received payment from the Japanese for the East Asia U-boats.

35 Herrmann, 25 May 1945.

36 Schirrmann, p. 32.

37 ibid. The USAF holds no records of a P-38 shot down during a raid on Singapore Harbour in May or June 1945 (letter, Air Force Historical Research Agency to author, 13 May 1994). Schirrmann may be confusing the incident either with a sweep made over Singapore by Far East Air Force P-38s on 4 August or another P-38 raid against shipping on 13 August—four days after the second and last atomic bomb was dropped.

38 Herrmann, 14 August 1945.

39 Schirrmann, p. 34.

40 ibid. p. 36. Otto Giese records that occasionally one of the Germans would be caught in the local dance halls dressed in civilian clothes, his position in the nightly roll having been taken by a friendly guard (Giese, p. 248).

41 Letters, Long to author, 9 January and 28 February 1995.

42 According to one account the move came after an article with the headline 'A German miracle in Changi Jail' appeared in the Singapore newspaper *Shonang Shimbun* (Schirrmann, p. 37).

43 W. Bulley, 'U 862—a coincidence' in *Naval Historical Bulletin*, vol. 20, no. 3. February 1990, p. 13.

44 Schirrmann, p. 37.

45 Herrmann, 28 July 1946.

46 ibid. 25 December 1946.

47 'But no we are in England. In the country of the esteemed democracy! It often feels here as if you have gone back around 100 years' (ibid., 25 August 1947).

Epilogue

1 Saville, pp. 80–92.

2 *I-124*, sunk by HMAS *Deloraine* off Darwin on 20 January 1942. Not included are the three midget submarines sunk in Sydney Harbour on the night of 31 May–1 June 1942 and *RO-33*, sunk by HMAS *Arunta* off Port Moresby on 29 August 1942.

3 The result bears comparison with the Canadian experience, where between 1939 and 1945 no submarine was sunk by the Royal Canadian Navy (RCN) anywhere near its own coast. Recognising RCN successes in other areas of the Atlantic and Mediterranean, recent research has noted a variety of reasons for the failure, including: a lack of experience and tactical training; too few assets for too big an area; the lack of shore-based operational staffs to coordinate searches; and poor Asdic conditions (Milner, pp. 263–264).

4 C. Sternhill & A. Thorndike, *Antisubmarine Warfare in World War* Office of the Chief of Naval Operations, Navy Department, 1946, p 86.
5 W. Frank, *The Sea Wolves: The Story of the German U-boats at war,* Weidenfield & Nicolson, London, 1955, p. 239.
6 Padfield, *Dönitz The Last Führer,* p. 492.
7 Letter, Dommes to RN Submarine Museum, 29 November 1980, NHB.
8 *I–13, I–14, I–400* and *I–401.*
9 C. Lockwood, *Sink 'Em All: Submarine Warfare in the Pacific,* E.P. Dutton, New York, 1951, p. 359.
10 'Nazis popped in for NZ milkshake'.
11 Another who rejoined the Navy and retired as a *Fregattenkapitän* was Helmuth Pich, who had sat out the remainder of the war as a prisoner of war in Australia.
12 An intelligence summary in August reported, 'The two ex-German U-boats renamed I.501 and I.502 are ready for trials. They are fully equipped and will carry 16 torpedoes each. Training is to be carried out during the last 20 days of August (NID SI Summary, 7 August 1945, ADM 223/230 IC SI J 176-314, PRO). A later report noted, 'They will have a transportation run to Andaman area and then will operate in Pacific and go to Japan to have torpedo tubes remodelled' (OPNAV Bulletin, 13 August 1945, ADM 223/54, PRO).
13 P. Elliot, *Allied Escort Ships of World War II,* Macdonald & James, London, 1977, p. 229.
14 The official sinking position for *U 862* is 003° 05'N, 100° 38'E. For *U 181* 003° 05'30N, 100° 41'30E, AWD 15 February 1946.

Bibliography

Archives

The following abbreviations are used in the notes and bibliography:

AA	Australian Archives, Canberra and Melbourne
ADFA	Australian Defence Force Academy Library, Canberra
ANL	National Library of Australia, Canberra
NA	National Archives, Washington
NHB	Naval Historical Branch, Ministry of Defence, London
NHC	Naval Historical Center, Navy Yard, Washington
NHS	Naval Historical Section, Russell Offices, Canberra
PRO	Public Record Office, Kew, London
UBA	U-boat Archive, Cuxhaven

Principal document collections

DEFE 3, 'Enemy signals decrypted by Government Code and Cypher School', Reel 730, PRO

Kriegstagebuch der BdU, 15 August 1939–15 January 1945, mfm 1699, ANL

Kriegstagebuch der Seekriegsleitung, 1939–1945, mfm 1712, ANL

Intelligence Reports on the War in the Atlantic 1942–45, MF 28, ADFA

Interrogation of Germans captured at Singapore, NHB

RG 457, Records of the National Security Agency, NA

The Magic Documents, mfm 1593, ANL

US Naval Technical Mission in Europe, NHC

U-boat data sheets, UBA

US Submarine Patrol Reports, MF 33, ADFA

Official histories and documents

B.R. 1736 (50) *War With Japan*, 4 vols, Historical Section Admiralty, 1953–57
B.R. 1736 (51) *The Defeat of the Enemy Attack on Shipping 1939–1945: A Study of Policy and Operations*, Historical Section Admiralty, 1954
B.R. 1736 (52) *Submarines*, 3 vols, Historical Section Admiralty, 1953–57
C.B. 3305(4) *Arctic Convoys 1941–45*, Naval Staff History, Battle Summary no. 22, Historical Section Admiralty, 1954
C.B. 04051 (103) Interrogation of U-Boat Survivors: Cumulative Edition, Naval Intelligence Division, London, June 1944, NHB
Bray, J. *Ultra in the Atlantic*, 6 vols, edited version of selected records from NSA Record Group 457, Aegean Park Press, Laguna Hills, 1994
Carter, K. & Mueller, R. *The Army Air Forces in World War II: Combat Chronology 1941–1945*, Office of Air Force History, Headquarters USAF, 1973
Gill, G. *Royal Australian Navy 1939–1945*, 2 vols, Collins, Sydney, 1985
Hessler, G. *The U-boat War in the Atlantic 1939–1945*, Ministry of Defence, HMSO, London, 1989
Hinsley, F. *British Intelligence in the Second World War: Its Influence on Strategy and Operations*, 4 vols in 5, HMSO, London, 1981–90
Odgers, G. *Air War Against Japan 1943–45*, Australian War Memorial, Canberra, 1957
Roskill, S. *The War at Sea, 1939–45*, 3 vols in 4, London, 1954–61
Spector, R., ed. *Listening To The Enemy*, Scholarly Resources Inc., Wilmington, 1988
The U-Boat Commander's Handbook, reprint of USN translation of 1943 edition, Thomas Publications, Gettysburg, 1989
'Submarine Operations in Second Phase Operations', Part I April–August 1942, Japanese Monograph No.110, Military History Section Headquarters Far East, Office of the Chief of Military History Department of the Army

Private documents

Schirrmann, A. & Peitel, F. *Freie Jagd Im Indischen Ozean*
Reiffenstuhl, G., Herrmann, R. *Kriegstagebuch von U 862*

Secondary sources

Alden, J. *U.S. Submarine Attacks During World War II*, Naval Institute Press, Annapolis, 1989
Bagnasco, E. *Submarines of World War Two*, Arms and Armour Press, London, 1977
Blair, C. *Silent Victory: The US Submarine War Against Japan*, J.B. Lippincott Company, Philadelphia, 1975

…yd, C. and Akihiko Y. *The Japanese Submarine Force and World War II*, Naval Institute Press, Annapolis, 1995

Brennecke, J. *Haie im Paradies*, Ernst Gerdes Verlag, Preetz/Holstein, undated

—— *The Hunters and the Hunted*, The Elmfield Press, undated

Bunker, J. *Liberty Ships: The Ugly Ducklings of World War II*, Naval Institute Press, Annapolis, 1972

Busch, H. *U-Boats at War*, Putnam, London, 1955

Cairns, L. *Fremantle's Secret Fleets*, Western Australian Maritime Museum, Fremantle, 1995

Chalmers, W. *Max Horton and the Western Approaches: A Biography of Sir Max Kennedy Horton, GCB, DSO*, Hodder & Stoughton, London, 1954

Churchill, W. *The Second World War*, 6 vols, Cassell, London, 1948–53

Compton-Hall, R. *The Underwater War 1939–1945*, Blandford Press, Poole, 1983

Creed, D. *Operations of the Fremantle Submarine Base 1942–1945*, Naval Historical Society of Australia, Garden Island, undated

Cremer, P. *U 333: The Story of a U-Boat Ace*, Bodley Head, Oxford, 1984

Dönitz, K. *Memoirs: Ten Years and Twenty Days*, Weidenfeld & Nicolson, London, 1959

Elliot, P. *Allied Escort Ships of World War II*, Macdonald & James, London, 1977

Erskine, R. 'Naval Enigma: The breaking of Heimisch and Triton' in *Intelligence and National Security*, January 1988.

Frank, W. *The Sea Wolves: The Story of the German U-boats at War*, Weidenfeld & Nicolson, London, 1955

Friedman, N. *Submarine Design and Development*, Conway Maritime Press, London, 1984

Fukui, S. *Japanese Naval Vessels at the End of World War II*, Greenhill Books, London 1992

Giese, O. and Wise, J. *Shooting the War: Memoirs of a World War II U-Boat Officer*, Naval Institute Press, Annapolis, 1994

Gunton, D. *The Penang Submarines*, City Council of George Town, Penang, 1970

Hackmann, W. *Seek and Strike: Sonar, Anti-Submarine Warfare and the Royal Navy 1914–54*, HMSO, London, 1984

Hadley, M. *U-Boats Against Canada: German Submarines in Canadian Waters*, Naval Institute Press, Annapolis, 1985

Herterich, W. 'Deutsche U-Boote in Südostasien 1943 bis 1945', in *Zeitdokumente*, no. 151, March–April 1994

Horner, D. *High Command: Australia's Struggle for an Independent War Strategy, 1939–45*, Allen & Unwin, Sydney, 1992

Howarth, S. (ed.) *Men of War: Great Naval Leaders of World War II*, Weidenfeld & Nicolson, London, 1992

Howarth, S. and Law D. (eds) *The Battle of the Atlantic 1939–1945*, Greenhill Books, London, 1994

Kimball, W. *Churchill and Roosevelt: The Complete Correspondence*, 3 vo
Princeton U.P., Princeton, 1984
Leggoe, J. *Trying To Be Sailors*, St George Books, Perth, 1983
Lockwood, C. *Sink 'Em All: Submarine Warfare in the Pacific*, E.P. Dutton & Co. Inc., New York, 1951
Mallmann Showell, J. *U-Boats Under the Swastika*, Ian Allan, Shepperton, 1973
——*U-Boat Command and the Battle of the Atlantic*, Conway Maritime Press, London, 1989
Marder, A. *Old Friends, New Enemies: The Royal Navy and the Imperial Japanese Navy—Strategic Illusions 1936–1941*, Clarendon Press, Oxford, 1981
Milner, M. *The U-Boat Hunters: The Royal Canadian Navy and the Offensive against Germany's Submarines*, Naval Institute Press, Annapolis, 1994
Ogle, B. *The History of HMAS Maryborough: Corvettes in World War II 1940–1946*, self-published, 1992
Padfield, P. *Dönitz: The Last Führer*, Victor Gollancz, London, 1984
Polmar N. and Carpenter D. *Submarines of the Imperial Japanese Navy 1904–1945*, Conway Maritime Press, London, 1986
Rahn, W. 'Japan and Germany, 1941–1943: No Common Objective, No Common Plans, No Basis of Trust' in *Naval War College Review*, vol. XLVI, no. 3, Summer 1993
Robertson, T. *The Golden Horseshoe*, Evans, London, 1955
Rohwer, J. *Axis Submarine Successes 1939–1945*, Naval Institute Press, Annapolis, 1983
Rohwer, J. and Hummelchen, G. *Chronology of the War at Sea 1939–1945*, Greenhill Books, London, 1993
Rössler, E. *The U-boat: The Evolution and Technical History of German Submarines*, Arms and Armour Press, London, 1989
Saville, A, 'German Submarines in the Far East', in *United States Naval Institute Proceedings*, August 1961
Sawyer, L. & Mitchell, W. *The Liberty Ships*, David & Charles, Newton Abbot, 1973
Schaeffer, H. *U-Boat 977*, William Kimber, London, 1952
Stern, R. *Type VII U-boats*, Arms and Armour Press, London, 1991
Terraine, J. *Business in Great Waters: The U-boat Wars 1916–1945*, Leo Cooper, London, 1989
Thomas, C. *The German Navy in the Nazi Era*, Unwin Hyman, London, 1990
Topp, E. *The Odyssey of a U-boat Commander*, Praeger, Westport, 1992
Ugaki, M. *Fading Victory: The Diary of Admiral Matome Ugaki*, 1941–45, trans. Masataka Chihaya, University of Pittsburgh Press, Pittsburgh, 1991
Vause, J. *U-boat Ace*, Naval Institute Press, Annapolis, 1990
Vincent, D. *Catalina Chronicle: A History of RAAF Operations*, The Catalina National Committee, 1981
Walker, F. *HMAS Armidale: The Ship That Had to Die*, Kingfisher Press, Budgewoi, 1990
—— *Corvettes—Little Ships for Big Men*, Kingfisher Press, Budgewoi, 1995
Watts, A. *The U-Boat Hunters*, Macdonald & Janes, London, 1976

..er, H. *Iron Coffins: A Personal Account of the German U-boat Battles of World War II*, Arthur Barker, London, 1970

/heeler, G. *Kinkaid of the Seventh Fleet*, Naval Historical Center, Department of the Navy, Washington, 1995

Winter, B. *The Intrigue Master: Commander Long and Naval Intelligence in Australia, 1913–1945*, Boolarong Press, Brisbane, 1995

Winton, J. *Ultra in the Pacific*, Naval Institute Press, Annapolis, Maryland, 1993

Index

Page numbers in *italics* refer to maps and illustrations.